Garden Birds
and other wildlife

By Kate Risely and Clare Simm

Looking out for birds

Published by the British Trust for Ornithology

British Trust for Ornithology
The Nunnery
Thetford
Norfolk
IP24 2PU

01842 750050
info@bto.org
www.bto.org
Charity Number 216652 (England & Wales), SC039193 (Scotland)

First published in 2016
British Trust for Ornithology

ISBN: 978–1–908581–68–6

Text: Kate Risely & Clare Simm
Maps and calendar wheels: Simon Gillings
Design and layout: Mike Toms
Front cover: Blackbird, by Laurie Campbell/NPL
Back cover: House Sparrow, by Edmund Fellowes

Environment: The paper used for this book has been certified as coming from well-managed forests and other controlled sources according to the rules of the Forest Stewardship Council.

This book was printed and bound in Italy by Printer Trento, an FSC certified company for printing books on FSC mixed paper in compliance with the chain of custody and on-product labelling standards. Printer Trento has an ISO 14001 certified environmental management system.

Garden Birds
and other wildlife

By Kate Risely and Clare Simm

Robin, by Edmund Fellowes

Contents

Introduction

Greenfinches, by Edmund Fellowes

Our gardens are more than open-air living rooms; they provide daily access to the natural world around us. Encounters with birds, butterflies and other wild animals in our gardens often kindle a natural interest in identifying, learning about and encouraging wildlife. Private gardens across the UK combine to form an important habitat for wildlife and, due to the increasing pressures of urbanisation on our countryside, it is now more important than ever that we record and conserve the birds, insects and other animals with which we share our gardens.

For many decades the British Trust for Ornithology (BTO) has successfully combined records collected by volunteer observers with high-quality scientific research, in order to deepen our knowledge of the natural world and inform conservation. One of the surveys run by the BTO is Garden BirdWatch (GBW), in which thousands of people record the birds and other wildlife they see in their gardens each week. Much of the information in this book is drawn from the collected observations of these thousands of Garden BirdWatchers, as well as the research on garden and urban wildlife carried out using GBW records. If you are not already a member of Garden BirdWatch, please consider joining, and sharing your garden sightings with us.

This book is aimed at people who want to start learning about the birds and other wildlife in their gardens, as well as existing Garden BirdWatchers who wish to deepen and update their knowledge. It begins with an overview of the lives of birds: their biology, nesting habits, daily and annual cycles and migratory habits; information that provides a context to

the activity we see in our gardens. Next we cover why gardens are important for birds, and provide practical information about managing a garden for wildlife. Following this is a section on the value of watching and recording birds, including the wider work of the BTO as well as information about how the data collected through Garden BirdWatch are used for research, both by BTO staff and others.

The main part of the book comprises individual accounts of over 60 garden birds, some very common, others less so, covering all the species that you are likely to see in your garden. Detailed maps combining summer and winter distributions, drawn from *Bird Atlas 2007–11*, allow you to see whether a bird is likely to be found in your area. Counts from Garden BirdWatch have been used to calculate a 'garden reporting rate', which gives the probability of seeing that species in your garden, as well as new 'calendar wheels', showing how the chance of seeing the species varies throughout the year. Facts about size, lifespan, population size and status are featured thanks to work going on through other

BTO surveys, including the Ringing Scheme and the Nest Record Scheme.

The accompanying text describes the identification features of the bird, interesting behaviours to look out for, and food preferences in gardens. We have also given wider information to add context to your garden sightings, such as migratory patterns or whether populations are increasing or declining. The accounts also feature photographs of the birds, showing different plumages (male, female or juvenile) where this would help with identification, as well as a photograph of the nest of each species.

While the main entries cover most birds likely to be seen in your garden, occasionally something completely different turns up! After the main accounts we have listed some unusual visitors that you may encounter, including escaped aviary birds and genuine rarities. Of course, a book on garden wildlife does not have the scope to cover all these species in depth, and for more information we recommend the *Collins BTO Guide to British Birds* and its companion the *Collins BTO Guide to Rare British Birds*.

Towards the end of the book we have covered how to recognise and identify other garden wildlife, including mammals, reptiles, amphibians, butterflies, dragonflies and bumblebees – the groups that can be recorded for Garden BirdWatch. The list is not exhaustive, but includes some of the more common species that you may see in your garden and explores the differences between similar species. If you want to find out more about garden wildlife, please have a look at the 'Resources' section where we have recommended books and websites for further reading and exploration. Whether you are a beginner or an experienced observer of garden wildlife, we hope that you learn something new from this book, and are inspired to record and contribute your sightings.

ABOUT THE AUTHORS

Kate Risely is the Garden BirdWatch Organiser, and has worked for the BTO in various roles since 2004. She is a strong believer in the value of wildlife recording for nature conservation, and aims to make the best possible use of information collected by Garden BirdWatchers. She enjoys wildlife gardening, as well as recording birds, moths, butterflies and marine life.

Clare Simm is the Garden BirdWatch Development Officer, working to raise awareness of Garden BirdWatch and its findings. She has always been fascinated by the natural world and, while she has been lucky enough to work in nature conservation abroad, she has always had a soft spot for British wildlife. She has a particular passion for birds, amphibians and reptiles.

Kate wrote the sections 'About birds' and 'Watching birds', while Clare wrote 'Gardens and wildlife' and 'Other wildlife'. The bird accounts were shared equally.

Using the species accounts

Calendar wheel: The calendar wheels show how the presence of each species in gardens varies throughout the year, and are derived from Garden BirdWatch data (see page 73). The amount of darker colour in each segment indicates the likelihood of seeing the species. An empty (all pale grey) segment means the bird is not usually seen in gardens during that month. A completely filled dark segment shows the month (or months) you are most likely to see the bird, and all other segments are scaled in size relative to the peak month. Note that a filled dark segment does not mean that the bird is seen in 100% of gardens; to find out the chance of seeing the bird at its most common please refer to the 'garden reporting rate' in the Spotlight box. Hence the peak month of February for Long-tailed Tit equates to 35% of gardens.

Swallow   Blackbird   Redwing

Spotlight: Information is mainly taken from the BTO's BirdFacts web pages, which contain further information and details of sources: www.bto.org/birdfacts.

Conservation status in the UK: Birds are red-, amber- or green-listed according to the listings published in *Birds of Conservation Concern 4* in December 2015.

Entries on the **breeding season, clutch size, incubation period, fledging period and number of broods** are mostly taken from *A Field Guide to Monitoring Nests*, mainly using information derived from the BTO Nest Record Scheme. The breeding season given indicates the period from which 90% of eggs and chicks are recorded; small numbers of birds may nest outside the main season. A second number in brackets after number of broods indicates the maximum number occasionally observed.

The **max lifespan** is the longest time an individual has been recorded carrying a ring, using data from the BTO Ringing Scheme.

The **typical lifespan** has been calculated using various published survival rates.

The **garden reporting rate** shows the percentage of Garden BirdWatch gardens reporting the species during the peak month for that species.

The highlighted **silhouette** gives a rough indication of the size of the bird, and whether it is closest in size to a Robin, Blackbird, pigeon, crow or chicken.

Long-tailed Tit, by Liz Cutting

Long-tailed Tit
Aegithalos caudatus

In gardens, Long-tailed Tits can be seen all year round, often in as family parties pass through, often attracted to suet products spring when birds are presumably splitting into their pairs and

Green-listed

Spotlight

Size 14 cm; Wingspan 18 cm; Weight 9 g

Food: Mostly arthropods, especially small bugs and insect eggs, plus the larvae of moths.

Breeds: March to June
Clutch size: 6–9 eggs
Incubation: 14–16 days
Young fledge: 14–17 days
Number of broods: 1 per year
Population: 330,000 territories
Max lifespan: 8 years, 11 months
Typical lifespan: 2 years
Garden reporting rate: 35%

A widespread specie
Long-tailed Tits can be
though they are large
Scottish islands. Due
woodland, they occur
areas. As they struggle
numbers can vary fro
fall quite dramatically.
and 1963 the Long-ta
as 80%. However, be
increased overall by 9
winters boosting over
success, with earlier la
produced.

Not a tit at all
Long-tailed Tits are no
same larger group tha
have very small, roun
more than half their le
black band that runs f
the crown, giving ther
throat and breast are
and flanks. The upper
and the long narrow t
orange or pink bare sk
Juveniles are duller
forehead and side of
the pink altogether. S
undergo a full moult o
indistinguishable fron

Long-tailed Tit nest in gorse, by Mike Toms

Maps: The maps present the likelihood of seeing each species throughout Britain and Ireland during summer and winter, and are based on data collected for *Bird Atlas 2007–11*. In purple areas the species is resident all year round, and is equally abundant in summer and winter. As the colour tends towards blue it means the bird is more common in winter than summer, and clean blues indicate birds present only in winter (e.g. Fieldfare). The change from purple to red indicates a tendency towards summer dominance, with pure reds for summer visitors (e.g. Swallow). Darker colours indicate greater abundance, while white areas mean the bird is absent or very rare. Distribution maps cover summer and winter periods only, and do not show occurrence during migration, when birds may turn up in other areas.

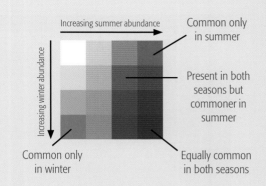

Increasing summer abundance

Common only in summer

Present in both seasons but commoner in summer

Increasing winter abundance

Common only in winter

Equally common in both seasons

...umbers increase in the winter ...feeders, and fall during the ...rby.

...oughout Britain and Ireland, ...om upland areas and some of the ...erence for nesting in deciduous ...ensities in wooded lowland ...through very cold winters, their ...ear and in severe winters can ...e in the winters of 1917, 1947 ...ulation was reduced by as much ...7 and 2012, their population ...bly due to progressively mild ...val and leading to better breeding ...and more fledglings being

...ut they are a member of the ...des warblers and swallows. They ...with long tails that make up ...ead is white and there is a wide ...e of the forehead back along ...arance of having eyebrows. The ...nd they have a light pinkish belly ...ack with pink on the shoulders, ...with white edges. They have ...eir eyes. ...nce than the adults, with a dark ...brown on their bodies, lacking ...aving the nest, however, they ...e plumage, making them ...

Family ties

During the spring, Long-tailed Tits are often seen only in pairs, but some breeding pairs do receive help raising their young from one or more close relatives. These 'helpers' may be birds whose own breeding attempts have failed. Up to eight helpers have been recorded feeding a single brood, strongly increasing the chances of the young fledging successfully.

Once the young have fledged, Long-tailed Tits come together in extended family parties, numbering several dozen individuals. This is especially advantageous in the winter as they are extremely susceptible to cold weather and so will huddle together in roosts during the night, very occasionally using nest boxes or commercially available roosting pouches.

Long-tailed Tits communicate with clicking calls that sound like they are chatting, along with a loud sharp 'srih srih srih' call. These calls can often alert you to the approach of a foraging party. They may also make a loud drawn-out trill when alarmed.

A thorny issue

Long-tailed Tits prefer to nest in areas of deciduous woodland that have dense undergrowth, though they seem equally happy in scrub or hedgerow habitats. Bramble bushes, Gorse and Blackthorn are all well used. If suitable vegetation is present they will nest in large suburban parks and gardens, but they only rarely penetrate more urban areas.

The nest is usually found attached to the outer twigs of a bush, especially one with thorns, but they will nest in climbing plants and in trees, often placing the nest up against the trunk, and within a fork. Built by both the male and the female, the nest is a dense ball of moss that is bound together with cobwebs and hair, and covered with grey lichen. The entrance is near the top, and the inside is thickly lined with hundreds of feathers. The pair take their time building the nest and it can be up to three weeks before they complete it. Once complete, the nest may be left for several days before egg-laying begins. This may reassure the pair that the nest-building activities have not attracted the unwelcome attentions of a nest predator. Certainly, Long-

tailed Tits can be fairly conspicuous when nest building, particularly when taking feathers to the nest. The birds rear one large brood from late March onwards. As the chicks grow, the nest stretches so that there is enough room for them all.

Rare visitors

Long-tailed Tits used to be rare visitors to gardens, but Garden BirdWatch results have shown an increase in the use of garden resources, including supplementary food. They will take fat products, small seeds, finely grated mild cheese and bread crumbs from both bird tables and hanging feeders. They are most likely to be seen at feeders during winter, when invertebrates are scarce. There are several different races of Long-tailed Tit in Europe and some look distinctly different from those found in Britain and Ireland. Occasional birds migrate here from northern Europe, mostly turning up in the east of England, and these individuals can be told by their entirely white heads.

Long-tailed Tit, by Ric Jackson

Nuthatch, by Edmund Fellowes

Acknowledgements

Firstly, the authors wish to thank Mike Toms for his tireless work planning and managing the production of this book, and for applying his considerable artistic skills to the layout and design of this publication.

This book benefits from the generosity and talent of the photographers who support the BTO through their contributions to our digital image library. These are: Adrian Dancy, Allan Drewitt, Amy Lewis, Anne Carrington-Cotton, Chris Knights, Christine M Matthews, David Hutton, David Tipling, David Waistell, Dawn Balmer, Dennis Atherton, Edmund Fellowes, Graham Catley, Graham Jarvis, Hazel Rothwell, Herbert & Howells, Howard Stockdale, Hugh Insley, Jeff & Allison Kew, Jeff Baker, Jill Pakenham, John Cranfield, John Dunn, John Flowerday, John Harding, John W Proudlock, John W Walton, Jonathan Tyler, Josie Latus, Les Foster, Liz Cutting, Mike Toms, Morris Rendall, Moss Taylor, Paul Newton, Paul Stancliffe, Peter Howlett, Ric Jackson, Richard Winston, Ron Marshall, Tom Wallis, Tommy Holden and Vic Froome. We are also very grateful to the following photographers for supplying the other photographs: Andrew Merrick, Ashley Jackson, Brian Small, Dpa Picture-alliance, Geoff du Feu, Hugh Clark, Juniors Bildarchiv, Laurie Campbell, Mark Watson, Michael Foord, NatureGuides, Owen Newman, Paul Sterry, Peter Castell, Richard Castell, Richard Revels, Roger Tidman, S C Bisserot, Steve Young and Tierfotoagentur. distribution maps, based on the data from the *Bird Atlas 2007–11*, by Dawn Balmer et al., were produced by Simon Gillings, who also created the calendar wheels based on BTO Garden BirdWatch data. Nigel Hawtin kindly produced the maps used on pages 35 and 107. Ben Darvill produced the artwork showing the size of each species.

We are particularly grateful to the proof-readers who gave their time to check the text. These were: Dave Leech, Dawn Balmer, Debbie Todd, John Marchant, Nick Moran, Sandra Sparkes, Sebastian Seely, Mike Toms, Nicky Ward and Ruth Walker. Remaining errors are our own.

Our understanding of the behaviour, ecology and health of garden wildlife is drawn from the work of countless scientists and observers, but we would particularly like to mention Kate Plummer, Nancy Ockendon, Gary Clewley and Becki Lawson for their work on Garden BirdWatch data that has enriched our knowledge.

We would like to thank our colleagues Heather Pymar, Donna Hobbs and Nicky Ward for all their work running Garden BirdWatch, as well as managing book orders and sales. Kate would like to thank her husband Dave Leech and baby son Rory for their support and forgiveness of time spent dedicated to writing. Clare would like to thank her fiancé Jonathan King for his support throughout her time spent working on the book.

We are grateful to all volunteers who provided data to *Bird Atlas 2007–11*, the BTO/JNCC/RSPB Breeding Bird Survey and the BTO Ringing Nest Record Schemes, from which the ecological information presented in this book is drawn. Finally, and most of all, we are indebted to all of the Garden BirdWatchers who support the project and send in their records, without whom none of this work would be possible.

House Sparrow, by Les Foster

About birds

Blackbird, by Edmund Fellowes

Bird biology

The birds in our gardens carry out their daily lives in full view – foraging, displaying to potential mates and raising their young – yet they remain wild and elusive. It is the power of flight that enables birds to live so visibly in a world full of potential predators. Understanding how their basic biology shapes bird behaviour can help to make sense of the patterns of activity we see in our garden birds across the seasons.

The challenges of life

The life of an individual bird is divided into distinct periods, shaped by the need to survive, to compete with other birds, to find a mate and to breed successfully. The study of these different parts of their life cycle, through statistics on annual survival and breeding success, helps us understand the changing structure of bird populations, and this knowledge then supports bird conservation and policy decisions.

One of the first challenges facing a young bird is surviving its first winter; mortality of first-year birds is often high, with as few as one in four individuals making it through to the following spring. The demands of flight mean that birds have high energy requirements, which is why in cold weather many are drawn to garden feeding stations, despite the attendant risks of cats, Sparrowhawks and uncomfortably close encounters with other birds. What appears as boldness to us should be seen as the result of a complex risk-benefit calculation that is inextricably linked to the prevailing environmental conditions and daily chances of survival.

Some birds, of course, fly south for the winter, exchanging the risks of extreme weather for the hazards of long journeys and sea crossings. Migration is an extraordinary natural phenomenon, requiring remarkable feats of endurance and navigation. Some of these movements are obvious, such as the Swallows which congregate on wires, ready to depart, or the first Bramblings that appear on the bird feeders in early winter. Other movements are more subtle, but watchful observers notice the differences in numbers and behaviour of their garden Blackbirds and Chaffinches as arrivals from northern populations join, and sometimes displace, local breeders. Strategies for making it through the winter can be fascinating to observers, and overwinter survival can have marked effects on the overall population size and trends.

Through the seasons

In the spring the struggle for survival eases, and the focus moves to reproduction. Warm weather, and associated increases in invertebrate numbers, see the return of our summer migrants, many of which need to feed on insects all year round. While resident birds generally eat seeds or fruit in winter, many switch to insects in the summer, and nearly all species take invertebrates to feed their nestlings; this seasonal shift contributes to a drop in popularity of garden bird feeders.

As food resources increase in the spring, birds pair up, spread out and set up territories. Males sing to defend their patch and attract a female, and, if successful, the pair will then build a nest, lay eggs and raise chicks. Every breeding season involves trade-offs; success today weighed against surviving to breed again another time. While small birds can live a surprisingly long time – the longevity record for a Blue Tit, according to ringing data, is 10 years – most individuals only survive a few years, so they breed first at one year old and invest heavily in each breeding season. A nest of eggs or chicks is extremely vulnerable to predators and bad weather, and many birds will attempt to raise several broods over the season, or at least will re-lay if their attempt fails early on.

Juvenile birds that make it to fledging are the lucky ones, and hatchlings grow quickly in order to leave the nest as soon as possible. Small birds reach their adult size faster than similarly-sized mammals, and by the time the youngsters leave the nest around two weeks after hatching they are the same size as their parents. However, some corners are cut to achieve this fast growth. All birds have extremely lightweight bones due to the need to keep weight down for flight, but juveniles have particularly flimsy skeletons as they are not fully developed by the time they leave the nest. Over the first few months of a bird's life it will gradually lay down more bone deposits until the skeleton is as strong as that of an adult bird.

The Robins breeding in your garden may have two or three broods over the breeding season, each reared in a nest constructed over several days from leaves, grasses and other material.

Robin, by Edmund Fellowes

Blue Tit nest, by Moss Taylor

Nests and eggs

Keeping nests well hidden is a matter of life and death for birds; the contents can be easy pickings for predators and failure rates can be high. It is therefore unsurprising that nests in gardens can be hard to find, but watching carefully for birds carrying nesting material, or food for young, can reveal the location of the nest.

The breeding season

The nesting season for most garden birds runs from March through to July, though there are many exceptions; Long-tailed Tits may be seen carrying nesting material in February, and Woodpigeons and Collared Doves will nest almost year round if conditions are suitable. Species differ in their nesting strategies, with most Blue Tits laying a single clutch of eight to ten eggs at the end of April, while Blackbirds may attempt to raise three or four clutches of around four eggs throughout the season, and may still have chicks in a nest into August.

Small birds only lay one egg per day, so it will take as many days as there are eggs to complete a clutch. The female will only start to incubate once the clutch nears completion, meaning that all the eggs start to develop at the same time. Around two weeks later the eggs hatch, and roughly two weeks after hatching the nestlings are ready to leave the nest and gain their independence. While small birds begin incubation from the penultimate egg, some larger birds (notably owls) start to incubate from the first egg, meaning that their eggs will hatch successively.

Making use of gardens

Gardens and houses provide a wide variety of nest sites. Dense shrubbery or Ivy is ideal for Blackbirds, Song Thrushes and Dunnocks, which all build open, cup-shaped nests. Chaffinches, Greenfinches and Goldfinches also build open nests, but these are often placed in high bushes or small trees. Robins and Wrens may nest in cavities, such as those present within log piles or tree roots.

Among the most obvious nests are those of Woodpigeons, whose untidy platforms of twigs are sometimes built completely out in the open. Blue Tits, Great Tits and Starlings will all nest in boxes, while other species get even closer to us; House Sparrows and Swifts breed in our roof spaces, Swallows use our outbuildings and House Martins construct their characteristic mud nests under our overhanging eaves. It's possible to safely observe the contents of most nests, and send in counts of eggs and chicks, by following the guidance of the BTO Nest Record Scheme. The observations gained through nest monitoring provide information that contributes to our understanding of why populations change.

Nest construction

As a general rule the nests of garden birds are temporary structures, built to contain a single clutch of eggs, and abandoned once the chicks have fledged. There are some exceptions; birds may choose to use the same nest for subsequent clutches if their first brood fledged successfully, and more permanent structures, such as House Martin nests, may be renovated year after year.

Different species have very different, specific ways of building their nests, but in general the outer, structural parts of nests built in the open (rather than in cavities) are normally made from thin twigs, grasses, or roots, and are variously insulated, decorated or supported with moss, lichen or dead leaves. The lining, which holds the eggs, is often a softer material, such as feathers, fur, moss or fine grasses, though Song Thrushes line their nests with a coating of chewed wood pulp and mud, which dries to a hard cup.

Often the female does the bulk of the work of collecting material and building the nest, though the male may also collect material for the female to work into the structure. In some species, such as Long-tailed Tit and House Sparrow, the males and females share the work equally, while in others, such as Starling, the male will build most of the nest, and the female will just complete the lining. Male Wrens, and a number of warblers, take this to extremes, and will build a number of unlined 'cock nests'. When a male Wren secures a mate, she inspects the nests, and then adds a lining to the one she will go on to use.

How is an egg formed?

An important requirement that female birds have during the egg-laying period is a supply of extra calcium. Birds' diets are generally poor in this important element; they have light, flimsy skeletons and, unlike mammals, do not store additional calcium in their bones. This extra calcium has to be sourced from the environment prior to an egg being laid. Sources of calcium that birds use include snail shells, hard-shelled arthropods such as millipedes and woodlice, the eggshells of other birds and grit.

Female birds lay one egg a day; most of the extra nutrients needed to create an egg can be consumed over a few days, but the calcium needed to create the eggshell is often only eaten last thing the night before. While the bird is roosting overnight the eggshell is completed, and the egg is then often laid at first light, so the female minimises the amount of time flying and foraging with a fully-formed egg on board. Birds that roost in the nest cavity overnight will often deposit the egg before they leave the nest in the morning, though sometimes birds return to the nest to lay later in the day, and some species, such as Woodpigeon, routinely lay in the afternoon.

THOSE FIRST STEPS

It's normal for young birds to leave the nest before their wing and tail feathers are fully grown. Until they are able to fly they stay hidden in vegetation near the nest, while their parents continue to feed them.

If you find a flightless young bird that is out of the nest, but hidden and uninjured, it should be left where it is. If it is out in the open and at risk, for example from cats or traffic, it should be moved into nearby dense vegetation. Nestlings without a full covering of feathers should not be out of the nest; if you find one, and can see an undamaged nest nearby, it is worth trying to put it back in.

Blue Tit fledgling, by Jill Pakenham

Behaviour

House Sparrow dust-bathing, by Edmund Fellowes

Watching birds can involve more than just identifying different species. Regular observation of the birds outside our windows can reveal a wide variety of fascinating behaviours, and even the commonest garden birds can surprise us. Particular behaviours may be apparent at certain times of the year, perhaps because they are only associated with certain activities or seasons.

Feeding behaviour

Centre stage, in most gardens, is the bird feeder. It doesn't take long to notice the different feeding preferences of different birds, and to link these to their ecology in natural habitats. Blue Tit, Great Tit, Starling and Great Spotted Woodpecker all have strong bills for digging and probing, and these birds often choose to gouge at peanuts or suet balls. Seed eaters, such as Greenfinch and Goldfinch, will favour delicately picking from seed feeders, particularly nyger or sunflower seeds, while Robin, Dunnock and Blackbird prefer to forage on the ground.

While each species may have a favourite food, it's interesting to watch what happens when several different species use the same feeder. Bird feeders present a highly artificial situation in which species that rarely interact in natural habitats compete for access and establish a pecking order. Interactions may take the form of physical disputes, with birds squabbling and pushing each other off perches, or they may be more subtle, with subordinate birds visiting the feeders only when the dominant species are absent. Size is

an important factor in establishing dominance, with Starlings and Great Spotted Woodpeckers often muscling out other birds, Greenfinches dominating Goldfinches, and Great Tits seeing off Blue Tits.

Due to their tiny size, Coal Tits almost never get time at a feeder before being chased off, but can be seen caching food to make the most of their access; darting to the feeder, retrieving a seed, stashing it for later, then back for another one. Jays also employ this technique, not due to subordinate status but to deal with a glut of food when acorns ripen, hiding hundreds for later retrieval. These and other birds that cache food, such as Nuthatches, can display a remarkable ability to remember exactly where they have hidden the seeds, even some time later.

Holding territory

While disputes between different species can be seen around a rich food source, such as a bird feeder or a bush of ripe berries, aggression between birds of the same species is often due to territoriality. In the winter months many birds flock together and roam in search of food.

The arrival of spring sees these flocks break up as individual birds establish a breeding territory, with each territory containing the resources needed to raise their young.

Some birds are much more territorial than others; House Sparrows nest in loose colonies and are happy to associate with other pairs even in the breeding season, while Robins are aggressively territorial and it's unusual for Garden BirdWatchers to see more than a single pair of Robins together, even in winter. Long-tailed Tits are cooperative breeders; relatives of a territorial pair (perhaps those whose own nesting attempt has failed) will join the territorial pair and help to raise their young.

Blackbirds will range into others' territories to access bird feeders or other food sources, but it is often possible to identify the resident male since he will be the one attempting to repel the intruders. Generally, contests between territorial birds are settled through display and chasing, rather than risking the serious injury that may come from direct aggression. However, a potentially injurious aspect of territorial aggression is birds attacking their own reflections in window panes; they believe their reflection is a rival to be seen off, but of course this rival will not fly away so the aggression escalates. Distressing to watch and exhausting for the bird, it should be short-lived and may be resolved by a temporary cover over the reflective surface.

Proclaiming ownership

The most obvious sign of territoriality is singing. As a general rule only male birds sing, as song

A number of garden birds, such as this Rook, may be witnessed exploiting food resources in unusual or 'clever' ways. Here, the bird has managed to remove the suet ball from the feeder in which it was held.

Rook taking a suet ball, by Moss Taylor

Juvenile Blackbird 'sunning' itself, by Moss Taylor

You may occasionally see Blackbirds, Robins and other birds 'sunbathing' in your garden. Exposing the feathers to the sun's rays is thought to increase the distribution of the oil that protects the feathers and drives out parasites that can damage the feather structure.

is designed to send a message to rivals and potential mates that a territory is occupied. Songs are generally more complex than calls, which are used for contact and signalling by both males and females. The distinction between call and song, however, is not always clear and some species, such as Long-tailed Tit and House Sparrow, do not have any obvious male songs.

Garden birds are most vocal at the start of the breeding season and many quieten when their mate is incubating a full clutch of eggs, since the risk of a rival male mating with the female has been reduced and lowering the volume of song lessens unwanted attention from would-be predators.

Courtship feeding and pair behaviour
An interesting behaviour to look out for at the start of the breeding season is courtship feeding, where a male presents food items to the female as if she were a nestling. This is thought to reinforce the pair bond, and possibly also increase the female's nutritional intake ahead of egg formation. It has been shown

that courtship displays and behaviours such as this may provide a potential mate with information on the quality of the displaying bird; for example, his ability to provide food for nestlings. In some species, the complexity of the male's song provides a signal of his fitness; the more complex the song, the better his quality as a prospective mate.

Once birds have paired, the male and female appear to work harmoniously together to raise their family. However, research has shown that 'marriage' in birds is rife with conflict and infidelity. Both parents want to produce as many healthy offspring as possible, and will not hesitate to mate with other individuals in order to achieve this. Male birds often look to mate with other females, thereby fathering some of the nestlings that will be cared for by another male. While this helps them to produce more offspring, it also means they do not have 'all their eggs in one basket'; if the male's own nest fails, there may still be some of his offspring in the nest next door.

However, the males do not have it all their own way; while they are in the next garden

Starling 'splash-bathing', by John W Proudlock

Many garden birds will visit the bird bath to 'splash bathe', wetting their plumage sufficiently but not giving it so much of a soaking that they are then unable to fly. Starlings often bathe in groups, which can make for animated viewing.

playing the field, their own partner may be mating with another male. Females will aim to mate with high-quality males in order to produce healthy, successful offspring, and for this they may look to males other than their partner. While it may appear that female birds can only raise a limited number of offspring – i.e. as many as they are able to care for and raise themselves – we now know that 'egg dumping', where a female sneakily lays an egg in another nest of the same species while the parents are away, is more common than previously thought.

Mixed parentage

The result of all this activity is that a brood of young birds may not all actually be related to the male parent, and sometimes not even to the female. Some studies have found that 40% of Blue Tit nests contain at least one chick that has been fathered by another male. Coal Tits have been shown to be even less faithful, with one study finding 75% of nests with at least one chick that is not related to the provisioning male, and overall a quarter of

chicks were being raised by a male that was not actually their father. House Sparrows and Starlings also show similar levels of 'extra-pair paternity', and nearly 30% of nestlings reared by a male Swallow will not, on average, be his own. In Swallows we know a little about what signs of quality the females are looking for in a male; the longer the tail of a male Swallow, the more likely it is that he will sire young in more than one nest.

We only know about these secret lives of our garden birds through genetic testing, but this knowledge gives insight into other behaviours that we are able to observe. Male birds do not want to unknowingly raise another's offspring, so when their mate is preparing to lay her eggs they will try to make sure she does not have an opportunity to mate with any other males by shadowing her every move. This 'mate guarding' is particularly noticeable in Robins and Dunnocks. On occasion a male will succeed in pairing up with two females; it is often hard to be sure if this is the case, but close observations may reveal this kind of 'ménage à trois' among your garden birds.

Gaining independence

A special sight is when the first juveniles of the year appear on lawns and bird feeders, often still dependent on their parents for food; this is a great opportunity to see the youngsters learn how to exploit hanging feeders, a source they wouldn't encounter in natural habitats. Adult Great Spotted Woodpeckers, for example, bring chicks to peanut feeders. A strange behaviour sometimes seen is a bird feeding fledglings belonging to a different species. This misfiring of a natural instinct can sometimes be triggered by the stimulus of a begging chick of the wrong species, perhaps when the adult bird has lost its own brood.

Taking care of yourself

As well as finding food and raising chicks, birds need to keep themselves clean, take care of their feathers and rid themselves of parasites. A bird bath will attract many different species to splash in the water, and some can also be seen 'sunbathing', drying their plumage and driving out parasites that live on the feathers. Somewhat counter-intuitively, some birds, such as House Sparrows, 'bathe' in dust or sandy soil, perhaps because the grains dislodge parasites. A rarer behaviour is 'anting', where birds seek out the kind of ants that spray formic acid. The bird crouches over their nest and the disturbed ants run over the bird's body. Formic acid kills feather mites without harming the bird. There have also been reports of birds sitting over smoking chimneys, presumably for similar reasons; a novel approach to an age-old problem.

Bright birds

While it's generally impossible to tell one bird from another, a few individuals do have distinguishing features, and it can be very interesting to watch how a particular bird behaves. Research has shown that Great Tits have different personalities, with some birds always bold, aggressive and willing to take risks, while others are more timid and slow to explore new opportunities. Researchers have discovered that these traits are heritable within families, being passed from one generation to the next.

Many Garden BirdWatchers have tales of particularly daring Robins or Blackbirds that have learned to beg for food at the kitchen door, or of birds that have figured out unusual feeding strategies. Members of the crow family, including Rooks, Jays, Jackdaws and Magpies, are especially famous for their problem-solving skills, and have been seen employing ingenious tactics to bring hanging feeders within their reach. One Garden BirdWatcher noted how one of the Rooks visiting her garden would haul up a bird feeder that was suspended on some string from a branch. The bird pulled up the string and then clasped it to the branch, before using its beak again to haul up another few inches, eventually reaching the feeder and the food contained within!

Whatever the species, careful observation of behaviour and interactions is sure to bring new discoveries for the Garden BirdWatcher.

Great Tit, by Amy Lewis

Goldcrest, by Mike Toms

The daily cycle

The old proverb tells us that the early bird catches the worm, and garden birds are certainly active in the early morning. However, bird feeders can be busy at other times throughout the day and into the evening, with birds' activity patterns shaped by the need to reduce competition and predation risk, as well as by their food requirements.

The costs of living

Flying requires huge amounts of energy, and small birds need to feed frequently to avoid exhausting their reserves. Fat stores are depleted overnight, and on long, cold winter nights small birds may lose up to 5% of their body weight, putting them at real risk of exhaustion or predation. Unsurprisingly, in the early morning many birds will prioritise feeding, and this burst of activity may continue for several hours after sunrise.

Feeders may also be particularly busy at the end of the day, as birds fuel up before nightfall. However, during these prime times the dominant species will crowd out smaller or subordinate birds, who need to wait and take their fill at quieter times. Bird feeders are stressful places for birds, with the risk of competition and predators, so individuals will actively avoid them during any time when feeding is not top priority.

Carrying around heavy fat stores may be a good way to guard against starvation, but fat birds are less manoeuvrable in the air and risk meeting an even quicker fate in the claws of a predator. Research into feeding patterns has shown that birds make some very complex choices about when and how much to feed, depending on the conditions. If the birds have assessed a food supply as reliable and predictable, they will often choose to keep a low 'flying weight', because they know they can top up whenever they need, including just before nightfall. Feeders in gardens are often a very reliable food source, and birds will time their visits just when their fat supplies are getting low.

Access to food

A study on Blackbirds showed that in winter, when energy requirements were high, birds prioritised feeding throughout the morning and into mid afternoon. In late summer, when the risk of starvation was much lower, birds split the day into two main foraging periods, and maintained lower fat stores. However, not all individuals can guarantee access to feeders whenever it suits them, which means that, somewhat counter-intuitively, dominant adult birds often have lower fat stores than subordinate juveniles, since the adults can guarantee access to feeders when they need. Of course, those species that rely on invertebrates, such as Robins, will tend to forage when opportunity arises throughout the day, since this food supply is by nature less predictable.

As well as evaluating the predictability of the food supply and their own position in the pecking order, birds also assess the risk of predation; a study on House Sparrows showed that birds carried significantly more fat in areas where Sparrowhawk numbers were low, as they could afford to be less manoeuvrable. The pattern of activity in one garden might, therefore, be very different from another.

Dealing with low light

While birds are driven to feeders as early as possible in the morning, it is risky and ineffective to attempt to feed before it's light enough to see properly. This is thought to be one of the reasons why birds spend the early half-light singing in the 'dawn chorus'; it's one of the only times of day when there is no choice to be made between foraging and singing. Birds will start to feed as soon as light levels are strong enough to forage efficiently, but this varies depending on their visual capabilities. A study involving BTO Garden BirdWatchers revealed that birds with large eyes relative to their body size start foraging earlier than those with smaller eyes. Large-eyed Blackbirds and Robins are the earliest to arrive at garden feeders, while, for example, Greenfinches tend to arrive much later.

Given that birds start to use feeders as soon as it is light enough for them to see properly, it's unsurprising that artificial light has been shown to affect foraging behaviour, particularly in winter. A study of Blackbirds in Germany, which involved fitting light-level recorders to a number of individuals, found that birds using areas with higher levels of light pollution started foraging earlier, and were active for longer, than those in areas where light pollution levels were lower, thus gaining important additional feeding time. Artificial lights can also stimulate birds to start singing earlier, and many a city dweller will have noticed Robins singing in the dead of night under city street lights.

Robin, by Jill Pakenham

The Robin has large eyes relative to its body size and this may be a reason why it is one of the first garden birds to arrive at bird tables early in the morning.

The early bird

However, this doesn't necessarily mean that birds in urban areas will appear earlier at bird feeders; BTO research, again involving Garden BirdWatchers, showed that arrival of birds at garden feeders during winter is delayed in more urban areas. This is thought to be because cities are generally slightly warmer than rural areas — the 'urban heat island' effect — meaning that birds don't need to use as much energy staying warm overnight. Urban and rural gardens are likely to have quite different patterns of activity, and, given all the conflicting factors that could influence each garden, it's impossible to predict exactly when birds will visit. It's always safe to assume that mornings are a good time for birdwatching, but garden feeders can be surprisingly busy in the afternoon or early evening.

Robin, by Paul Sterry/NPL.

HOT IN THE CITY TONIGHT!

It's clear that urban warmth and artificial light can have significant effects on the daily cycle of garden birds, although these effects might sometimes work in opposite directions. Garden BirdWatch participants are ideally placed to collect data on birds and urbanisation, with thousands of recorders distributed across urban, suburban and rural landscapes; this is why records from city plots are needed as much as from big rural gardens.

To help with BTO research into the possible effects of artificial light and temperature on birds, Garden BirdWatchers were recruited for the BTO Shortest Day Survey, which took place on 21st December 2004. Nearly 5,400 responses were received from the volunteers, and it is from these that we learned that birds with larger eyes (relative to their body size) arrive at garden feeders earlier in the morning, and that urban birds arrive at garden feeders later than those living in more rural areas.

This kind of research into the effects of artificial light and urbanisation will become increasingly relevant as more of our landscape becomes urbanised, and Garden BirdWatchers can contribute directly by taking part in the targeted research projects organised through the BTO's Garden Ecology Team.

Robin, by John Harding

Spring

Our garden birds respond to the seasons, fitting their breeding attempts, replacement of flight feathers and other important things into a defined seasonal cycle. Spring delivers a chorus of bird song, underlining that this is the time of year when the establishment of breeding territories is at its peak. Many birds will have already initiated their first nesting attempts, and some may be incubating eggs.

The trigger for breeding

The focus for birds in spring is reproduction; they defend territories and the resources that these contain, build nests, and bring provisions to their nestlings. Food supplies, in the form of invertebrates, are abundant, and the temperatures are generally kind, so nearly all birds in the temperate UK have evolved to rear their chicks during the spring.

Seasonal changes in bird activity are often triggered by changing day length, rather than by temperature, and some of our garden birds can start nest-building as early as February. For our winter visitors, such as Fieldfare, Redwing and Brambling, the initiation of breeding-season song may sometimes begin before the birds leave our shores. This means that it is sometimes possible to hear these birds singing in our gardens, even though they won't go on to breed here.

Getting going

Some of the earliest-nesting species are Long-tailed Tit, Blackbird and Robin, all of which can have completed nests containing eggs in March. As residents, these species do not have

to travel to their nesting areas, and can take early advantage of food and nesting sites as soon as the weather conditions are suitable. By April the breeding season is in full swing, with Goldfinch, Greenfinch, Chaffinch, Song Thrush, Dunnock, House Sparrow and Wren all nesting. During the early stages of nest building, birds can be seen carrying pieces of grass or fine twigs to weave the main structure of their nests, but for the lining, and other finishing touches, birds will seek out feathers, animal fur, spider webs and lichen; a wire mesh dispenser filled with sheep's wool or pet fur often proves popular! Great and Blue Tits can be seen bringing material to garden nest boxes from March, with their main nesting season in April.

Our migrants return

Throughout April, House Martins, Swallows and Swifts arrive back from their African wintering grounds, and many will return to individual nest sites under eaves, in outbuildings and in roof spaces respectively. Spotted Flycatchers are one of the last migrants to arrive, appearing in gardens at the end of April, though numbers of this once-common bird have plummeted by nearly 90% since the 1960s and few gardens can now boast a breeding pair. The spring migration brings the chance of unusual visitors on their way north; Wheatear, Ring Ouzel, Redstart and Pied Flycatcher are all known to drop in to gardens during migration season. Examination of arrival dates underlines that many of our summer visitors now arrive a week or more earlier than they did just a few decades ago. This pattern has been linked to our changing climate.

A quiet time in gardens?

While springtime sees an increase in nesting behaviour, the actual numbers of birds seen can be low. At this time of year birds spread out onto breeding territories, with many individuals leaving gardens for more-natural habitats, and the remaining individuals often becoming more retiring during the breeding season. Most Garden BirdWatchers see an average of just two or three Blackbirds together in their gardens during spring, and the season sees a pronounced dip in the counts of other species, such as Starling, Goldfinch, Chaffinch, Great Tit and Blue Tit. Long-tailed Tits have virtually disappeared from most gardens by late spring, although they may remain to breed in large rural gardens with scrubby areas.

While the feeders may be quiet, spring is the best time to listen to birds; most species sing only at this time of year. Blackbird, Robin, Wren and Dunnock are common garden songsters, and their songs consist of complex fluting or whistling phrases, distinguishable by their timbre and by patterns within the song. Chaffinch, Greenfinch, Great Tit and Blue Tit have much simpler songs that are easy to recognise by the pattern of the notes, while Song Thrush sings in repeated phrases. Starlings sometimes build mimicry into their stuttering, chattering songs, including the calls of other birds and human noises, such as phone ringtones!

Other garden wildlife

Spring is a great time to enjoy other garden wildlife; Peacock, Brimstone, Comma and Small Tortoiseshell are the first butterflies to appear, as these species, unlike others, overwinter as adults, and emerge from hibernation when the weather is warm enough, normally in late March or April. Queen bumblebees will also emerge from hibernation and can be seen foraging for nectar from early flowers, building up energy stores before searching for a suitable nesting site, often in dry cavities under a bank or in grass tussocks.

Common Frog, Common Toad and Grass Snake emerge in March, and the amphibians will spawn in garden ponds from April. Newts will also become more evident, returning to ponds from their overwintering sites elsewhere within the area. Both dragonflies and damselflies overwinter as larvae, and need to complete their final moult before they can emerge in adult form; species that are likely to be seen in spring include Azure Damselfly and Large Red Damselfly.

Brimstone, by John Flowerday

One of the first butterflies to emerge come spring, the Brimstone overwinters in its adult form, hidden away in Ivy or green cover.

Juvenile Robin, by John W Proudlock

Summer

The summer months from June to August can deliver an increase in activity at garden feeding stations, as recently fledged youngsters are introduced to the reliable offerings available from bird tables and hanging feeders. It is at this time of the year that we also see a seasonal peak in insect activity, with garden-visiting butterflies, bees and dragonflies much in evidence.

The next generation

In summer recently fledged juvenile birds start appearing at garden feeders, boosting counts after the springtime lull. Garden records of Great Spotted Woodpecker peak at this time of year, as the adults escort their young to peanut feeders, and increases are also seen in Blue Tit, Great Tit, House Sparrow and Starling as young birds discover garden food supplies.

These youngsters often look quite different to their parents because they are still in their first set of feathers. Feathers grown in the nest are relatively poor quality and loose-textured, as flightless nestlings are extremely vulnerable and need to grow their flight feathers as quickly as possible, with some species taking as little as two weeks to do this.

As well as this difference in quality, juveniles have no need to show their colours to attract a mate, so their first plumage is often drab, lacking the distinguishing features of the parent birds, although sometimes spotted or streaked to aid camouflage. Newly fledged Blue and Great Tits have washed-out yellow cheeks rather than bright white patches, young Greenfinches are streakier, duller versions of

their parents, while juvenile Blackbirds have light brown spots, and are sometimes mistaken for Song Thrushes. Juvenile Goldfinches lack the red face of their parents, giving them a completely different appearance, and young Robins have no red breast and are entirely covered in light brown speckles.

The need to moult

A bird's first feathers are good enough to allow them to leave the nest, but they are worn out by the end of the summer and need to be replaced. A newly fledged bird also lacks the downy under-feathers needed for warmth and weatherproofing. By the time the weather turns cold young birds of most garden species will have moulted into their adult plumage, with red feathers gradually appearing on the breasts of Robins and the faces of Goldfinches until their livery is complete.

At this point the youngsters are generally indistinguishable from the adults, although juveniles of most species do not immediately replace the large flight feathers of the wings and tail; these will have to last until next year, and by then may look relatively dull and faded.

This is particularly noticeable in first-year male Blackbirds, with their black body plumage and brown wing feathers; in other species the differences tend to be more subtle.

Adults of most garden bird species complete their full annual moult, including flight feathers, in late summer after the breeding season. By this time many adult birds look distinctly tatty after the demands of nest building, provisioning nestlings, and diving in and out of nest sites. Their feathers need to be replaced in readiness for the autumn, when many birds will migrate or disperse and need their plumage to be in good condition. Feathers are moulted in sequence, so garden birds are never flightless, but many lay low during their moult.

A long breeding season

Though the first juveniles normally appear by June, this doesn't mean the breeding season is over. Swallows, House Martins, Wrens, Robins and House Sparrows may all breed a second or third time once the chicks from their first attempt have fledged. Blackbirds and Song Thrushes routinely nest three times in a season, and may even raise four broods in particularly good years. Swifts raise just one brood per year, but are unusual in having a long and variable fledging period; chicks can be in the nest for 50 days, and normally emerge in late summer.

Wildlife delights

Summer, of course, is the best time for enjoying butterflies, bumblebees and dragonflies in the garden. Most butterfly species overwinter as caterpillars or pupae, and emerge into their adult form in the warm summer months. Some, such as Holly Blue and Large White, fit two generations into the summer and adults may be absent for several weeks before the second generation emerges.

In early summer the first worker bumblebees will hatch from eggs laid by the queens, and later in the summer new bumblebee queens, together with some males, will leave colonies to mate. Amphibians can also provide a mini wildlife spectacle in summer, with tiny froglets and toadlets emerging in huge numbers from suitable garden ponds. Some of these may fall victim to predatory cats or Grass Snakes, the latter often targeting garden ponds for the Common Frogs that may be present there.

Grass Snake, by Paul Newton

Robin, by Jill Pakenham

Autumn

The 'season of mellow fruitfulness' sees a change in the levels of garden activity. With so much food on offer elsewhere, many birds leave our gardens, shunning the food provided in hanging feeders. By late autumn, however, a change in the weather can see an upturn in the numbers of birds visiting gardens; included among these individuals may be the first of the winter migrants, arriving from overseas.

Autumn bounty

As the year turns, berries ripen in the hedgerows and seeds and nuts are abundant. Plant food supplies are at their peak and our garden birds, their breeding over and no longer tied to a territory, are free to seek out the richest pickings. At this time of year gardens can seem empty of birds, since in good years every fruiting bush is a richer and less crowded feeder than any artificial offering.

Fruits and berries, such as blackberries, sloes, rose hips, hawthorn berries, Elder berries and crab apples, form an essential part of the diet of many birds in autumn, particularly thrushes. Other birds feed on nuts, such as Beech mast, hazelnuts and acorns, as well as plant seeds, which is why leaving garden plants to set seed can benefit birds at this time of year. Energy-rich food sources are necessary as birds are laying down fat stores, either to buffer against freezing temperatures to come or to fuel their migration to warmer climes. The result of this focus on natural foods is that we lose some of our most familiar birds from gardens; Blackbird numbers fall in September and October, with Garden BirdWatchers seeing an average of just one or two birds together. Garden counts of Dunnock, Robin and Great Spotted Woodpecker all hit their annual lows in autumn, a pattern repeated across the years.

Fickle nature

The success of the natural crops depends on the weather during the previous spring and summer. Mild sunny weather early in the year gives shrubs time to flower, be pollinated and set fruit or seed, but late spring frosts or summer storms can lead to bare hedgerows come autumn. In years when natural pickings are slim, birds will turn to gardens, and the yields of local hedgerows can be used to predict which birds will be seen at home.

As natural food supplies are depleted over the course of the autumn season, times get harder for birds, and they turn back to garden feeders to see them through. Birds that seem to abandon gardens in early autumn have often returned by November, and may be joined by species like Stock Dove, which often only turn to supplementary food at this time of year. The timing of this return will depend, in part, on the weather.

In early autumn Swallows line the wires and House Martins pass overhead, with most having departed by the end of October. The Swifts have already gone; this species is one of the earliest summer migrants to leave, with just a few stragglers lingering into September. Spotted Flycatchers are also on the move in early autumn, and may be seen stopping in gardens for a day or so on passage. This is the time of year that Garden BirdWatchers are most likely to discover off-course rarities, with jewels such as Yellow-browed Warbler or Wryneck blown in from the Continent on autumn gales.

Autumn arrivals

While many birds pass through gardens in autumn, others are here to stay. The first Redwings are heard overhead in September, and Fieldfares and Bramblings are seen in gardens from October. Less conspicuously, the ranks of many of our year-round residents are swelled by arrivals from continental Europe; the Chaffinches and Goldcrests present in October may well be Scandinavian breeders. At this time of year first-year birds outnumber adults,

as winter mortality has not yet reduced their numbers, so the counts of winter visitors and residents alike will generally reflect the success of the preceding breeding season.

Autumn can be a time for increased activity for our other garden wildlife. Young Grass Snakes hatch in early September from eggs laid in leaf litter or compost heaps, while Hedgehogs will start searching for hibernation sites in which to spend the winter.

Most adult butterflies die off at the end of the summer, with the next generation already hibernating in larval form or as eggs. However, a few overwinter as adults and, like birds and mammals, they need to lay down fat stores in order to survive the cold weather and the long period without feeding opportunities that lies ahead. Brimstone, Comma, Peacock and Small Tortoiseshell can be seen feeding on late flowers in preparation for hibernation. Later into the autumn they may be disturbed from outbuildings, where they will have been seeking shelter from the elements and from predatory birds and small mammals, for which they would make a welcome meal.

Redwing, by John Harding

Some of the first Redwings to reach our shores during the autumn months may visit gardens to feed on berries, though they tend to do this only if feeding conditions elsewhere are unfavourable. Overnight frost can restrict access to soil- or surface-dwelling invertebrates and push birds into our gardens instead.

Robin, by John Harding

Winter

Garden feeding stations become busy with the arrival of the first winter frosts and we usually see a sharp upturn in the reporting rates that emerge from the weekly counts of BTO Garden BirdWatchers. Just how busy the gardens will continue to be throughout the rest of the winter is very much driven by the size of natural seed and berry crops and the vagaries of the winter weather.

A busy time of year

Though gardens may seem lifeless in winter, this is traditionally the busiest time of year at bird tables and hanging feeders, since many birds will rely on supplementary food to survive. Energy-rich foods such as peanuts, fat products and sunflower hearts are particularly popular with birds throughout the winter, and during spells of freezing weather any open water in a pond or bird bath can also attract birds to drink. Most birds do not hold territories at this time of year – though Wrens may hold small feeding territories in some habitats – and will congregate around reliable food sources. Often this will lead to increased conflict for birds, as well as potentially spectacular sightings for Garden BirdWatchers.

When the cupboard is bare

Natural winter food supplies for birds include invertebrate larvae, seeds, and the remains of the autumn fruit. During mild winters much of this food remains accessible, but if the ground and vegetation are covered in snow, or frozen solid, birds are unable to forage and survival rates can be very low. Conifer and Alder cones provide food supplies for birds such as Coal Tit, Nuthatch and finches, but the size of cone crops naturally varies from one winter to the next. At times, natural food supplies may be extremely scarce, and this is when birds can flock to gardens in huge numbers. In some winters Siskins hardly come into gardens at all, but in other years numbers peak in late February. Some species not normally associated with gardens, such as Pied Wagtail and Black-headed Gull, come in search of food during cold weather, and Long-tailed Tit numbers peak in gardens around the turn of the year.

Filling the 'hungry gap'

Later in the winter many Garden BirdWatchers are surprised to see species under the bird feeders that are normally thought of as farmland birds. Research into farmland birds has identified a 'hungry gap' in late winter when modern arable systems do not leave enough food for seed-eating birds in the wider countryside, and this is when Yellowhammers, Reed Buntings and Tree Sparrows move into gardens. These sightings, interesting in themselves, also prove the value of garden resources in buffering changes in the countryside. Most farmland visitors turn up at more rural gardens which are, after all, closer to the farmland habitats where these species breed, though some do reach our suburbs.

Foreign visitors

Redwing, Fieldfare and Brambling are common winter visitors that do not generally breed here, arriving mostly from northern Europe and Scandinavia in autumn and departing in March. As is the case for resident birds, the numbers seen are controlled by natural food supplies. In years with good tree and berry crops in Scandinavia relatively few migrants will travel to the UK, but if these natural food supplies fail the numbers will be higher.

The Waxwing takes this to extremes; most winters very few Waxwings are seen in the UK, but when a productive breeding season is followed by a failure of the berry crop in their normal wintering grounds, entire populations of this exotic bird will fly south, with thousands arriving in the UK in 'irruption years'. Easterly winds and particularly cold snaps can result in one-off movements that may surprise Garden BirdWatchers, with birds such as Woodcock turning up on suburban lawns in midwinter.

Other wildlife

While many mammals lay up during cold weather, December to February is the best time to see Foxes in gardens. This is their mating season, and they can be particularly vocal. Frogs, toads, newts, bats, Hedgehogs and queen bumblebees are normally hibernating or dormant during the winter months, but all of these species can be seen to emerge and forage should temperatures rise for a few days in a row.

It's predicted that our winters will continue to be warm and that the pattern of extended periods of cold weather, with associated snow and frost, may become the exception rather than the rule over the coming years. These changing weather patterns could have implications for many garden inhabitants and, in particular, for the numbers of winter visitors that we see using our gardens.

CHANGING FACES AT BIRD TABLES

It's not just cold snaps that bring birds to the garden in winter; warming temperatures can also mean unexpected visitors. Blackcaps — normally summer migrants — have started to overwinter more frequently, and are often seen at garden feeding stations.

Information from bird ringing shows that our wintering Blackcaps, rather than being resident breeders deciding to stay put, actually originate from central Europe. These birds have evolved a new migration strategy, which sees some of them migrate north-west to the UK rather than heading south to the Mediterranean. Examination of the BTO Garden BirdWatch data set shows that where these individuals spend the winter within the UK is influenced both by winter temperatures and by food availability, particularly the increased amounts of fats and sunflower hearts provided in gardens. It is the first time that a bird has been shown to evolve a new migration strategy in response to food provided by humans.

Male Blackcap being ringed, by Dawn Balmer

Swallow, by Laurie Campbell/NPL

Movements and migration

Birds are highly mobile, and the power of flight is fundamental to how they use the landscape. All are capable of migration, but there are huge differences in how far they normally fly. Some birds seen in British gardens are very unlikely to have moved more than a few kilometres from where they hatched, some never fly over water, while others will fly thousands of kilometres around the globe every year.

Why do birds migrate?

The reason birds migrate is ultimately to increase their reproductive success. Birds travel to the best areas to find a territory, a mate, and resources to feed themselves and raise their chicks. At other times of year, when they are not tied to a nest site, their aim is to stay in the best condition possible. For some species this means staying put and saving energy, while others travel to the areas with the richest food supplies; strategies which take into account competition for resources and the costs and risks of the journey.

Migratory habits are linked to body shape. Wrens, with their short wings, are clearly adapted for burrowing around in vegetation rather than transoceanic flights. Another related factor is diet: birds that feed on invertebrates can take advantage of a glut of protein-rich food during the British summer, but the bounty soon passes, and species that feed on flying insects must switch to other food supplies or travel south to tropical climates. Most garden birds tend to be seed-eaters or generalists, attracted to seed-based bird food, so garden bird lists tend to include relatively few insect-

eating summer migrants. The main exceptions are Swift, Swallow and House Martin, all of which are attracted to gardens for the nesting opportunities rather than the food supplies. However, a number of garden species are winter visitors; these are mainly plant-eating or generalist species that breed in northern Europe, and which migrate to Britain when conditions on their breeding grounds become inhospitable in winter.

Finding the way

Migrating any significant distance has to involve feeding up to build fat supplies beforehand – some small song birds may even double their body weight – and possibly also finding places to refuel on the way. The fact that tiny birds can physically manage to travel immense distances is incredible, but even more so is how they find their way. Many theories have been proposed as to how birds can navigate, unguided by parents, to their wintering grounds and back again, and the current research suggests that a number of methods are used in combination. In some species the start of migration is triggered by dwindling resources, in others by changes in day length. However, departures from equatorial latitudes cannot be prompted by day length since this does not change, so it is believed to be entirely internally controlled.

Most song birds migrate at night, and experiments have shown that they orientate by the stars and the earth's magnetic field, while following pre-programmed flight distances and directions. While the general route can be flown by innate instinct, birds can return to a previous nesting or wintering site with remarkable accuracy, which has to also involve remarkable feats of memory. Migrating birds also need to take into account weather conditions, delaying their journeys until the weather is suitable, and re-orientating, if possible, after being blown off course.

TRACKING BIRDS

The BTO Ringing Scheme involves fitting uniquely-numbered metal rings to the legs of birds so that individuals can be identified. Today this information is used to calculate survival rates and breeding success, to help us understand changes in bird populations, but one of the initial aims of marking birds in this way was to find out where they went. Birds have been ringed in Britain and Ireland for over 100 years, and many thousands have been reported from other parts of the world, building an enormous database of movements.

While marking birds with numbered metal rings is an effective way to study migration routes, many ringed birds are never found, and the finding locations are biased towards areas with human observers. Modern technology means that individual birds can now be fitted with tiny tags to record their movements.

Smaller tags called geolocators record the location of a bird over its migration but need to be retrieved to download the data, while larger tags can transmit their location via satellites. The technologies involved are getting ever smaller, and birds as light as Swifts have been fitted with geolocators, revealing new information about time spent at stopover areas in the Congo Basin.

A BTO bird ringer processing a Greenfinch, by David Tipling

Migratory strategies

A number of typical British garden birds can be classed as sedentary. Once established in a breeding territory, adults of these species will not make significant seasonal movements, though they may range over several kilometres throughout the year. Birds that are likely to remain in the same area all year round include House Sparrow, Blue Tit, Great Tit, Long-tailed Tit, Nuthatch, Treecreeper and the woodpeckers. All of these species are well adapted to the British winter, feeding either on nuts and seeds, or foraging for overwintering invertebrate larvae, and have no need to migrate. Wrens and Dunnocks are insectivores that are sedentary in Britain as they are able to find enough food year round, but in other, colder parts of their range the invertebrate life is insufficient to sustain them in winter, and they are migratory.

Even sedentary species normally need to establish their own territories away from their parents and thereby avoid inbreeding. In their first autumn and winter young birds set out for pastures new, and during this dispersal period even the most unadventurous species are capable of making long movements, with Blue Tits and Wrens occasionally travelling overseas. It is for this reason that 'vagrant' rare birds are quite often juveniles, perhaps getting it very wrong on their first migration.

Should I stay or should I go?

Many British bird populations are partially migratory, meaning that some individuals will migrate southwards during the winter while others will stay close to their breeding grounds. Chaffinch, Goldfinch and Greenfinch are partial migrants, as are thrushes, including Blackbird and Robin, as well as Goldcrest, Pied Wagtail and Starling. British populations of many of these birds are substantially augmented in winter by migratory individuals from Scandinavia and elsewhere within northern Europe. Studies of migratory behaviour have shown that this is genetically controlled; migratory individuals are more likely to have offspring which themselves migrate. This genetic variation means that populations can quickly change behaviour in response to changing environmental conditions, as the genes for migration or for staying put can spread through the population depending on which is more advantageous at the time.

Alongside the migratory Blackbirds, Robins and Chaffinches that arrive from northern breeding populations in the autumn are birds that are seen in Britain only in winter. Redwing, Fieldfare and Brambling are the commonest winter migrants seen in gardens, arriving from September and departing in April. The numbers vary from winter to winter as birds respond to the severity of the conditions and available food supplies further north. When particularly cold weather coincides with food shortages, counts can rocket in British gardens, with winter thrushes congregating under bird feeders. Migration in response to environmental conditions is taken to extremes by Waxwing, which makes very irregular winter migrations, known as irruptions, when compelled by food shortages.

Always on the move

The most predictable and obvious migrations are made by our summer visitors; Swift, Swallow, House Martin and Spotted Flycatcher will return to the same nesting sites year after year, often arriving around the same date, in order to optimise their breeding success. These birds travel the longest distances, with Swallows spending the winter 6,000 miles to the south in South Africa, and British-breeding Swifts reaching Mozambique. While their journeys may be disrupted or delayed by adverse weather, these long-distance migrations are not controlled by environmental conditions to the same extent as those of winter or partial migrants.

However, these long-distance migrations involve crossing the Mediterranean and the Sahara desert, and migrant birds rely on important 'stop-over sites', where they can rest and build up fat supplies during these arduous journeys. Loss of these sites can be devastating, and overgrazing, drought, deforestation and agricultural intensification all affect the habitats that vulnerable migrant birds need, both in their wintering areas and during their demanding journeys.

This map shows the complex migration patterns of two familiar garden birds. Goldfinch is a partial migrant and some individuals from our breeding population migrate south to winter in France, Spain and Portugal. Some of our wintering Blackbirds originate from further east, while others pass through during autumn on their way to wintering areas located further south.

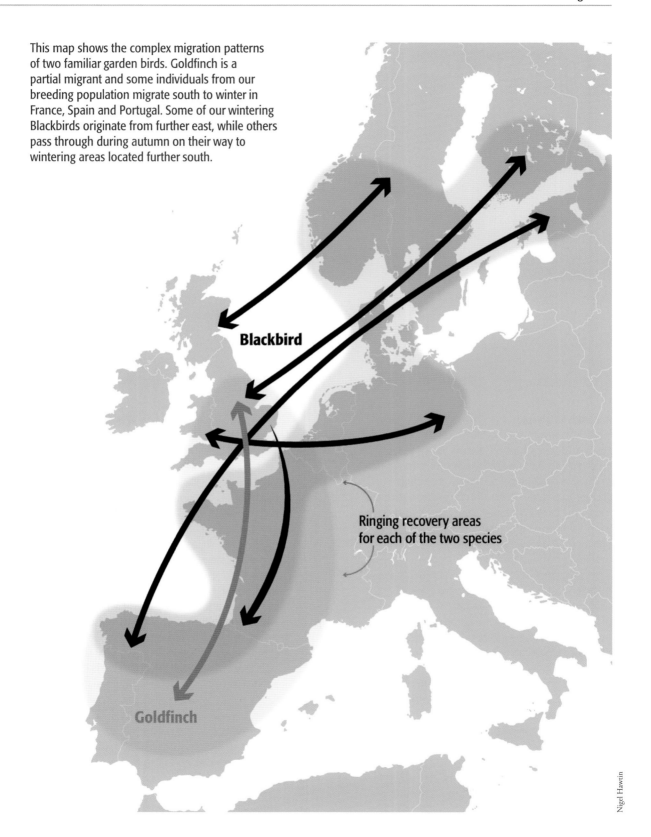

Blackbird

Ringing recovery areas
for each of the two species

Goldfinch

Nigel Hawtin

Sparrowhawk, by Edmund Fellowes

Life and death

Given the very large numbers of birds that live around many of us, it is perhaps surprising that we do not see more evidence of the life and death struggles that they face on a daily basis. Predation, disease and starvation are just some of the risks that impact individual birds and shape the size of their populations.

A short existence

House Sparrows can live for 12 years, Great Tits for 13 years and Blackbirds for 14 years, according to bird ringing studies, but the lives of most individual garden birds are much shorter than that. Many don't make it out of the nest, and generally fewer than half of fledglings will survive their first year, meaning they never produce offspring themselves.

This high mortality of nestlings and young birds is normal in wild populations of smaller birds, and is the reason why birds have a relatively high reproductive rate. A single pair of Blue Tits might lay 10 eggs in a single nest, and a pair of Blackbirds might produce four clutches of four eggs over the course of the breeding season. If all eggs hatched, all the resulting chicks fledged, and all survived to breed themselves the following year, in just a few years we would be overrun with unimaginable numbers of birds. This doesn't happen, because their breeding strategies take into account that only a fraction of the young will survive to breed themselves.

The fact that high mortality is normal, however, does not make it easy to watch.

It can be distressing to see Magpies raiding Blackbird nests and Sparrowhawks taking juvenile Blue Tits off the bird feeders. It may seem logical to assume that the loss of these eggs, nestlings and juveniles will result in a reduction in the size of next year's breeding population, and will therefore affect the overall numbers of the species.

However, it should be remembered that bird populations are generally limited by other natural processes, such as competition for food over the winter, and individuals taken by predators reduce the numbers that are lost to other causes. This has been confirmed by research into bird populations, which has shown that the total numbers are not generally affected by the local densities of predatory birds such as Sparrowhawk, Magpie and Jay.

Causes of mortality

While predation is the most noticeable form of mortality, birds are killed by starvation and exposure as surely as by predators. Survival is hardest during the winter, when garden birds struggle to meet their daily energy requirements, and hardest of all for inexperienced first-year birds that have never had to cope with winter conditions. Once an individual bird has survived its first winter this experience stands it in good stead, and overwinter survival rates are often higher for birds entering subsequent winters. Nevertheless, harsh conditions take their toll even on adults; on average, only six or seven adult Blackbirds out of every 10 are expected to make it through each winter, and only the very lucky or successful ones will make it to the ripe old age of 10 years or more.

Breeding-season conditions are kinder, but food supplies can still limit bird numbers. While many adult birds feed on seeds, nearly all our common garden species supply their nestlings with invertebrates, such as worms, caterpillars and flying insects. Parent birds aim to raise as many young as possible, but any change in conditions which reduces the availability of invertebrate food will mean that not all the young will survive.

The challenges of urban living

Bird populations may be well adapted to natural predators and weather conditions, but our modern human-dominated environments present both novel opportunities and unprecedented challenges. British householders spend an estimated £200 million a year providing supplementary food for wild birds, a significant and novel resource. We know that Blackcaps have evolved an entirely new wintering strategy fuelled by garden food supplies, and it's thought that garden bird feeding may have helped to boost the numbers of other species, such as Goldfinch, by reducing the numbers that die from lack of food over the winter. As well as supplementary food, the provision of nest boxes may help populations in areas where they are limited by lack of suitable nest sites.

However, human environments also contain significant hazards for birds. There are an estimated eight million domestic cats in the

Greenfinches, by Jill Pakenham

The 2006 outbreak of the disease trichomonosis brought about a pronounced decline in our Greenfinch population, reducing numbers in the regions of peak mortality by 35% in just over a year.

UK. The populations of most predators are both sustained and limited by the amount of prey they are able to catch, but there are no such limits on cat numbers, so they are capable of disproportionately affecting their prey populations. While the effect of cat predation on overall bird numbers has not been fully quantified, research has shown that the survival rates of young fledglings are much lower in neighbourhoods with lots of cats.

Human environments contain many other hazards for birds, including collisions with vehicles or buildings. However, the most serious effects that human activities have on bird numbers are indirect, through large-scale degradation of their natural habitats. Agricultural intensification, development, changes in management, climate change and pollution have all reduced the suitability of natural habitats for birds, both in this country and on their migration routes and wintering grounds. These factors are also thought to have been behind large-scale declines in the invertebrates that many birds rely on, and lack of food has been linked to declines in many common bird species, due to reduced survival of both adult birds and chicks in the nest.

Parasites and disease can also limit bird numbers. For example, avian malaria is widely found in birds across the world, including the UK, and while its presence does not always cause direct mortality, it is thought that an infection will reduce an individual's chances of survival during difficult times. Some diseases do cause direct mortality, particularly when a new strain emerges. In the UK Greenfinches suffered high mortality due to the trichomonosis epidemic, caused by a protozoan parasite. Although known from pigeons and doves, the disease has spread through finch populations since 2005, causing large-scale declines in Greenfinch populations.

Blackbird, by John Harding

Winter can be a tough time for many garden birds, with cold weather and snow restricting access to food and water and leading to increased mortality.

WHAT IS HAPPENING TO OUR BIRDS?

The first step in conserving our bird populations is to understand what factors cause their numbers to go up or down. The BTO runs a number of surveys in which volunteer birdwatchers collect valuable information about birds, including the overall population trends, the number of young produced, and the number of adult birds that survive from year to year. This information can help with conservation action; for example, if we know a species is declining due to low overwinter survival, it's clear we need to direct our efforts towards boosting winter food supplies, rather than improving nesting habitats.

HOW ARE NUMBERS CHANGING?

The BTO/JNCC/RSPB Breeding Bird Survey (BBS) measures how the numbers of common birds vary over the long term. Each year volunteers make two springtime visits to an allocated 1-km square and count all the birds seen or heard using standardised methods. These survey sites are randomly chosen, and form a network covering the whole country, meaning that the changes in bird numbers recorded are representative of the national population. This survey tells us how the breeding populations of common birds are increasing or declining across different parts of the country, which may stimulate further investigations.

BIRD SURVIVAL

To understand how well birds survive we need to be able to identify individuals, so for over 100 years Ringing Scheme volunteers have been marking birds with numbered lightweight metal leg rings. Today we have two ringing surveys that collect detailed information on birds; firstly, the Constant Effort Sites (CES) scheme involves the capture and marking of birds to investigate how the numbers of adults and juveniles change over time. The other, the Retrapping Adults for Survival (RAS) scheme, involves standardised monitoring of individual bird populations to calculate survival rates. Ringing also tells us about bird movements.

BREEDING ECOLOGY AND PRODUCTIVITY

The BTO Nest Record Scheme (NRS) involves volunteers finding and following the progress of nests, which gives us information on the numbers of eggs laid, hatching rates, timing of breeding and survival of nestlings. When combined with the information on annual survival of adult birds, collected by ringing surveys, this can be used to identify the causes of population declines. Information from the Nest Record Scheme provided some of the first evidence of the impacts of a changing climate on bird populations, revealing that birds had begun nesting earlier than they did a few decades previously.

HOW LONG DO BIRDS LIVE?

Since adult birds of one species generally all look alike, it's often hard to know whether the individuals we see in our gardens are the same ones as in previous years. Occasionally birds will have distinctive plumage features or behaviours that allow them to be identified as individuals, and, given good luck, may be seen to survive for many years. However, mortality rates are high, and on average most individual birds only survive for a few years.

Species	Longevity record	Typical lifespan
Grey Heron	23 years 9 months 2 days	5 years
Sparrowhawk	17 years 1 month 11 days	4 years
Woodpigeon	17 years 8 months 19 days	3 years
Collared Dove	18 years 2 days	3 years
Swift	17 years 11 months 5 days	9 years
Great Spotted Woodpecker	11 years 1 month 15 days	not known
Goldcrest	4 years 2 months 24 days	2 years
Blue Tit	10 years 3 months 10 days	3 years
Great Tit	13 years 11 months 5 days	3 years
Coal Tit	9 years 2 months 25 days	2 years
Long-tailed Tit	8 years 11 months	2 years
Nuthatch	9 years 9 months 9 days	2 years
Wren	7 years 3 months 6 days	2 years
Starling	17 years 7 months 25 days	5 years
Blackbird	14 years 9 months 15 days	3 years
Robin	8 years 4 months 30 days	2 years
Dunnock	11 years 3 months 7 days	2 years
House Sparrow	12 years 12 days	3 years
Chaffinch	13 years 11 months 26 days	3 years
Greenfinch	12 years 8 months 26 days	2 years
Goldfinch	8 years 8 months 4 days	2 years

Goldcrest, by John Dunn; Woodpigeon, by Paul Newton; Grey Heron, by Edmund Fellowes

Robin, by John Harding

Gardens and wildlife

Mike Toms

The importance of gardens

Step outside your back door and there is a good chance that you will be stepping into a garden that is visited by birds and other wildlife. Just how well this garden is used will depend on where it is located, what habitats are present nearby and what features it contains. If there is bird food on offer and a place to nest then it is more likely to be visited by birds.

An important contribution

Gardens are the place where many people first encounter wildlife and learn to love it. Until recently, however, their importance was underestimated as a habitat for birds and other wildlife. Part of the problem was that protecting common species was not a priority but now that it has been realised some common species, such as House Sparrow, are under threat, people have turned their attention to gardens. The other issue was that gardens used to be somewhere to grow food or to display exotic plants. While these two things are still a major feature of many gardens, managing them for wildlife has also become more important.

Within the UK, about 87% of households have some sort of a garden, which means that there are approximately 23 million gardens. While these vary in size depending on where they are, overall they cover around 4,330 square kilometres of the UK, which is an area one-fifth the size of Wales and is larger than the total area of sites designated for the protection of wildlife. Gardens are extremely important in built-up areas, providing a corridor for mobile urban species and a refuge for others. In addition, in contrast to the perception of some of the public, wildlife will still use neat gardens as long as they provide key resources.

Habitat

No bird species in Britain or Ireland can be said to rely solely on gardens but a large number of bird do use them to a certain degree. Depending on the species, gardens can provide resources for nesting, feeding and shelter; with changing practices in land use and increasing urbanisation, these resources are becoming increasingly important for a large range of birds.

Nesting

Whether in the form of a purpose-built nest box or Ivy on a fence, nesting opportunities are extremely important in gardens – though some species use them more than others. The BTO Garden Nesting Survey, which ran in 2010, found that over half of the gardens which took part in the study recorded Blackbirds nesting, closely followed by Blue Tit. These two birds do have conspicuous nesting habits, unlike other common garden species like Dunnock which are more furtive, but it is clear that gardens can provide the right nesting resources. Interestingly, the survey found that there has been a significant underestimation of the number of birds that do breed in gardens, especially for some of the commonest British bird species.

Feeding

As with nesting, some birds are more likely to use gardens for food resources than others but even with our more common garden bird species, such as Blackbird, we see seasonal patterns of use. Garden BirdWatch data show that Blackbirds exhibit an 'autumn trough' in reports, during which they move out of gardens into the wider countryside. This coincides with their moulting period, but also when the berries are at their best outside gardens. Garden BirdWatch data also provide clues as to when natural food crops are good or when they are not. Siskins, for example, are reported from more gardens in years when the Sitka Spruce crop, which makes up a large part of their diet, is poor. Garden bird feeding stations offer a reliable source of food and one that is usually used by birds when it is the best option available. Birds can experience hardship at any time of year, which is why they can be seen using our garden bird feeders year round. Supplementary food takes the pressure off adult birds in the summer if invertebrates are hard to come by; it helps birds in the autumn when seed or berry crops are poor and it provides resources in harsh weather. Providing supplementary food also helps species that would traditionally have been making the most of other resources in the countryside. These birds rely on seeds for most of the year but with changing farming practices food can be harder to come by in late winter. We often see a peak in garden reports of Reed Bunting and Yellowhammer in February and March, especially in colder winters.

Importance for other wildlife

It is not just for birds that gardens provide important resources. Pollinators benefit from the flowers that are planted and food plants can be provided for their larvae. By encouraging invertebrates, food is provided for insectivores including reptiles and mammals. Garden ponds are also becoming increasingly important. Ponds in the countryside are constantly being filled in or polluted and there are now fewer than 430,000 left in Britain. It is estimated that 16% of gardens contain ponds, which could mean over three million ponds, providing an important resource for amphibians.

Male Blackbird, by Mike Toms

Roughly a third of our Blackbirds now breed in our towns and cities, living alongside humans and exploiting the opportunities on offer.

Starling, by Edmund Fellowes

Attracting birds

If you provide food and water, and manage your garden in a wildlife-friendly manner, then you will increase your chances of attracting a range of birds to your garden. Of course, you cannot conjure up just any bird, since those that visit will be determined by which species occur locally and by which of these are likely to make use of a garden and the opportunities on offer.

Attracting birds

To attract birds to a garden all year round, four things should be provided: food, water, resources for nesting and shelter. Encouraging birds to use gardens has many positives. It can improve the nesting prospects for some species, provide valuable food resources at different times of year and be an oasis in urban areas. On top of this, it is great for humans, allowing close encounters with species that might not normally be seen at close quarters. There are hazards in gardens, however, that need to be thought about; these include the risk of disease, predators and window strikes.

Local habitats

The community of birds that uses a garden will, in part, be determined by where the garden is and by what habitats are around it, so it is important to consider what birds might be in the area before adding features to a garden. Many gardens are isolated from what would be regarded as 'natural' habitats, and are usually surrounded by other gardens, but they can still act as refuges for birds and many other species of animal and plant.

While rural gardens attract a wide range of species, they also tend to attract more location-specific species as well. For example, gardens near farmland may see an influx of farmland specialists such as Yellowhammer or Reed Bunting in late winter. Gardens closer to woodland may see more Great Spotted Woodpeckers or Great Tits. However, rural gardens may also see a much larger turnover of birds, as there are more choices for food and nesting resources in the surrounding habitat.

Gardens in suburban areas attract a wide range of species, but these may be more regular visitors, as options here are reduced. Urban gardens are often overlooked as valuable habitats for birds and other wildlife, but they become increasingly important as green spaces are destroyed for development. These gardens attract their own community of birds, with Feral Pigeon, Black-headed Gull and Woodpigeon overwhelmingly seen in urban areas. Bird communities can change, however, as seen with the declines of House Sparrow and Starling; they used to be more common in urban and suburban areas, but now are seen more in rural gardens.

Location

A large part of what determines a garden bird community is where the garden is located in the country. While many of the common garden bird species are found throughout the UK, there are others that are scarce in parts of the country. Nuthatch, for example, has been expanding its range slowly northward, but is still scarce across large parts of Scotland; Nuthatch has yet to reach Ireland and seems unlikely to do so soon. Tree Sparrows, on the other hand, are now absent from large swathes of southern and western Britain but have been increasing further north. Other species, seen across the country, are more likely to be seen in some areas than others – such as Blackcap, which favours southern and western gardens, especially in the winter.

Internal features

While the habitat around a garden does play a part in determining what birds will visit it, internal factors, such as its size, plants and water features, are also important. Larger gardens are likely to attract more birds but this is generally for two reasons. Firstly they are usually found in rural areas, and secondly there is more space to create micro-habitats within the garden.

Whatever size a garden is, there are key features that should be provided so that birds are catered for all year. Food sources are vital, whether supplementary food provided at feeding stations or natural foods. Natural food sources can be provided in many different ways, ranging from berries to seeds to plants that encourage insects. Food is important all year round and can be a lifeline to a range of different species depending on the season. Water is also a valuable resource in gardens and may attract birds that would not normally feed in a garden. Water can be supplied in the form of a bird bath or a pond.

Cover is extremely important for garden birds for both nesting and shelter. BTO research found that Wren, Robin and Woodpigeon were more likely to be found in gardens that provided year-round cover, rather than those that provided it just for the summer. While hedges or shrubs are ideal for nesting, for smaller gardens evergreen climbing plants such as Holly and Ivy fulfil the same role.

Busy bird feeders, by Edmund Fellowes

Gardening for wildlife

Cuckoo bumblebee, by Mike Toms

Wildlife-friendly gardening has never been more popular, and more and more of us are making the effort to manage our gardens in ways that benefit birds and other creatures. The amount that you choose to do for wildlife is up to you, and even small things – such as putting in a pond or creating a woodpile – can make a big difference.

Get gardening

With a growing interest in gardening for wildlife, it is not hard adapting or starting a new garden to benefit a whole range of different species. It doesn't matter if the garden is a balcony, one in the middle of the city or a large garden in the countryside; wildlife can be encouraged in. The key is to provide choice in the form of microhabitats, so that there are areas for wildlife to breed, shelter, feed and bathe. A range of microhabitats will also provide a stable, diverse system that is less likely to be overtaken by just one species or group of organisms, meaning there should be fewer problems with pest and weed species.

Encourage birds

While supplementary food and a bird bath or pond are obvious ways to attract birds to a garden, providing suitable nesting habitat is also crucial. Birds that breed early in the season often do so before deciduous trees are in leaf, so evergreens provide crucial cover. Native bushes such as Holly and Yew are ideal but, if starting from scratch, introduced conifers may grow more quickly. If space is limited, Ivy is good as a climbing plant on a wall or fence and it also provides nectar for insects and berries for birds, making this a good all-round plant to have in your garden.

Broad-leaved trees come into their own later in the breeding season, providing structures favoured by species such as the finches, which like to nest in the fork of a branch or against a tree trunk. Shrubs with thick, thorny cover are often popular as they provide an extra deterrent to predators. Hawthorn is an ideal native – there are a couple of different species – as it also provides berries later in the year, but the non-native *Berberis* and some of the *Pyracantha* species are also good.

Berries are a great way to attract birds in the autumn and winter, especially migrant thrushes that normally visit only when the weather is particularly harsh or berry crops elsewhere are poor. Different fruits are available at particular times of year and different birds have specific preferences so, if there is space, plant a few different varieties. Some fruits are around for a while, such as Holly, partly because they're long-lasting but also because they may be less popular than others.

If space is limited, hawthorn haws seem to be the most popular berries, according to scientific studies, liked by Blackbird, Redwing and Fieldfare. However, Song Thrush and Mistle Thrush seem to prefer sloes. Yew and Elder berries will also be taken by Blackbird and Song Thrush. Birds have been shown to use berry colour as an indicator of nutritional value, favouring red and black berries in the UK, so some introduced plants will also be used, but you may wish to avoid those with white berries as these seem to be less attractive to birds.

Attracting invertebrates

Providing the right habitats for invertebrates will not only help them but also benefit the insectivorous birds, mammals, amphibians and reptiles that feed on them. Providing pollen and nectar sources throughout the year is key as both are important to a range of pollinators. Research published in 2015 showed that, while native plants are preferable for attracting a large abundance and diversity of invertebrates, the best strategy for supporting pollinating insects in gardens is to use a mix of flowering plants from different countries and regions. Exotic plants from the southern hemisphere can be used to extend the flowering season as they tend to flower later in the year. It is advised to avoid certain cultivars though, especially those with double flowers, as they have been shown to be less beneficial.

It is not just flowers that attract invertebrates to the garden. With butterflies, it is important to think about the whole life cycle and to provide food plants for the butterflies to lay their eggs on. Consider the location and habitat surrounding the garden to determine which species might visit your garden. There is no point in using specific plants for Holly Blue, for example, if the garden is in northern Scotland. Location of the plants is also important within the garden; butterflies prefer to feed in sunny, sheltered parts of the garden with large visible displays of flowers. Red Valerian and Goat Willow are attractive to both butterflies and moths, and moths also like plants which produce their scent in the evening such as honeysuckle and jasmine species.

A patch of wilderness

Wild patches in the garden are great for encouraging invertebrates that amphibians, reptiles and Hedgehogs like to feed on. They also provide cover for a range of species whether they are passing through the garden, or staying. Leaving log piles, decaying wood and fallen leaves will also encourage more wildlife to use the garden. Avoid using chemicals such as insecticides, molluscicides and herbicides, as these are likely to have knock-on effects on non-target species, perhaps by reducing prey populations. Many wildlife gardeners prefer to garden organically.

Slow-worm, by Amy Lewis

House Sparrow, by John Harding

Foods and feeding

Food is perhaps the most important thing when it comes to attracting birds into your garden. By providing a range of different foods, and by using different feeders and feeding locations, you can provide for many species of bird, meeting their needs and feeding preferences. Understanding what the birds prefer to feed on is key to deciding what to feed and where.

History of feeding

While the history of feeding birds started here in the early 19th century, the practice of feeding garden birds really took off at the beginning of the 20th century with people throwing out kitchen scraps and bread during the winter. Even in the late 1980s leftovers were still the main foods being provided for garden birds, though peanuts were also encouraged outside the breeding season. It is only relatively recently that the garden bird food industry as we know it has taken off.

The variety of bird foods and feeders that we see today has dramatically influenced which species of birds now visit our gardens. The industry has been estimated to be worth over £200 million a year with over half of British adults providing supplementary food in their gardens. This expansion in the availability of bird food has succeeded in attracting new bird species to our gardens. Data from the BTO's Garden Bird Feeding Survey (GBFS), which started in the winter of 1969/70, show that in the 1970s an average garden attracted 16 species to food between October and March. By 2010 this figure had risen to 23 species.

Feeding all year round

Longstanding advice to not feed birds during the breeding season was based on the fact that many foods were thought to be unsuitable for growing chicks, whereas the young of most garden bird species are fed on insects and nest studies show that adults rarely bring in supplementary food. This additional food is important for the adults, however, as it provides a quick and easy energy source. It is now widely accepted in the UK that year-round feeding can be beneficial, because birds can face challenges throughout the year. Food provision in late winter is crucial for many species as natural foods become scarce; in the breeding season supplementary food supports adult birds and newly independent young; feeding in the autumn can be especially helpful in years where natural food crops are in short supply.

Does it have an impact?

Fat-based bird foods are thought to help birds with a calorific boost, especially in the winter, and attract a wide range of species. Recent scientific studies, however, found that these fat-based products might not be good for all bird species. Two studies into the effects on tit species found that there was a link with lower productivity in the following breeding season. In contrast, a study looking at Great Spotted Woodpecker showed that productivity increased. More work is needed on the overall effects of fat-based foods; it might be that over longer periods of time these foods actually have a positive effect on bird populations through improved survival.

Supplementary feeding does appear to have affected which species now feed in our gardens. BTO research found that there was a strong link between the provision of bird food in gardens and the increasing numbers of overwintering Blackcaps. This study found that garden supplementary food has helped Blackcaps to evolve a successful new migration route, as traditionally most would head south from central Europe rather than north-west.

Different types of feeders

There are many different types of feeders available on the market now. Hanging feeders are ideal for providing seed and peanuts; they should be well made and easy to take apart for cleaning. Metal feeders are best, though more expensive, as they usually last longer and are less easily damaged by squirrels and corvids. There are also different feeders for specialist foods such as nyger.

Blue Tits feeding on peanuts, by Ric Jackson

Bird tables are great for providing mixed seed and suet pellets for ground-feeding birds. The simpler they are the better, and easier to clean. To avoid larger birds, such as pigeons, monopolising all of the food, cages can be bought that allow access for smaller birds only.

Where and when to feed

To avoid creating a surplus of food that might go off or attract unwanted visitors, such as rats, try to match the amount of food provided to the number of birds coming in to feed. If food won't be put out for a certain period of time, the amount of provided should be reduced in the days leading up to it so that birds do not find that the supply has suddenly disappeared. They will come back once food is being provided regularly again.

It is better to have a number of smaller feeders scattered around the garden, if there is space. This allows birds to feed under less competitive conditions, but also allows different foods to be provided. Feeders should be placed close to vegetation that will provide cover if a predator appears. However they should not be placed near low cover which may hide cats, or near nest boxes. In addition, to avoid window collisions, they should be placed away from the house.

Mixed seed

There are many different seed mixes available on the market which vary in content and quality. Cheaper mixes tend to be bulked out with cereals, which are popular with sparrows and pigeons. Those with lower grain content are often more expensive but are particularly suitable for finches and buntings. Some now contain added suet pellets, fruit or pieces of mealworm, but the best ones are those that have been balanced to cater for a range of species.

Sunflower seeds

Sunflower seeds attract a wide range of species, from tits to finches. They come in two different forms. Black sunflower seeds still have their shells on but these are thinner than the

Tree Sparrow, by John Harding

The size of a bird's bill should give you an idea of what it feeds on. The large and robust bill of the Tree Sparrow enables it to tackle larger seeds.

traditional striped sunflower seeds. They are popular but the discarded husks do create a lot of mess under the feeder. Sunflower hearts are more expensive but produce little waste and are favoured by birds as they do not have to spend energy de-husking them.

Peanuts

Peanuts are high in oils and proteins and have been a popular food choice for birds for many years. They should be of high quality, from a reputable source and provided behind a wire mesh if whole. Peanuts can be contaminated with a naturally occurring poison known as aflatoxin, produced by mould, so peanuts are best stored in a cool, dry environment and not kept for too long.

Fat products

There is a huge range of these energy-rich foods and many different species enjoy them, especially in winter. Some are better quality than others so buy them from a reputable source. Nets should be removed from fat balls as these can pose a danger to birds, whose tongues (which have an arrowhead-shaped barb towards their rear) or feet may become entangled in the netting.

Nyger seed

This specialist, oil-rich food is suited to birds, such as Goldfinch, Siskin and Lesser Redpoll, adapted to feeding on small seeds, though other species may eat it. Ideally nyger seed should be provided in a specifically-designed feeder as the seeds are so small that they are easily lost from normal feeders. Nyger used to be sought out by Goldfinches but it seems that the seed has fallen out of favour, especially in those gardens where sunflower hearts are also available to these birds.

Live foods

Live foods, including mealworms, are great for species such as Robin, Starling and Blackbird. Mealworms are not actually worms but are the larval stage of a beetle. They can be scattered on the ground or provided on bird tables.

Starling, by John Harding

Suet and other fat-based products are a firm favourite with Starlings, often being demolished rather quickly, but they are also used by woodpeckers, Wrens and Long-tailed Tits.

Common Frogs, by John Harding

Water in gardens

Water is an extremely important element to provide in gardens for birds and other wildlife. Water provision doesn't have to be in the form of a pond – a bird bath or even a plant saucer will do. The important thing is that birds and other species can access it safely, and that it is clean. If you have the space then a pond will attract a much broader range of wildlife.

Water in gardens

Unlike mammals, birds have no sweat glands so need to drink less water than mammals. However, they do lose water in their droppings and through respiration, which is why on a hot day you may see birds panting to cool down. While most birds drink by scooping up water and throwing their heads back, Woodpigeons do not have to – they suck water through their beaks like a straw. Drinking water is particularly important in gardens where seeds are provided as seed-eating birds, such as finches, do not get moisture from their food. Birds which eat invertebrates obtain more moisture, but still need to drink as their diets often incorporate other foods.

For birds, water is vital not only for drinking but also for keeping their feathers clean, as damping feathers loosens dirt and makes them easier to preen. It is particularly crucial in the winter, as preening spreads the oil that waterproofs feathers, insulating birds from the cold. Some birds, such as Blackbird, Robin and Woodpigeon, bathe more than others so do not be surprised if you see these splashing around more frequently.

Bird baths

The simplest way to provide water is with a bird bath. There's a wide range of bird baths available to buy, or you can create one yourself from a dustbin lid or plant saucer. A good bird bath should mimic a shallow puddle – not too deep and with low, sloping sides. Birds should be able to perch on the sides or above the water (e.g. using stones) so that they can drink without getting wet, or have a perch on which to preen.

The downside to bird baths is that they dry out quite often in the summer and freeze in the winter. A water source is particularly important to birds in the winter when natural sources may have also frozen over. Do not, however, top your bird bath up with boiling water or use antifreeze. The best thing to do is to empty the bath at night and then refill it with tepid water in the morning.

Like feeders, bird baths must be placed with predators in mind. Whether placed on the ground, to attract mammals as well, or hung from a tree, make sure that it is close enough to cover to make the birds feel safe, but not so close to low cover where cats can hide. Bird baths also need to be cleaned out regularly to prevent the spread of disease and the build-up of algae.

Ponds

A pond is an easy way to attract many different species to your garden, benefiting everything from birds to invertebrates. It doesn't have to be large – an old washing-up bowl dug into the ground will do. Two-thirds of freshwater plants and animals are supported by ponds in the UK, making them a highly important part of our environment. It is estimated that, in the last 50 years or so, we have lost about a third of them from the countryside. Some have been filled in or drained for agriculture and development and others have been neglected, left to become silted up or polluted.

If you don't already have a pond, the best time to put one in is during the autumn or winter. At least one side of the pond should have a long, shallow slope that allows easy access for birds and mammals to the water. If restricted by the type of pond (e.g. a washing-up bowl), a wooden or stone ramp can be created to provide the same effect.

Ponds do not have to be planted up – they can naturally be colonised by plants and wildlife surprisingly quickly, depending on their location. However if you do wish to add plants to your pond, mid-spring to early summer is the best time. If you want to encourage wildlife, do not keep fish in your pond as they will eat the larvae of many species, including amphibians.

Starling, by John Harding

Health and welfare

Chaffinch, by John Harding

Disease in the garden can be a serious issue for wildlife. It can cause major population declines (for example that seen in the British Greenfinch population following the outbreak of trichomonosis), welfare issues – namely those that may arise if caused or exacerbated by human activities – and some diseases that can affect human health. It is, therefore, important to understand and be aware of potential diseases.

Health and welfare

Within the garden environment, disease is most likely to be transmitted at feeding stations. These attract bird species that would not normally mix, and often creates greater densities than might be seen in the wider countryside. Both of these can increase the risk of disease transmission, through contaminated food, saliva or droppings. Understanding these risks is important, since it should reinforce the message to keep your bird tables and hanging bird feeders clean.

Diseases

There are many diseases that affect garden birds. Four of the most commonly reported are salmonellosis, avian pox, trichomonosis and leg abnormalities.

Salmonellosis is typically caused by the bacterium *Salmonella* Typhimurium and is most commonly seen in Greenfinch and House Sparrow. It affects the oesophagus and other internal organs but has non-specific symptoms, including lethargy and fluffed-up plumage, which are seen in a number of other diseases. It tends to occur in the winter and

is likely to be spread by infected droppings contaminating food or water sources. It does have the potential to affect humans and domestic animals, notably cats that predate sick birds, so personal hygiene is also important.

Avian pox is caused by a virus which has various strains. Most commonly affected birds include Dunnock, House Sparrow and Woodpigeon, but since 2006 it has also been seen in birds from the tit family and especially in Great Tit. Avian pox exhibits itself in warty or tumour-like growths, often on the head but also elsewhere on the body. These growths can be relatively mild and may disappear but in some cases, notably in Great Tit, they can be very large and may affect sight and the ability to move around. It is thought to be spread by biting insects, direct contact between birds and indirect contact via contaminated surfaces, such as bird tables.

Trichomonosis historically affected pigeons, doves and the birds of prey that fed on them. However in 2005 it was first seen in finch species, and rapidly spread across Britain and Europe. Greenfinch and Chaffinch are most frequently hit by the parasite, which affects the back of the throat and the oesophagus. While they often show general signs of illness, affected birds may also drool, regurgitate food and have difficulty swallowing. Most likely spread through birds feeding each other or through contaminated food or water, it is the cause of the largest-scale mortality of British birds through infectious disease, having caused a 35% decline in the Greenfinch population within the first few years of emergence.

Leg abnormalities are most often seen in Chaffinch, where they are caused either by a virus called Chaffinch papillomavirus or by *Cnemidocoptes* mites. Both affect the feet and toes, and sometimes the leg. Birds often cope well, though severe cases can result in lameness or loss of digits or the foot. It can be spread via direct contact between birds or via shared surfaces. These leg abnormalities are usually fairly obvious, the legs and toes appearing white and enlarged.

For more details on these diseases, or other potential diseases that may affect garden wildlife, please visit the Garden Wildlife Health website (see below), which also provides advice on hygiene measures.

PREVENTION

By the time a bird is obviously ill, it is usually too late to help, making prevention, rather than cure, key to reducing disease in gardens. Things that can be done:

- Increase the number of feeding stations to reduce the density of birds in any one place.

- Avoid placing feeding stations under areas where birds congregate.

- Clean away uneaten food and droppings from bird tables.

- Provide clean drinking water regularly.

- Clean and disinfect feeders, feeding stations and bird baths every two weeks. This can be done using a suitable vet-safe disinfectant, then rinsing and air-drying.

- Maintain careful personal hygiene to reduce risk to human and domestic animal health.

When sick birds are seen in the garden, it can be quite distressing. In areas where there is plenty of natural food around, it is likely that birds will disperse to lower densities and it can be beneficial to stop feeding for a short time (two to four weeks). Feeding can then be reintroduced gradually. Treating sick wild birds is rarely an option though, if worried, the local vet or wildlife rehabilitation centre can be called.

If sick wildlife is seen in the garden, report it to the Garden Wildlife Health project, which monitors trends in wildlife diseases to identify their impact and underlying causes and to identify new and emerging threats.

Garden Wildlife Health website: **www.gardenwildlifehealth.org**

Greenfinch, by Jill Pakenham; Siskin, by John Harding; Great Tit with avian pox, by Hazel Rothwell

Nest boxes

Pied Flycatcher nest, by Mike Toms

Nest boxes provide nesting opportunities for those species that use natural cavities, making them a very good way of attracting birds into the garden environment – where natural cavities tend be less abundant. Bird species vary in the types of nest boxes they prefer, so understanding these requirements is an essential first step when looking to provide nest boxes in your garden.

Why put up a nest box?

With increasing urbanisation, the lack of suitable nesting sites may be limiting for some birds. Few gardens contain old trees with cavities or hedges with thick cover, and even if a garden does, a nest box provides an additional choice. For birds that nest in holes in buildings, such as House Sparrow and Starling, nest boxes could be of particular value, as the loss of nesting options might have contributed to the declines seen in their populations.

Nest boxes are also regularly used for roosting during the winter as they provide a relatively warm, sheltered space. There is a record of 61 Wrens sharing a Norfolk nest box in 1969, where they would have had to sit on top of one another in order to fit.

What to look for in a nest box?

Each species has its own nesting requirements, though they can be versatile and will often occupy holes not designed for them, including post boxes and upturned plant pots. However there are basic elements that nest boxes should have, whether they are homemade or shop-bought:

- **Materials:** hard-wearing, insulating material such as wood or special waterproof wood/concrete compound. Should be no less than 15 mm thick. Boxes made from thin wood, plastic or solid ceramic materials should be avoided as these can be dangerous.

- **Predator-safe:** avoid boxes with perches as these may provide a foothold for squirrels or Weasels as they reach into the box. Entrance holes can be reinforced with metal plates to reduce access by squirrels and Great Spotted Woodpeckers.

- **Easy access:** boxes should be easy to open without disturbing the nest, for monitoring purposes.

When and where to site:

If the hope is to attract birds to the nest box for the breeding season, it is best to put it up in late winter, as some birds (e.g. House Sparrow) start to look from mid February onwards. However, any time of year is fine as the box may be used for roosting in the winter or by birds that have multiple broods. Boxes may not be used in their first year, so be patient, but if a box has not been used for several years then check that it is of an appropriate design and that it has been put up in a suitable location.

Different species have different requirements when it comes to location of nest boxes but as a general rule:

- Nest boxes with small holes should usually be placed 1–3 metres above the ground, away from easy access to predators. Usually a tree, the side of shed or a wall will do.

- Nest boxes should not be placed too close to other nest boxes unless they are specifically for colonially nesting birds such as House Sparrows. They should also be placed away from bird feeders as constant activity nearby could disturb the nesting pair.

- If open-fronted, nest boxes should be hidden from view by shrubs or creepers as they are easier for predators to access.

- Shelter from extreme weather is important. The front of nest boxes can be angled slightly down to prevent rain from getting in but it is important to place them in areas that are sheltered from high winds and strong sunlight.

Even if a bird does not use your nest box for nesting, it may be used for roosting in the winter or by a number of other non-bird species, including Tree Bumblebee, a recent colonist that has developed a liking for hole-fronted nest boxes.

Cleaning out

According to wildlife legislation, nest boxes can be emptied and cleaned only between 1st September and 31st January. However, some species, such as House Sparrow, may have second or third broods in the same nest box, so boxes occupied by these species should be left until later in the autumn to be certain that the nest box is no longer in use. Nest boxes can contain fungi or parasites harmful to human health, so disposable gloves and a dust mask are advisable when cleaning them out at the end of the breeding season.

Checking a nest box, by David Tipling

NEST BOX DESIGNS FOR GARDEN BIRDS

The shape, size and design of a nest box will determine which species will use it. The familiar 'hole-fronted' nest boxes have a small circular entrance hole, the diameter of which will restrict access to certain species. Some of those available commercially have holes that are so small no bird will ever use them. The following guidelines should help you to select your box, or build your own:

- **Blue Tit:** Readily takes to nest boxes. Small nest box with 25 mm hole, erected more than 1 m above the ground with clear flight path to entrance.

- **Coal Tit:** May lose out in competition to other tit species. Small nest box with 25 mm hole, placed 1 m or less above the ground.

- **Great Tit:** Readily takes to nest boxes. Small nest box with 28 mm hole, sited more than 1 m above the ground with clear flight path to entrance.

- **House Sparrow:** Likes to nest colonially so needs more than one box, or a purpose-made House Sparrow terrace. Small box with 32 mm hole, placed 2 m or more above the ground.

- **Tree Sparrow:** Relatively easy to attract. Nest colonially so boxes can be placed close together. Small box with 28 mm hole, placed 2 m or more above the ground.

- **Nuthatch:** When using nest boxes, usually plasters mud around entrance hole and the roof. Small nest box with 32 mm hole, positioned 3 m or more above the ground and with a clear flight path to the box entrance.

- **Pied Wagtail:** Best sited where there is water and a lawn nearby. Readily takes to nest boxes in suitable areas. Open-fronted nest box, placed up to 5 m above the ground.

- **Robin:** Likes to nest in thick, overhanging vegetation. Open-fronted nest box, front 100 mm high. Height above the ground is less important than the amount of cover around the box.

- **Starling:** Favours a large nest box with 45 mm entrance hole, sited 2.5 m or more above the ground. Prefers higher sites, with a clear flight path to the box.

- **Tawny Owl:** Needs a very large nest box with at least a 150 mm entrance, placed at least 2.5 m above the ground. Favours a quiet secluded spot, but will nest in well-wooded gardens.

- **Swift:** Requires a medium-sized nest box with special oval hole, placed as high as possible on a building, with an entrance sited under eaves or within loft space (with entrance through wall). Needs a clear drop below entrance. Colonial, so installing several boxes is recommended.

- **Wren:** Favours a small open-fronted box, 140 mm high, and placed within cover, such as thorny undergrowth, up to 5 m above the ground.

- **Spotted Flycatcher:** Likes a good view from its nest, hence favouring an open box with a low front (60 mm), ideally placed within overhanging vegetation that still affords the bird a good view. The box should be placed 2–4 m above the ground.

- **House Martin:** Requires a special cup-shaped nest, placed under eaves and at least 2 m above the ground. Colonial, so installing several boxes is recommended.

Blackbird chicks, by Mike Toms

NEST RECORD SCHEME

The next step after installing a nest box in the garden is to monitor it for science! The BTO Nest Record Scheme gathers important information on the breeding success of birds in the UK. Whether monitoring a single nest box in the back garden or monitoring nests of a whole range of species, the survey simply requires that volunteers find and record the progress of individual nests. This information is then used to measure breeding performance trends which help to determine whether populations are declining due to failure during different nesting stages. Monitoring nest boxes will not disturb breeding birds as long as they are approached carefully. For more information, and to read the Nest Record Scheme Code of Conduct, please visit www.bto.org/nrs.

Plants for birds

Redwing taking berries, by Tom Wallis

A wide range of different plants can be used to encourage wildlife into your garden. Birds will use garden plants for nesting or roosting cover as well as for foraging, and insects will be attracted to a wide range of different flowering plants in search of nectar and pollen. By bearing the various life-stages and needs in mind, you can easily create a wildlife-friendly garden, no matter what size it is.

Plants for nesting and roosting cover

When considering plants for nesting and roosting cover, it is important to think about evergreen plants as well as deciduous ones as some birds, such as Robin and Blackbird, will nest before deciduous plants come into leaf. There are various conifers and shrubs that can provide nesting opportunities ranging from native species, such as Holly (*Ilex aquifolium*) and Yew (*Taxus baccata*), to introduced ornamental species.

If you are willing to wait, Holly and Yew will both provide thick cover for nesting birds such as Dunnock early in the season. If you have both male and female plants, Holly has the added advantage of providing flowers for pollinators and berries for thrushes. It is also the preferred food plant of the Holly Blue butterfly. Yew may attract nesting Goldcrests and also provides berries later in the year, though note that these are toxic to mammals. If you want cover more quickly, however, consider an introduced species like a variety of Lawson Cypress (*Chamaecyparis lawsoniana*) which, depending on the variety, can grow into low cover or tall trees. Shorter versions

of ornamental conifers are more likely to be used by species like Dunnock, whereas taller varieties may attract nesting finches.

For climbing cover, you could consider the native Ivy (*Hedera helix*). This is useful if you don't have space for trees or bushes, as you can grow it against trees, walls or fences. Bear in mind, however, that it will only flower if it is in the sun. Its flowers attract a wide range of invertebrates in the autumn and the berries are eaten by thrush species. Another option is *Lonicera henryi*, a semi-hardy evergreen species of honeysuckle. The native British honeysuckle is deciduous.

For deciduous options, consider what birds you may wish to attract. Finches usually nest in shrubs or small trees, including hedging species and fruit trees, as they like to nest in the fork of a branch or against the trunk. Lower, scruffy vegetation, such as Bramble (*Rubus fruticosus* agg), can provide cover for Robin or Blackcap. Thorny shrubs provide an extra level of protection against predators. A native option are the hawthorns (*Crataegus*) which grow in a wide variety of soils and provide nesting opportunities as well as roosting. In addition, their flowers attract a wide range of insects and they provide berries for birds from September onwards. Other options include *Berberis* or *Pyracantha* species which can be grown up walls and also provide berries. If you live by the coast, Sea-buckthorn (*Hippophae rhamnoides*) is a good option as it is tolerant of salty conditions, though if you want berries you will need both male and female plants. Don't forget, as well, that if you have a dead or dying tree that is safe to leave standing, you could provide a cavity nest for Great Spotted Woodpecker or Starling.

If you have the space, a good option is to plant a mixed hedge, as this will provide a wide range of different options for attracting birds and invertebrates. For example, a hedge of hawthorn, Blackthorn (*Prunus spinosa*), Holly, Yew, Elder (*Sambucus nigra*), Spindle (*Euonymous europaeus*) and Dog Rose (*Rosa canina*) would provide nesting cover, song posts, flowers and berries!

OTHER PLANTS FOR COVER:

Berberis darwinii
Berberis gagnepainii
Buxus sempervirens (Box)
Ceanothus spp
Clematis spp
Cotoneaster lacteus
Elaeagnus x *ebbingei*
Humulus lupulus
Laurus nobilis (Bay Laurel)
Ligustrum vulgare (Wild Privet)
Lonicera periclymenum
Prunus laurocerasus (Cherry Laurel)
Prunus lusitanica
Rosa rubiginosa
Viburnum fragrans
Viburnum tinus

As well as providing evergreen nesting and roosting cover for birds, Ivy also provides nectar and pollen for visiting insects and, late in the year, fruits for birds and other species.

Ivy and Red Admiral, by Paul Sterry/NPL

Sea-buckthorn, by Laurie Campbell/NPL

Plants for berries and seeds

A great way of attracting birds into the garden is to provide fruit- and seed-bearing plants. Different plant species will provide berries at different times of the year. Some berries will only be around for a short time whereas others can last for quite a while. For example, Holly berries can first ripen in September, but can be found through until the following July thanks to their durability.

The nutritional value of berries can also vary. For example, as the season goes on, the water content of the pulp can decline. On the other hand, as the season progresses the average lipid content of berries increases. This is important as lipids produce more energy (per gram of dry weight) than the protein and carbohydrates also found in berries. Birds will make a choice and select berries that offer the greatest rewards. Evidence shows that one thing they consider is the amount of anthocyanin, a well-known antioxidant. The more anthocyanin, the darker or more ultraviolet-reflecting the berry (which birds can

see well), and birds should select these berries first. It is important to bear in mind, therefore, that, if you want to provide non-native or cultivated berry-bearing plants, birds are more likely to choose berries that are similar to native ones. Plants that bear white berries, for example, may prove less attractive.

If you have a space for a tree or shrub, consider native Rowans (*Sorbus* species) with red berries, which are particularly attractive to thrush species. In addition, their flowers attract invertebrates. Elder, a native tree, has berries popular with thrushes and warblers, with the added bonus that both their berries and flowers can be used by humans. Native Crab Apple (*Malus sylvestris*) grows well in sunny spots and produces small green apples that are attractive to Robins, Starlings, Greenfinches and thrushes – and humans – and the spring blossom attracts a wide range of bees.

For smaller shrubs or climbing plants, consider Dog Rose and honeysuckle species (e.g. *Lonicera periclymenum*) which both provide fruits in the autumn and attractive flowers. Bramble is also popular with a wide range of birds and mammals, and is important for a wide range of invertebrates. While berries will attract a wide range of birds (and mammals too), don't forget that you can also encourage winter thrushes by leaving windfall apples or pears, if you have them.

Seeds

While fruits attract a wide range of birds, some will come into gardens looking for seeds. One way you can provide these is simply by not deadheading your flowers, such as Lemon Balm (*Melissa officinalis*) or dandelion species (*Taraxacum*), and allowing them instead to set seed. Goldfinches, in particular, will take advantage of these as well as Teasel (*Dipsacus fullonum*) and lavenders (*Lavandula*).

Alternatively, you can plant trees that provide seeds. Conifer trees are good for Siskins and Coal Tits, and Alder (*Alnus glutinosa*) and Silver Birch (*Betula pendula*) will attract Siskins, Lesser Redpolls and Goldfinches. If you have the space, Beech (*Fagus sylvatica*) mast is popular with Chaffinches and Bramblings. Many of these trees also attract insects.

Devil's-bit Scabious, by Paul Sterry/NPL

OTHER PLANTS FOR BERRIES:

Crataegus monogyna (Hawthorn)

Daphne mezereon

Euonymus europaeus (Spindle)

Hedera helix (Ivy)

Hippophae rhamnoides (Sea-buckthorn)

Ligustrum vulgare (Wild Privet)

Lonicera caprifolium

Prunus padus (Bird Cherry)

Prunus spinosa (Blackthorn)

Pyracantha spp

Sorbus aria (Whitebeam)

Sorbus torminalis (Wild Service Tree)

Taxus baccata (Yew)

Viburnum opulus (Guelder Rose)

Viscum album (Mistletoe)

OTHER PLANTS FOR SEEDS:

Carduus/Cirsium (Thistles)

Carpinus betulus (Hornbeam)

Centaurea cyanus (Cornflower)

Centaurea scabiosa (Greater Knapweed)

Corylus avellana (Hazel)

Echinops bannaticus (Globe Thistle)

Erysimum cheiri (Common Wallflower)

Helianthus annuus (Sunflower)

Knautia arvensis (Field Scabious)

Larix decidua (European Larch)

Lavendula (Lavender)

Lunaria annua (Honesty)

Oenothera spp (Evening primrose)

Solidago canadensis (Goldenrod)

Succisa pratensis (Devil's-bit Scabious)

Plants for pollinators

Attracting insects into your garden helps to pollinate your flowers, and also to provide food for insectivorous birds. One of the most important things to think about when trying to attract pollinators is to ensure that pollen and nectar are available through as much of the year as possible. As a general rule, native species are best but introduced plants come into their own in parts of the year when other sources of nectar are hard to come by. Ensuring that you have plants in flower early in the season is especially important for butterflies that overwinter as adults (e.g. Brimstone, Small Tortoiseshell, Peacock) and early emerging bumblebees (e.g. Buff-tailed and Early Bumblebees). Flower form is also important – plants with heavily modified blooms that have been specifically bred for appearance are often not suitable.

While some bumblebees and butterflies are restrictive about what plants they will visit, there are quite a few plant species that will attract a range of pollinators. Red Clover (*Trifolium pratense*) and Common Bird's-foot Trefoil (*Lotus corniculatus*), for example, will attract a number of bumblebee species.

Wallflower species (*Erysimum*) are good for bees and butterflies as an early source of nectar, and *Salvia* species tend to flower between May and July. *Sedum* and *Verbena* species can flower as late as October, providing much-needed late nectar.

Schedule 9 plants

The problems associated with the invasive Japanese Knotweed (*Fallopia japonica*) and Himalayan Balsam (*Impatiens gladulifera*) are well known due to high-profile media stories. Other plant species, however, are also causing problems for our native wildlife, including some that have been widely promoted for their wildlife benefits in gardens.

There is a list of plants known as Schedule 9, which features species that have been classed as invasive non-natives; it is illegal to plant species listed on Schedule 9, or allow them to become established, in the wild. Some popular berry-bearing plants, including a number of *Cotoneaster* species, are on the list and, as they can be dispersed by birds, it is worth bearing this legislation in mind when planting. You can find a full list of Schedule 9 plants online; try the RHS website.

Small Tortoiseshell on *Verbena*, by Josie Latus

Blue Tit, by Edmund Fellowes

Watching birds

Chaffinch, by Edmund Fellowes

Watching birds

An interest in garden birds unites many thousands of people across the country. Some may be well-travelled birdwatchers, familiar with many British species; others may never pick up binoculars. Supermarket aisles and garden centres are well stocked with bird food, and grandchildren help their grandparents with the ritual of filling up the bird feeders.

A growing interest

Access to a garden provides one of the best opportunities in our daily lives for close-up views of wildlife, and there is growing evidence that regular access to green spaces and nature benefits our physical and mental health.

The most basic element of enjoying garden birds is telling apart the different species. Our common cultural knowledge means that nearly everyone can recognise at least a few different kinds, such as Robin and Blackbird, and many people have no trouble identifying a range of common garden birds without referring to a guide. Some garden birdwatchers are content to simply take pleasure in watching the birds they recognise, while others enjoy learning how to identify new birds, and take an interest in their ecology and behaviour.

The value of regularly watching garden birds comes through familiarity with their normal routines and behaviours, and being able to notice patterns, changes or anything out of the ordinary. Keeping a record of these observations, and submitting them to a national project, captures this value and adds purpose to the enjoyment of watching garden

birds. In this way a simple activity can quickly become a hobby, a learning experience, and a rewarding way of contributing to our collective knowledge of garden ecology.

What you need

All that's really needed to be a garden birdwatcher is an interest and a pair of eyes! However, unless the birds are very close, a pair of binoculars is normally necessary to get good views and to confirm identification. Some way of taking notes, whether a notepad and pen, tablet or smartphone, is also essential to record on-the-spot observations.

Another important item to have to hand is a good bird guide. Some feature photographs of birds while others contain illustrations; both can vary in quality, and the choice is mainly down to personal preference. Photographs are, of course, a very accurate way of reproducing an individual bird in a particular light and position, but ambient light and angle may mean birds in real life can look different to photographs in a book. Illustrations may seem less true to life, but should be thought of as signposts to important identification features.

Many experienced birdwatchers prefer guides with illustrations, but learning to use these to identify birds can take a little practice. Another feature to consider is the range of species covered; many available books cover the birds of Britain and Europe, and include many species that will never be seen in a British garden. Choosing a guide that contains only British birds should avoid confusion and misidentifications. Finally, look for what other information is included, such as how likely the species is to be seen, its feeding habits, behaviour, and a description of its call and song; all of these are likely to be very helpful in learning to identify different birds.

In addition to books, online resources such as videos and recordings of songs and calls can be extremely useful for bird identification, and the potential for accessing expert opinion online should not be overlooked. Keeping a small digital camera or camera phone to hand makes it easy to snap any unfamiliar birds, and these can be shared with online communities or sent to the BTO. Even a very poor-quality picture is worth a thousand words; it's far easier for an expert to identify a bird from an out-of-focus picture than from a description, and should the bird in question turn out to be a genuine rarity, a photo will be valuable proof.

BINOCULARS

Binoculars for the kitchen windowsill can be picked up for £10 or £20; these are better than the naked eye but likely to be frustratingly poor quality. Many manufacturers of birdwatching binoculars do pocket models for around £50, and these are generally more than good enough for watching birds on garden feeders. A full-size pair of birdwatching binoculars can cost hundreds of pounds. Good deals on second-hand binoculars can often be found from reputable dealers.

The magnification and lens size of a pair of binoculars is represented by two figures, for example 8x32. The first figure is the magnification, and is normally between 7 and 10. The second figure is the diameter of the large lens in millimetres, and is normally between 30 and 50. A higher magnification (the first figure) will result in a larger image, but one that is harder to focus and hold still. A larger lens size (the second figure) will result in a brighter image, but will normally mean the binoculars are larger, heavier and more expensive. Small 8x32 binoculars are normally a good choice for garden birdwatching, though the quality of the lenses should be taken into account. Other factors to bear in mind are how easy they are to hold, and whether they will focus on objects closer than a few metres away, as this can be useful for looking at butterflies and dragonflies. Glasses-wearers will want to look for binoculars with retractable eye cups.

Buzzard, by Edmund Fellowes

Citizen scientists, by David Tipling

Citizen science

The partnership between professional scientists and 'citizen scientists' can be a powerful one, delivering important knowledge that could not be collected without the help of enthusiastic volunteers. The BTO has been championing 'citizen science' throughout its 80-year history, setting the standard for this approach to broadening our understanding of birds and the environment.

A measure of health

Wild birds are important indicators of the health of our environment, as well as being valued for their own sake. In order to conserve bird populations we need to know how many there are, where they are, and whether numbers are increasing or declining. We need to understand what resources different species need, how they interact with their environment, and how our actions are affecting them.

We cannot find out any of these things through isolated observations; much of our knowledge of the ecology of wild birds relies on sightings collected by thousands of observers. The UK has a long tradition of 'citizen science' projects, through which observations made by members of the public, working in partnership with professionals, contribute to knowledge of the natural world.

The work of the BTO

The British Trust for Ornithology carries out ecological research using data collected by large-scale volunteer bird surveys. The longest-running BTO survey is the Heronries Census, for which volunteers have counted

nests at Grey Heron colonies since 1928, without a break even during wartime. Today BTO scientists work in partnership with many thousands of volunteer birdwatchers to collect data on a scale that would not be possible by professional researchers.

Long-term bird-monitoring schemes run by the BTO involve standardised counts made by birdwatchers at specific sites across the country, which are then compared to provide a picture of whether species are increasing or declining. Other traditional projects involve collecting sightings to map the distribution of birds across the landscape; over the years the BTO has published four atlases of bird distribution maps, the first covering the period 1968–72 and the most recent 2007–11. These maps have been published online as a free resource for those interested in the changing status and distribution of our breeding and wintering birds. The atlas projects are run as partnerships.

Volunteers who catch and fit metal rings to birds' legs, or record the contents of their nests, are also coordinated by the BTO, and these schemes provide valuable information on the movements, survival and productivity of birds.

The role of technology

Modern technologies have greatly simplified the communication and data collection needed for traditional volunteer bird surveys, and have also enabled new ways to participate in citizen science schemes. Over 33,000 people are registered for BirdTrack, the online bird recording system that allows people to store and submit their own personal bird sightings. The speed and flexibility of online and mobile data-collection systems allows up-to-date monitoring of the movements and distributions of birds from anywhere in the world. As new technologies continue to emerge, so even more will become available to citizen scientists, enabling them to make an even greater contribution to our knowledge.

How citizen science data are used

Once the survey data and bird records have been collected, BTO scientists use this information to carry out research into birds and their relationships with the environment and with people. The aim of this research is to provide conservation decision-makers, including UK government agencies and non-governmental organisations, with high-quality scientific evidence.

The BTO has used volunteer survey data to analyse the causes of farmland bird declines, to produce indicators of the status of wild bird populations, and to identify the species that are conservation priorities. Records collected by volunteers have enabled the BTO to carry out broad-scale research into the effects of climate change and habitat loss on bird populations, and also to predict the environmental effects of specific proposed developments, such as new ports. In this way, data collected by volunteer birdwatchers can have a real and significant impact on conservation decisions.

The combination of volunteers, long-term data sets and professional ecologists gives the BTO a unique, impartial and knowledgeable voice in nature conservation. The 'citizen scientists' provide the data needed for the research, thereby playing a part in conservation policy, and the partnership also works to inspire and educate BTO volunteers about birds and the state of our natural world.

ABOUT THE BTO

The BTO is a research charity dedicated to increasing our knowledge of birds to inform the conservation of nature. We combine long-term data sets collected by volunteer birdwatchers with high-quality, relevant and independent science. Our aims are to understand and communicate the status of bird populations and their ecosystems, the causes of change and how to sustain biodiversity. BTO research is funded through charitable donations, membership subscriptions, sales of goods, contracts and commercial consultancy work.

The BTO operates a broad range of surveys, enabling volunteers to contribute to our understanding: e.g.

BirdTrack:
www.birdtrack.net
Breeding Bird Survey:
www.bto.org/bbs
Garden BirdWatch:
www.bto.org/gbw
Nest Record Scheme:
www.bto.org/nrs
Ringing Scheme:
www.bto.org/ringing
Wetland Bird Survey:
www.bto.org/webs

Citizen scientists, by David Tipling

Robin, by John W Proudlock

Garden BirdWatch

Garden birdwatching can be a rewarding hobby and many people keep lists of the birds that they see using their gardens. It is easy to take this interest a step further and to become a 'citizen scientist' contributing your records to the BTO's Garden BirdWatch scheme; this is a weekly survey that has been running year-round since 1995.

Make your garden count

The BTO's Garden BirdWatch (GBW) is a long-running project, started in 1995, that captures weekly garden bird records from many thousands of participants across the country. The food and resources available to birds in garden and urban habitats are very different from natural habitats, and in a time of increasing urbanisation it's important to understand how our wildlife uses garden resources. The aim of Garden BirdWatch is to capture the annual patterns of garden use by birds and other wildlife, which can then be linked to environmental conditions, such as weather and food availability.

Garden BirdWatch is one of the largest citizen science schemes run by the BTO, drawing on the huge number of people who enjoy watching the birds and wildlife in their gardens. One of the aims of citizen science projects is to inform and educate the participants, to stimulate a deeper understanding of the natural world. For this reason, Garden BirdWatch volunteers receive a quarterly magazine, *Bird Table*, containing the findings of the survey, articles on bird identification and

wildlife gardening, and interesting observations from participants' gardens.

The year-round cost of administering the paper and online data-collection systems, carrying out research using the data and producing a quarterly magazine is substantial. Urban wildlife monitoring programmes have not traditionally been priorities for public-sector funding, but BTO Garden BirdWatch is able to operate independently at a large scale as it is funded by the participants themselves, who pay a small annual subscription. The BTO is extremely grateful to all Garden BirdWatchers who support the survey in this way.

The presence of supplementary food is one of the most important factors influencing which birds are seen in gardens. While it's not necessary to provide bird food to take part in the survey, the vast majority of GBW participants do feed the birds in their gardens, and they are asked to make a note of what food they put out for the birds each week.

Many garden birdwatchers are also interested in the other wildlife seen in their garden, and the recording system built for Garden BirdWatch can also be used to collect records of other species. GBW participants can, optionally, submit records of the mammals, butterflies, dragonflies, bumblebees, amphibians and reptiles seen in their gardens, in exactly the same way as for birds. These records are used for research, and shared with other relevant organisations.

Taking part in BTO Garden BirdWatch

First register your garden, and enter some basic details on its size, age, composition and the nature of any surrounding habitat.

Think about the area you would like to watch, such as the part of the garden visible from the living-room window, as well as how much time in an average week you spend watching this area, and try to keep your observations generally consistent in most weeks. Clearly, it's not always possible to spend exactly the same amount of time watching the birds every week, but the idea is that the records should reflect bird activity, and not how much time the observer has to watch the birds that particular week!

Keep a note of the birds you see in your garden every week. You can choose to just record a list of birds, but most people also record the maximum count of each species. To record counts, make a note of the maximum number seen together at one time during that week. For example, if you see four Goldfinches on your bird feeders on Monday, and six on Thursday, the maximum count for Goldfinch in that week would be six. Do not add the counts from different days together, because this may be the same birds visiting your garden at different times. Start a new list each week.

Records should be submitted every three months if using the paper forms, or more regularly if using the online system. All records are held on a database which can be accessed online, allowing all users to view all the records they have submitted, regardless of whether they were submitted online or on paper forms.

Garden BirdWatchers, by Paul Stancliffe

House Sparrow, by Edmund Fellowes

Understanding patterns

Collecting weekly records allows us to see how the numbers of birds in gardens change through the year, and from one year to the next, depending on their preferences and environmental conditions. Variation in annual patterns can often be linked to the amount of natural food available in the wider countryside, as a poor crop of seeds or berries will mean more birds need to visit garden feeders.

If you look carefully you will begin to notice patterns in the times of the year when particular species of bird visit your garden. Some of these patterns tend to remain consistent from one year to the next, such as the peak in Great Spotted Woodpecker sightings in early summer as young birds visit garden feeders for the first time, while others will vary markedly depending on conditions. The size of the peak of Coal Tit sightings at garden feeders in late autumn is very variable, depending on the amount of natural food available elsewhere. Some birds normally found in the wider countryside, such as Yellowhammer and Reed Bunting, can often be seen visiting garden feeding stations in late winter, indicating that seed supplies in farmland habitats have run low.

Nesting preferences also play a large part in when we are likely to see birds in our gardens. Long-tailed Tits rarely nest in gardens, but often visit peanut feeders in winter, and these habits are reflected in the annual reporting rates. On the other hand, birds such as House Sparrows, which nest around or near our houses, are most often seen during the breeding season.

The annual patterns revealed by Garden BirdWatch data can tell us about the times of year that birds make use of the food, shelter and nesting sites available in our gardens, and help us to provide for their needs.

Garden BirdWatch records can be presented in several ways. The simplest is the reporting rate, which is the percentage of gardens from which a particular species is reported. More detail can be gained from count data, using the peak counts divided by the number of gardens to give an average number of birds per garden for each week of the year. Looking at data from different parts of the UK can often show a subtly different pattern to the overall national picture. As records are received they are loaded onto the online database, and up-to-date graphs and maps are available for all to view via the Garden BirdWatch website, allowing garden birdwatchers to compare their own observations with the bigger picture. These charts and maps can be generated for mammals, insects, reptiles and amphibians as well as birds, revealing annual variation in abundance and showing, for example, when animals emerge from hibernation.

ANNUAL PATTERNS

These charts use Garden BirdWatch data to show the probability of recording a species in your garden in every month throughout the year, and the same information has been represented on the individual species pages as circular 'calendar wheels'. The charts show the average reporting rate for all years combined, and do not capture the variation between different years, but this information can be explored on the Garden BirdWatch website.

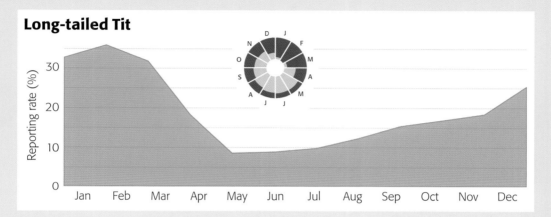

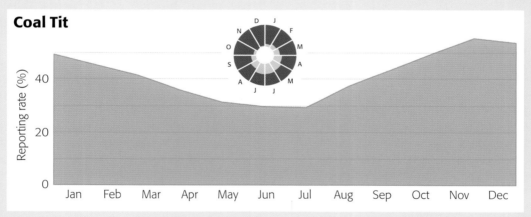

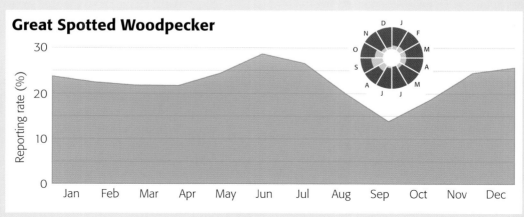

Woodpigeon, by John W. Proudlock

Long-term changes

As well as providing information on annual patterns of garden use, Garden BirdWatch also gives us important information on longer-term changes in bird populations. The data set collected since the survey began in 1995 is a great resource for showing how birds' use of gardens has changed over time. Understanding the reasons for these changes can aid conservation efforts elsewhere.

Reasons for a change

An increase, or decrease, in the number of a particular species seen in gardens does not necessarily mean that the actual numbers of that species have increased, or declined, overall. It may be that numbers in the countryside as a whole have remained stable, but a change in behaviour has changed the numbers that are seen in gardens. Nevertheless, long-term trends from GBW, such as the increase in Goldfinch numbers or the decline in House Sparrows, do mirror the results shown by the Breeding Bird Survey, which measures the national population changes of British birds.

Other garden wildlife

Large-scale collection of butterfly, mammal, reptile and amphibian records began in 2007, with bumblebees added in 2008 and dragonflies in 2011. These large data sets of other wildlife sightings have potential for generating valuable population trends for a variety of species. The aim of collecting information on garden birds is to add to our scientific knowledge; peer-reviewed papers enable BTO science to reach a wide audience and to inform environmental policy. Garden BirdWatch records have been used to answer questions on the ways birds use the landscape; as the data set grows over time these records will become ever more valuable. Understanding how birds make use of resources in gardens may, in the long term, help to explain how the urbanisation of our landscape will affect bird populations, and reveal whether garden resources can compensate for the other changes we are making to our environment.

Habitat associations of garden birds

Analysis of how garden features affected the likelihood of seeing different bird species showed that the surrounding environment was more likely to predict species seen in the garden than the features within the garden itself. Even particularly rich gardens will not attract many birds if the surrounding habitat is not bird-friendly. However, Wren, Robin and Blackcap were all more likely to be found in gardens with more vegetation cover than in gardens with bare walls and fences.

CHANGING FORTUNES

The weekly observations of BTO Garden BirdWatchers have revealed (a) the increasing use of gardens made by Goldfinch, a species that has responded to the food available at garden feeding stations, (b) the steady loss of House Sparrow, whose population has halved since the 1970s, and (c) the impact of the disease trichomonosis on our Greenfinches, the outbreak hitting the species in 2006 and 2007. Systematic weekly monitoring of this kind reveals long-term changes in garden bird populations.

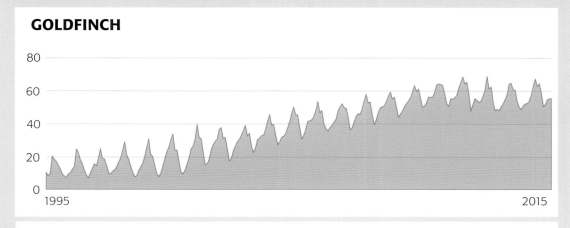

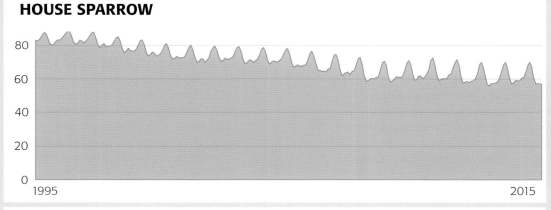

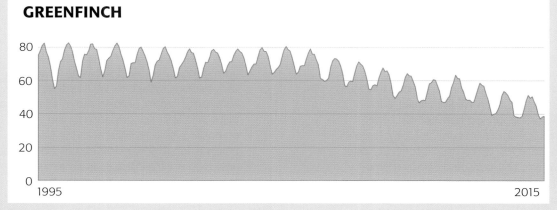

Sparrowhawk, by Paul Newton

GBW projects

Garden BirdWatch isn't just about weekly recording; from time to time the survey team run other projects as they attempt to answer questions about garden birds and the wider garden environment. These projects have delivered much new information, published in the first instance through peer-reviewed scientific papers.

While Garden BirdWatch is the largest survey run by the BTO's Garden Ecology Team, the capacity and enthusiasm of garden birdwatchers make it possible to periodically run smaller, supplementary investigations. These may cover a single species, a short timescale, or a particular aspect of garden wildlife biology or behaviour not covered by the standard GBW method. These additional surveys, open to the general public as well as Garden BirdWatch recorders, are designed to educate and engage, and ultimately to produce meaningful scientific results.

Garden Wildlife Health

Diseases of wild animals are often poorly understood, but gardens offer a valuable opportunity to monitor the disease threats to wildlife. Garden Wildlife Health is a collaborative project between BTO, the Zoological Society of London (ZSL), Froglife and the RSPB, which uses records of sick or dead wild animals submitted by members of the public to monitor the health issues affecting our garden wildlife. Dead garden birds, reptiles, amphibians and Hedgehogs can also

be submitted for post-mortem examination, after consultation with Garden Wildlife Heath veterinarians, allowing large-scale surveillance of wildlife diseases.

This surveillance has led to new discoveries about health issues affecting garden wildlife. The parasitic disease trichomonosis was first noted in British finches in 2005, and initial epidemics occurred in 2006 and 2007, mainly affecting Greenfinches and Chaffinches. BTO records were used to establish the extent of the outbreaks, and have shown that the disease went on to cause a longer term decline of around 50% in Britain's Greenfinch population.

Collecting reports of sick and dead wildlife from gardens has been shown to be a valuable early-warning system for wildlife disease. This knowledge can be used to inform conservation plans, and to create guidance for the public on possible ways to minimise disease transmission. The project website also provides advice on wildlife disease, and measures to reduce its impact, such as optimal hygiene at garden feeders and bird tables.

Abnormal plumage and bill deformities

Familiarity with their garden birds means that garden birdwatchers will often notice birds with deformities or other abnormalities. Plumage abnormalities include albinism and leucism, which involve a lack of melanin pigment, melanism, involving raised levels of melanin pigment, erythrism, where a chestnut-red pigment replaces certain other pigments, and flavism, an excess of yellow pigment. Beak deformities are caused by abnormalities in the keratinous parts of the beak, and include crossed, elongated, upcurved or downcurved mandibles.

It is possible that bill deformities are triggered by disease or malnutrition, and may be more common in urban environments than in natural populations. Plumage abnormalities, which are likely to have a genetic component, could affect the behaviour or breeding success of birds. The BTO runs simple online surveys for collecting sightings of birds with abnormalities, and recording their behaviour. Records collected by these surveys show that the rate of bill deformities appears to be highest for Blue Tit, and the rate of plumage abnormalities is highest for Blackbird.

Shortest Day and Early Bird surveys

Two one-off surveys that have been used to examine the effects of urbanisation on bird behaviour are the Shortest Day and Early Bird surveys. The Shortest Day Survey was carried out in 2004, when nearly 6,000 participants recorded the time in the morning that different species arrived at their garden feeders on a winter's day. Analysis of the data found that species with larger eyes arrived earlier in the morning, suggesting that birds start foraging on winter mornings as soon as it is light enough for them to see. Results from this survey also showed that birds appeared at garden feeding stations later in the morning in urban areas than in rural areas. This suggests that urban heat pollution may be helping birds survive cold winter nights, reducing the urgency for them to 'refuel' first thing in the morning.

This was followed in 2014 by the Early Bird Survey, which aimed to investigate how artificial light affected birds' early-morning foraging patterns. Surprisingly, birds did not appear to arrive at bird feeders any earlier in areas with artificial lights, which could be due to differences in food availability or predation risk in areas with more artificial light.

House Sparrow with abnormal plumage, by John Harding

House Sparrow surveys

One species inextricably bound to human habitation is the House Sparrow. This familiar bird is now a red-listed species of conservation concern, making it a prime subject for study. In 2002 the BTO launched the House Sparrow Project to investigate the problems facing House Sparrows in urban areas.

First, information about House Sparrows was collected from over 11,000 households via a questionnaire. This revealed that House Sparrows were more likely to occur at sites with gaps in the roof tiles, but also that a quarter of respondents had previously blocked up tile gaps. The questionnaire was followed by the House Sparrow survey, in which random 1-km squares were surveyed for House Sparrows. This study revealed the importance of the suburban landscape for this species: houses with gardens supported some of the highest densities, and allotments were also shown to be particularly important. The survey concluded that measures to prevent the loss of urban House Sparrow breeding colonies should concentrate on the maintenance and enhancement of the quality of urban gardens and the resources they contain.

Garden Bird Feeding Survey

The companion to Garden BirdWatch is the long-running Garden Bird Feeding Survey (GBFS), which has charted the use of garden bird food since 1970. This is run at a relatively small number of sites, carefully selected to provide representative geographical coverage of both suburban and rural habitats. The methodology of standard weekly winter counts has remained constant over the survey period, revealing the long-term patterns in feeder use by garden birds and how these relate to their overall long-term population trends.

The GBFS survey period has seen the return of Sparrowhawks to gardens following their recovery from declines caused by organochlorine pesticides; increased Sparrowhawk counts were associated with reduced abundance of some other garden bird species, but with no evidence that Sparrowhawk recolonisation was linked to long-term declines in population size.

Analysis of GBFS data has also supported the theory that woodland species that feed on Beech seeds are seen in lower numbers at garden feeders in years with a good Beech mast crop.

Blue Tit, by Tommy Holden

Great Spotted Woodpecker, by Edmund Fellowes

Species accounts

Mallard
Anas platyrhynchos

Mallards, by Edmund Fellowes

This familiar species is an occasional garden visitor and one that has been known to put in an appearance within even the smallest suburban garden. Some of these visits happen when the females move away from local waterbodies to seek out a quiet location in which to make their nest.

Amber-listed

Spotlight

Size 58 cm; Wingspan 90 cm; Weight 1.2 kg

Food: Omnivorous and opportunistic, taking a wide range of plant and animal material.

Breeds: March to August

Clutch size: 9–12 eggs

Incubation: 27–29 days

Young fledge: c.7–8 weeks

Number of broods: 1 per year

Population: 100,000 pairs

Max lifespan: 20 years, 6 months

Typical lifespan: 3 years

Garden reporting rate: 3%

Female Mallard on her nest, by Mike Toms

Rich in its variety

The Mallard is our most familiar duck, and the bottle-green head, white neck ring and yellow bill of the male's breeding plumage are unmistakeable. These bright colours are lost for about a month in late summer when the males take on a drab 'eclipse' plumage during their moult, making them look similar to the mottled brown females. Even then, both the females and eclipse males can be told from other ducks by their relatively large size and white-bordered blue wing panel. This is a very vocal species; loud repeated quacks are made only by females, while males make softer, more nasal calls.

Most breeds of domestic duck are descended from wild Mallards, and escaped domestic strains will freely mingle and interbreed with their wild cousins. This mixed stock results in a confusing variety of feral birds, which may be white, black, or patchwork, have feathery plumes on their heads, a noticeably upright stance, or may also be considerably larger or smaller than true wild Mallards. Domestic duck breeds include Aylesburys, Call Ducks and Indian Runners, but all of these breeds and mixtures are nevertheless the same species.

A garden visitor

While normally associated with large bodies of water, Mallards can also be found in gardens with small ponds, or away from water altogether, particularly during the breeding season in early spring. In the wild they feed by dabbling, upending to forage on aquatic plants and invertebrates, but they are opportunistic feeders, and will take advantage of grains on the ground under garden feeding stations. Long association with humans means that Mallards are comfortable around habitation, and this is the only species of duck likely to be seen in small or medium-sized gardens, or in very urbanised areas. They can damage plants in garden ponds; blocking access to the water may be necessary to discourage them.

Bringing up baby

Mallards are ground nesters, and have been known to nest in garden flowerbeds or borders, often well concealed by vegetation. They can lay up to 16 eggs in one clutch, and only breed once a year. It may be hard to see the nest as the female is very well camouflaged, and she covers the clutch with down and other nesting material to hide the eggs when she is not incubating. After about a month the eggs will hatch, and the ducklings can immediately begin to forage for themselves. Their mother will lead them to the nearest water to find food, and for some protection from land predators, though they are still vulnerable to aquatic hunters such as Pike.

In urban areas the journey between the nest site and the nearest water may be perilous, but it is normally best not to interfere, as disturbance may risk the mother taking fright and abandoning her ducklings. The female will brood the young to keep them warm overnight while they are small, but the father takes no role in caring for his offspring.

Origins

Mallards are very widely distributed across Britain and Ireland, absent only from remote mountainous areas, and there are thought to be around 100,000 breeding pairs in the UK. The breeding population has increased steadily since the 1960s, which may be partly due to annual releases of large numbers of captive-bred birds for shooting.

The wintering population is much larger than the breeding population, being estimated at nearly 700,000 individuals. However, the numbers of wintering birds have declined, predominantly due to a reduction in migrants from continental Europe, Fennoscandia and Russia. This decline in the non-breeding population has led to the Mallard being added to the amber list of birds of conservation concern during the latest review.

A female Mallard with her brood, by John Harding

Pheasant

Phasianus colchicus

Pheasant pair, by Jill Pakenham

The Pheasant is a familiar sight across much of the countryside, its numbers boosted each year by the release of young birds for shooting. Individuals may appear in rural and suburban gardens from time to time, where they can become regular visitors if suitable food is available.

Not listed

Spotlight

Size 71 cm; Wingspan 80 cm; Weight 1.4 kg

Food: Omnivorous, taking seeds, berries, leaves, roots and insects; may also dig into ground for food.

Breeds: April to September

Clutch size: 8–15 eggs

Incubation: 22–28 days

Young fledge: 10–11 weeks

Number of broods: 1 per year

Population: 2.2 million females

Max lifespan: 2 years, 1 month

Typical lifespan: unknown

Garden reporting rate: 6%

Pheasant nest with eggs, by Mike Toms

Variation on a theme

Pheasants are unmistakeable large birds with long, barred, brown tails. Males have a glossy greenish-purple head, with bare red wattles on either side of the face. Overall they have brownish-orange plumage and many have a narrow white collar around their neck. There are different varieties, however, which have been interbred with each other and produced quite a range of different plumage types. One popular variety is the 'blue-back' which can be slightly smaller. Females are more nondescript, with buff-brown plumage and dark spots in the feather centres. Juveniles have similar colouring to females, with shorter tails. Pheasants have a characteristic alarm call which is a series of 'ku-tuk' noises.

Habitat and breeding behaviour

In Asia, from where they originate, the preferred habitat of the Pheasant is grassland near water with areas of trees. In Britain, however, they will also use habitats with dense vegetation, such as deciduous woodland with scrub, and farmland areas containing copses with dense undergrowth. They will visit large gardens and parks, especially those in the countryside. Males are polygynous, with up to 18 females in a 'harem'. They start to establish their breeding territories from February and then attract females by performing an impressive display in open areas, raising their tails and craning their heads upwards while calling out, followed by an audible drumming of their wings. They will stay with their females until eggs are being incubated.

The nest, built by the female, is usually on the ground under Brambles, Bracken and other vegetation, or in nettles and tall grasses along the edges of fields. In gardens, they can be found in flowerbeds with thick vegetation. The nest is very simple, consisting of a scrape lined with grass and leaves. They have large clutches of 8–15 eggs. Occasionally two females will lay their eggs in the same nest, resulting in what looks like a larger clutch. They usually only have one brood, but with many eggs and chicks lost to predation they will sometimes have another attempt. To increase their chances, chicks are able to get up and walk away from the nest with their mother soon after hatching. During the winter, most Pheasant groups are made up of just one sex with females typically forming larger groups than males.

Omnivorous birds, Pheasants readily eat seeds, berries, leaves, roots and small invertebrates; these are taken from the ground where the birds forage. Very occasionally they will also take small vertebrates such as snakes and lizards. They are often attracted to garden feeding stations by fallen seeds and grain, usually feeding on the ground. Many have also learned to jump up at seed feeders to knock the seed out, or even how to feed directly from the feeders themselves. This behaviour is thought to have been transferred from their ability to jump up at berries that are hanging just out of reach.

Origins

The first documentary evidence of Pheasants in the UK dates from Norman times, though it's not known when they started to form feral populations. They spread through England and Scotland during the Middle Ages but did not really colonise Wales until the late 19th century and are still fairly uncommon in Ireland. Now it is estimated that at least 35 million Pheasants are released every year, and around eight million of these survive the shooting season, resulting in high densities of this species in some areas. Given the numbers of birds involved, it is thought that their presence may have negative effects on native species, though such effects have been poorly studied and more research is needed.

RED-LEGGED PARTRIDGE

Another introduced gamebird that frequents gardens is Red-legged Partridge. They were brought to Britain from continental Europe in the 18th century and here are most numerous in England. Females and males are alike and are instantly identifiable by their red bill and legs.

These sedentary birds have heavily marked faces with a white stripe above the eye, a black stripe through the eye, a white throat and a black 'necklace'. They feed on seeds and other plant material, and come into gardens in search of the spilled seed found under garden feeding stations.

Red-legged Partridge, by Paul Newton

Grey Heron, by John Harding

Grey Heron
Ardea cinerea

While not always a welcome visitor, the Grey Heron may exploit garden ponds and the fish and amphibians that they support. These large birds are solitary in their habits, except during the breeding season, when pairs come together to nest communally in treetop heronries.

Green-listed

Spotlight

Size 94 cm; Wingspan 185 cm; Weight 1.5 kg

Food: Fish and amphibians mainly, but also small mammals, insects and reptiles.

Breeds: April to July

Clutch size: 3–4 eggs

Incubation: 25–28 days

Young fledge: 42–55 days

Number of broods: 1 per year

Population: 12,000 pairs

Max lifespan: 23 years, 9 months

Typical lifespan: 5 years

Garden reporting rate: 1%

Grey Heron eggs, by Hugh Insley

The patient fisherman

Grey Herons can be distinguished in flight, even at a distance, by their large bowed wings and drawn-back head. The males and females cannot be told apart on plumage, but young birds can be identified by their grey crown and neck, while adults have a white forehead flanked by black stripes that continue into long black plumes at the back of the head. Their only call, away from their breeding sites, is a harsh, echoing 'kah-AHRK', uttered in flight.

These accomplished predators mostly feed on fish, which they catch with lightning-fast jabs with their 12 cm, dagger-like bills. This hunting technique also works on amphibians, water beetles, small mammals, snakes and even smaller birds, though they rarely forage far from water. They are sometimes attracted to garden ponds, and can decimate collections of expensive ornamental fish if these are unprotected by netting, especially as these ponds tend to be shallow with little vegetation, offering the fish nowhere to hide. Since Grey Herons are known to defend feeding territories, some people position replica plastic herons near their fish ponds in the hope of deterring other individuals from feeding in the same spot, but there's no evidence that this works.

Gardens and herons

Grey Herons are unlikely to be seen in gardens without water features, and they are recorded in only around 1% of Garden BirdWatch gardens each week. There is no clear pattern of occurrence, but in most years there is a small peak in garden sightings in April, presumably of parent birds foraging for their newly hatched young. Their hunting success is, of course, severely affected by frozen conditions, so at these times they may be forced to seek out unfrozen water sources such as garden water features. While our Grey Herons are generally sedentary, some birds from populations located further to the north and east may move to Britain and Ireland. Many of these individuals will be birds seeking to escape the Scandinavian winter.

Colonial breeding

Heron colonies are normally formed in trees – sometimes near water, but not always – and are widely distributed throughout Britain and Ireland. Many heronries are at traditional, well-known sites, and hold dozens or hundreds of pairs of birds, now in many cases joined by Little Egrets.

National colony counts have been carried out by volunteers annually since 1928 for the BTO's Heronries Census, the longest-running annual bird-monitoring programme in the world. These counts show that back in 1928 numbers were considerably lower than they are today, partly due to the fact that before the advent of wildlife protection laws Grey Herons were killed in large numbers in order to protect fish stocks in rivers.

Grey Heron numbers gradually increased over time, but in the 1960s there was a severe decline in the breeding population, falling from approximately 11,000 pairs down to around 7,000, the lowest level ever recorded by this long-running annual survey.

Hit by hard weather

The main cause of this decline was thought to be a series of particularly harsh winters, but organochlorine pollution may also have played a part. The population soon recovered from this dip, and from other fluctuations, and increased to around 13,000 breeding pairs in the early 2000s. This has been attributed to reduced persecution, improvements in water quality, the provision of new habitat as new lakes and gravel pits mature, and increased feeding opportunities at freshwater fisheries. However, numbers have been declining slightly since 2001, and this downturn is as yet unexplained.

In the time since monitoring started the average egg-laying date has shifted earlier due to warming springs, and Grey Herons now lay their eggs around a month earlier than they did at the start of the century.

Grey Heron, by Edmund Fellowes

Red Kite, by John Harding

Red Kite
Milvus milvus

Red Kite is one of the largest birds that you are likely to see over or in your garden. Their numbers and distribution have increased dramatically over recent years, following a very successful reintroduction programme aimed at bringing this bird back to its former haunts.

Green-listed

Spotlight

Size 63 cm; Wingspan 185 cm; Weight 1 kg

Food: A scavenger on carrion and other scraps, but will also take small live prey on occasion.

Breeds: March to August

Clutch size: 1–3 eggs

Incubation: 31–32 days

Young fledge: 50–60 days

Number of broods: 1 per year

Population: 1,600 pairs

Max lifespan: 23 years, 11 months

Typical lifespan: 4 years

Garden reporting rate: 1%

Red Kite nest with eggs, by Mark Watson

An urban bird?

Originally, Red Kites were found mostly in the lowlands of Britain, including in city centres such as London, where they were deemed valuable thanks to their habit of removing refuse. Along with other raptors, however, they were persecuted and the species was lost from most of the UK.

Red Kites have a wide habitat tolerance. Outside the breeding season they can gather in flocks of up to several hundred to spend the night together. In the autumn, these groups are initially made up of young birds and those that failed to breed. They do not usually breed until they are two or three years old but when they do they generally pair for life, though only meeting up to breed. They build their nests in trees that are fairly accessible and adorn their nests with scraps ranging from animal dung to items taken from washing lines. The breeding season starts in March, with most pairs having two or three, occasionally four, eggs. Their diet is dominated by scavenged carcasses, including roadkill, but they will take fish and insects and rummage around in refuse as well. They will land in gardens where meat scraps are provided, but remain wary.

Back from the brink

Red Kites are now part of a success story. Whereas there was a surviving population in Wales, in other parts of Britain and Ireland they had to be reintroduced. In 1989 they were released in the Chilterns and Scotland, and since then they have expanded their range. Since 1995 further successful reintroductions have taken place across Britain and Ireland, and they are now found across much of central and southern England. Outside these areas, breeding is localised, but this should change with time. Currently there are about 1,600 breeding pairs nationally.

Buzzard
Buteo buteo

Buzzard, by Edmund Fellowes

Rare garden visitors, Buzzards will occasionally visit when the weather is poor, and then are usually only seen in large open gardens in rural areas. They are often seen circling overhead, however, their presence perhaps revealed by a loud mewing call, underlining that this is one of our more vocal birds of prey.

Green-listed

Spotlight

Size 54 cm; Wingspan 120 cm; Weight 780 g

Food: Mostly small mammals, but also birds, reptiles, large insects and earthworms.

Breeds: April to September

Clutch size: 2–3 eggs

Incubation: 36–38 days

Young fledge: 42–56 days

Number of broods: 1 per year

Population: 67,000 pairs

Max lifespan: 28 years, 1 month

Typical lifespan: 12 years

Garden reporting rate: 1%

Buzzard nest with chick and eggs, by Richard Castell

Return of the native

One of the most numerous European raptors, Buzzards are found across Britain and the eastern half of Ireland throughout the year. Their population took a hard hit due to persecution during the 18th to early 20th centuries, reduced prey availability with the outbreak of myxomatosis and the impacts of organochlorine pesticides in the mid-20th century. Due to this, their strongholds remain in Wales, south-west and northern England and southern Scotland, with the highest densities associated with mature woodland. Following a reduction in persecution, and the increasing availability of nesting habitat in the form of woodland and plantations, their population is expanding again.

An open-country bird

Buzzards prefer areas that have forest or woodland with access to open land, farmland, meadows or marsh. They now breed in most counties in the UK, but densities are highest in the west. When nesting they often choose trees covered with Ivy, though they will also nest on cliffs. The nests that they build are large and often quite flat in outline, made of sticks and twigs, and lined with greener branches. A pair will often use the same nest from year to year, though sometimes they rotate between a few different sites, adding new material to the nest each year. Buzzards establish their breeding territories in February, and lay eggs from late March, having just one brood of two to three eggs.

Like Red Kites, Buzzards are opportunistic feeders, taking advantage of any chance to scavenge. Earthworms make up a surprisingly large part of their diet, these being taken from the soil surface on wet days, but they will also catch mammals as large as a Rabbit and birds as large as a Carrion Crow if the opportunity arises, underlining that this is a bird of prey.

Sparrowhawk
Accipiter nisus

Sparrowhawk, by Edmund Fellowes

A bird of prey seen in a garden is very likely to be a Sparrowhawk. These small predators are now widely distributed across Britain and Ireland, and are reported by around 10% of Garden BirdWatchers in any given week throughout the year. Sparrowhawks are not always welcome visitors to gardens, but smaller birds are well prepared for this natural hazard.

Green-listed

Spotlight

Size 33 cm; Wingspan 62 cm; Weight 150 g

Food: A specialist predator of small birds, up to the size of a pigeon.

Breeds: May to August

Clutch size: 4–5 eggs

Incubation: 32–36 days

Young fledge: 24–28 days

Number of broods: 1 per year

Population: 33,000 pairs

Max lifespan: 17 years, 1 month

Typical lifespan: 4 years

Garden reporting rate: 13%

Sparrowhawk nest with chicks, by John Harding

A specialist predator

Sparrowhawks are specialist predators of birds, and while they normally take tits, finches and sparrows, the larger females have been recorded taking prey up to the size of Jays, Lapwings and even Pheasants. They are stealthy hunters, approaching unseen then appearing suddenly from behind cover, so sometimes the only sign that they have been through a garden is the smaller birds scattering and falling silent. However, once they have lost the element of surprise they can be surprisingly bold, sitting out in the open on a fence, or plucking their prize after a successful hunt, and this gives the best opportunity most people have of watching a wild hunter at close quarters.

The sight of a predator feeding on other garden visitors is not a welcome sight for everyone, and tactics such as occasionally varying the position of bird feeders, and siting feeders near cover, can tip the balance in favour of the smaller birds. However, Sparrowhawk attacks are a natural hazard for small birds, and research has shown that they are capable of weighing up for themselves the advantages of bird feeders against the increased risk of predation, so there's no need to stop feeding if a Sparrowhawk is present.

A recovering population

The national Sparrowhawk population increased by over 100% between 1975 and 1995, but since the 1990s numbers have been stable or slightly declining. Their increase is thought to be a return to previous levels after a crash caused by organochlorine poisoning and predator control, and the population now numbers around 33,000 breeding pairs.

The increase in Sparrowhawk numbers coincided with a decline in the populations of many smaller birds, but a number of studies have concluded that Sparrowhawks are not the cause of these reductions, either locally or nationally. Research shows that the number of birds able to survive from year to year is limited by the food and other resources available, and the proportion taken by Sparrowhawks simply reduces the numbers that perish through other causes.

Battle of the sexes

Female Sparrowhawks are normally around the size of a Woodpigeon, while the much smaller males are only a little larger than Collared Doves. It's been suggested this size difference, often seen in birds of prey that engage in fast, active hunting, could enable the agile males and weighty females to specialise on different kinds of prey, thus increasing the range of food items they bring to their young and reducing the competition between the two sexes. While the smaller male Sparrowhawk is more agile than his mate, the female can carry the additional body reserves that she needs to produce a clutch of eggs.

Occasionally Sparrowhawks are mistaken for Merlins or Goshawks, but these are both very unlikely to be seen in gardens. Goshawk is a much larger bird, although the difference in size between the two sexes, which is also seen in Goshawk, means that a small male Goshawk is not that much bigger than a large female Sparrowhawk. Kestrels are sometimes seen in large, rural gardens, but these small falcons can be easily told from Sparrowhawks by their barred or chestnut back and shoulders.

Age and Sparrowhawks

Juvenile Sparrowhawks of both sexes have dark brown upperparts and coarse brown-and-white horizontal barring on the underside. Adult females can look superficially similar to juveniles, but the upperparts are brownish-grey and the barring on the underside is finer and paler, and they often show a distinct pale stripe above the eye (see below). Adult males have pure slate-grey upperparts, and the barring on the underside and cheeks ranges from pale brown to a rich red (see opposite). In all cases look for the relatively long, barred tail, upright stance, and slim yellow legs.

Sparrowhawks hatch with brown eyes, but these turn lemon yellow within a few months. With age, the eyes turn from yellow to orange, and some older adult males may have wine-red eyes. If you get a good view of an individual then do look at its eye colour.

STACKING THE ODDS

You can tip the odds in favour of the small birds visiting your garden by positioning your bird feeders close to tall, thick cover, into which the birds can dive should a Sparrowhawk appear. However, be mindful of other predators – if cats are a threat in your garden be aware that these ambush predators may take advantage of cover near bird feeders.

Sparrowhawks tend to follow a favoured route when hunting, so moving your bird feeders around the garden every so often will stop the predator from being able to predict where the smaller birds will be gathered.

Place feeders at some distance from your windows, as this reduces the chances of birds being flushed into the glass when a predator appears.

Sparrowhawk, by Paul Newton

Kestrel, by John Harding

Kestrel
Falco tinnunculus

Kestrels are one of the most widespread and abundant raptors in Britain and Ireland. They are found in highest densities in central and eastern England, and in south-west Ireland. Their population declined by almost a third between 1995 and 2010, but the reasons are poorly understood. They are occasionally seen in gardens, usually in rural areas.

Amber-listed

Spotlight

Size 34 cm; Wingspan 76 cm; Weight 190 g

Food: Chiefly small mammals (voles) but also insects, small birds and lizards.

Breeds: April to August

Clutch size: 4–5 eggs

Incubation: 27–29 days

Young fledge: 27–32 days

Number of broods: 1 per year

Population: 45,000 pairs

Max lifespan: 15 years, 11 months

Typical lifespan: 4 years

Garden reporting rate: 1%

Kestrel nest with eggs, by Richard Castell

An adaptable bird

Kestrels nest in a wide range of sites near suitable hunting habitat and will use ledges on buildings, large cavities in trees and large open-fronted nest boxes. The nest itself is a simple scrape with no additional material added, and pairs will often return to the same site each year. Young Kestrels can be rather vocal in the nest, particularly when a parent has returned with prey, and it soon becomes obvious if you happen to have a pair of these delightful birds nesting nearby. Pairs may sometimes use nest boxes erected in large rural gardens overlooking farmland.

Identification

The Kestrel is a medium-sized falcon with reddish-brown upperparts contrasting with dark flight feathers. The male has a pale grey rump and upper tail, a dark terminal band to the tail and a greyish head. The female has a brown, barred rump and upper tail, a brown terminal band to the tail and a brownish head. Juveniles have similar colouring to that of females, but their upperparts are more barred. Kestrels are often seen hovering, with their tail spread like a fan, a behaviour not generally seen in our other breeding birds of prey.

Diet and hunting behaviour

In the countryside, the diet of Kestrels consists mainly of small mammals, such as voles, but they will also take large insects. In urban areas they will also take small birds, and these also tend to feature in the diet more during the winter months than at other times of the year. Kestrels are most commonly seen hunting over open areas, such as along roadside verges and rough grassland, but they will very occasionally come into larger gardens for food, perhaps looking for roosting birds.

Moorhen, by John Harding

Moorhen
Gallinula chloropus

Adult Moorhens are nervous birds and prone to scattering noisily if disturbed, but occasional pairs will set up territory in larger gardens if they have a suitably large pond. The gardens chosen tend to be located fairly close to some other waterbody, be it a lake, river or old gravel pit.

Green-listed

Spotlight

Size 34 cm; Wingspan 52 cm; Weight 320 g

Food: Omnivorous, taking a wide range of plant and animal material.

Moorhen nest with eggs and chick, by Mike Toms

Breeds: April to September

Clutch size: 5–8 eggs

Incubation: 19–21 days

Young fledge: 6–7 weeks

Number of broods: 2–3 per year

Population: 260,000 territories

Max lifespan: 11 years, 4 months

Typical lifespan: 3 years

Garden reporting rate: 1%

Where there's water

Moorhens can be found almost anywhere with still or slow-moving fresh water including lakes, ditches and large garden ponds. They like to breed in or near dense vegetation, but their nests can be built either on the water, on land or, occasionally, in trees. Along with the nest that they build for their eggs, Moorhens will also build 'brood platforms' on which they will sit and sometimes mate. Nests consist of a platform of plant material, with a cup of the same or finer plant materials and often lined with dead leaves. They will have multiple broods and can lay eggs from mid March. Nests suffer from high rates of predation, with rats, American Mink, Otter and Carrion Crows thought to be the main culprits. However, if the first brood survives, they will sometimes stay with their parents and help to rear the second. This not only improves the chances of the second brood, but also gives the older young experience of raising chicks.

On the move?

Our resident Moorhens are highly sedentary, but winter numbers are increased by birds migrating from elsewhere in northern Europe. Although they can be seen in gardens all year round, it is usually only those with a large pond that are favoured. The population decreased between the mid 1970s and mid 1980s before partially recovering, but since 2000 has declined once again. These declines may be due to cold winters, but could also result from the loss of ponds or predation by the introduced American Mink.

Moorhens have a varied diet taken from both aquatic and terrestrial habitats, including plant material, berries, invertebrates, fish and the eggs of other birds. In gardens, they will feed on scattered bread and grain from the ground or low bird tables.

Black-headed Gulls, by John Harding

Black-headed Gull
Chroicocephalus ridibundus

This small gull will make use of gardens on occasion, visiting to take scraps from the ground or from uncovered bird tables. Greater use is made during the winter months and it is clear from Garden BirdWatch results that some gardens can attract very large numbers.

Amber-listed

Spotlight

Size 36 cm; Wingspan 105 cm; Weight 330 g

Food: An opportunist, taking insects, earthworms, plant material and various scraps.

Black-headed Gull nest with eggs, by Moss Taylor

Breeds: April to August

Clutch size: 3 eggs

Incubation: 23–26 days

Young fledge: c.35 days

Number of broods: 1 per year

Population: 130,000 pairs

Max lifespan: 32 years, 4 months

Typical lifespan: 11 years

Garden reporting rate: 6%

A winter visitor

Black-headed Gulls are the gull species most commonly seen in urban and suburban gardens. They prefer open areas and may be attracted to food scraps left out on lawns, sometimes descending in large, noisy flocks of fifty or more. In confined spaces they may swoop down to snatch pieces of food from the ground without landing. In the wider countryside they will eat worms, insects, fish and carrion, often following the tractor and plough, and in gardens they will take a wide variety of kitchen leftovers, including meat and bread.

These small gulls are most commonly seen in gardens in winter, the time of year when they are widely distributed throughout lowland areas of Britain and Ireland. At this time our resident birds are joined by a large number of winter immigrants from around the Baltic and as far east as Russia, possibly more than doubling the size of the population. However, in recent years there has been a reduction in the wintering population, and due to this decline they are an amber-listed bird of conservation concern.

Identification

One of our smaller widespread gulls, Black-headed Gulls can be easily recognised in summer by their dark heads. Despite their name, in good light it can be seen that the head is actually dark chocolate-brown rather than black. In winter, however, they have white heads, with the black shrinking to just a small dark shadow behind the eye. They have small red bills, and all ages can be recognised in flight by the white blaze along the forewings and the dark smoky grey on the underwings. Birds that are under two years old still show some juvenile plumage mixed in with the pale grey feathers on the upper wings, as well as a black band at the end of the tail.

On the move

Black-headed Gulls are ringed in large numbers at European breeding colonies, and many of these birds migrate to Britain and Ireland in the winter. Close examination of the legs of birds in parks or gardens will often reveal ringed birds, and with the investment of some time and food scraps it's often possible to photograph the rings with a digital camera and read the ring numbers. Wintering flocks are often found to contain birds from Denmark, the Netherlands, Germany, Finland, Sweden, Poland and many other countries, alongside British-ringed birds.

In summer they breed at a wide range of coastal and inland, natural and man-made wetlands, in colonies that can be as small as 10 pairs or as large as 10,000. This adaptability allows a very wide breeding distribution, including colonies in central London, though they are sparsely distributed in other inland parts of southern England. During the breeding season they are less likely to visit gardens, appearing on only around 2% of Garden BirdWatch weekly lists.

For hundreds of years Black-headed Gull colonies were a major source of eggs and young birds for the table, which may have been the cause of the decline that led to

Winter-plumage Black-headed Gull, by John Harding

their near extinction in the 19th century. Since then the reduction of the egg harvest, as well as the creation of new wetland habitats, has resulted in a remarkable increase to the population levels we see today. Some recent local declines could be due to the loss of safe nesting sites, drainage of wetland areas and predation by introduced American Mink.

COMMON GULL

Though Common Gulls breed in northern Scotland and in Ireland, they are most commonly seen during the autumn and winter when numbers are swelled by an influx from the Continent. Common Gulls are similar in colouration to the much larger Herring Gulls, and wintering birds can be distinguished from wintering Black-headed Gulls by their streaky heads and different bill colour: dull pink with a black tip in first-winter birds, or greenish-yellow with a dark band in adults.

Common Gull, by Allan Drewitt

Lesser Black-backed Gull
Larus fuscus

Lesser Black-backed Gull, by Edmund Fellowes

Like most large gulls, Lesser Black-backed Gulls usually nest on cliffs along the coast. However, in 1945 they started to nest on rooftops, a behaviour which caught on rapidly. They usually nest in colonies, and the largest urban one, in Gloucester, is thought to be made up of 1,000 pairs!

Amber-listed

Spotlight

Size 58 cm; Wingspan 142 cm; Weight 830 g

Food: Omnivorous, often seen feeding at rubbish dumps.

Breeds: May to August

Clutch size: 3 eggs

Incubation: 25–27 days

Young fledge: 35–40 days

Number of broods: 1 per year

Population: 110,000 pairs

Max lifespan: 34 years, 11 months

Typical lifespan: 15 years

Garden reporting rate: 1%

Lesser Black-backed Gull chicks, by Allan Drewitt

An opportunist

Lesser Black-backed Gulls will take a wide range of food. In the winter they feed more on fish and shellfish, though they will scavenge on rubbish dumps and agricultural land to supplement their diet. In the summer they will take invertebrates, eggs and young of other birds, fish and small mammals. They will also come into gardens for scraps. Increased opportunities for finding food inland, and nesting opportunities on rooftops, have seen the population increase. However, the birds are affected by culling and changes in landfill and fisheries practices.

On the move

Lesser Black-backed Gulls are traditionally migratory birds. Typically during the winter the gulls that breed in Britain leave for south-west Europe and north-west Africa. The numbers of gulls overwintering here has risen in recent decades. Many of these are local breeders that are perhaps reacting to milder winters and the ability to exploit a wide range of feeding opportunities and roosting places. They are also joined by birds from Iceland and north-west Europe which also benefit from the milder conditions. It is at this time of year that Lesser Black-backed Gulls are most likely to be seen in gardens, looking for food.

Identification challenges

This is the smallest of the large gulls, being less bulky than Herring Gull, with longer, more pointed wings and a thinner bill. Its legs are yellow, unlike those of Herring Gull which are pink. The call of Lesser Black-backed Gull is similar to that of Herring Gull's 'kyow', but is deeper and rougher sounding. Their nests usually contain grass, seaweed and debris, but inland they will often add moss, heather and lichen as well.

Herring Gull
Larus argentatus

Herring Gull, by John Harding

Traditionally found in coastal areas, Herring Gulls were the first large gull species to nest inland in Britain. While the majority still nest on rocky coasts, many now use buildings and are the main gull species to do so – the first Herring Gulls nested on roofs in the 1920s.

Red-listed

Spotlight

Size 60 cm; Wingspan 144 cm; Weight 1.2 kg

Food: Omnivorous, but mostly animal material; also scavenges and steals food from other seabirds.

Breeds: April to August

Clutch size: 2–3 eggs

Incubation: 28–30 days

Young fledge: 35–40 days

Number of broods: 1 per year

Population: 130,000 pairs

Max lifespan: 32 years, 10 months

Typical lifespan: 12 years

Garden reporting rate: 2%

Herring Gull chick, by Anne Carrington-Cotton

An urban colonist

In the winter Herring Gulls can be found throughout lowland areas of Britain, though their highest concentrations are found close to the coast. It is at this time of year that they are most likely to come into gardens looking for food. In the summer they are widely distributed around the coast of Britain, but have also colonised urban areas. They are a declining species, though are found in higher populations than in the early 20th century. Suggested reasons for their decline include a reduction in feeding opportunities such as from fishing industry discards and changes in intertidal ecology.

Age and plumage

The plumage of Herring Gull changes with age. Adult Herring Gulls are larger than other common gulls, and have pale grey upperparts. They have a yellow bill with an orange-red spot and pink legs. In the summer the head is white and in the winter it is streaked with grey-brown. The species most similar to Herring Gull within a garden setting is the Lesser Black-backed Gull, which has a much darker back and wings, and yellow legs. The classic Herring Gull call is a 'kyow' repeated several times, and very loudly when used as an alarm.

Food and feeding

Like most gulls, Herring Gulls are opportunistic feeders and will take a wide range of food including fish, earthworms, offal, roadkill, eggs and the young of other birds. As well as taking advantage of human food, they will feed on fields and in dumps, which unfortunately often leads to the ingestion of human rubbish. They will venture into gardens, especially in coastal areas, to take scraps from bird tables and the ground.

Feral Pigeon
Columba livia

Feral Pigeon, by Moss Taylor

Feral Pigeons come in many different colour forms, and urban flocks of these birds can look somewhat worse for wear, with individuals often showing some form of injury or evidence of disease. Despite this, these small pigeons have existed alongside humans successfully for many thousands of years.

Spotlight

Not listed

Size 32 cm; Wingspan 66 cm; Weight 300 g

Food: Seeds of cereals and weeds; urban and suburban birds also take scraps extensively.

Feral Pigeon nest with eggs, by Richard Castell

Breeds: March to October

Clutch size: 2 eggs

Incubation: 17–19 days

Young fledge: c.25 days

Number of broods: 2–3 per year

Population: 540,000 pairs

Max lifespan: 7 years, 9 months

Typical lifespan: 3 years

Garden reporting rate: 14%

What's in a name?

There is no clear-cut biological difference between pigeons and doves, just a naming habit, and the birds we call Feral Pigeons are descended from the species known in the wild as the Rock Dove. Everyone is familiar with the feral 'town pigeons' that inhabit urban areas. Overall they tend to be dark grey, but they can be variegated white and grey, reddish-grey, piebald, or very similar to ancestral Rock Doves, with a dark grey head and pale back with two dark wing bars. Some varieties of Feral Pigeon can look like Stock Doves, but they can be told apart by the eyes; Stock Doves have dark eyes that appear quite large, while Feral Pigeons have smaller, amber-coloured eyes.

Ancient origins

Wild Rock Doves are cliff nesters, but they have easily adapted to nesting in dovecotes or, later, ledges on urban buildings. They are thought to have been semi-domesticated since as early as 4500bc, and have been kept for the table in Britain since Roman times. Both the adults and chicks were consumed, and at the peak of this industry there are thought to have been 26,000 dovecotes in Britain. In more recent times domesticated pigeons have been bred for racing, for carrying messages, as ornamental white doves and myriad forms of 'fancy' show pigeons, with long legs, short beaks, turkey-like fanned tails, head plumes or enormously feathery feet.

Over time domesticated birds have escaped or simply moved from dovecotes into the wild, and the interbreeding of all these varieties has resulted in the hotchpotch of forms we see in the Feral Pigeons inhabiting our cities and towns. This process is ongoing, as can be seen by the occasional colour-ringed racing pigeon that has forsaken its loft for urban street life.

Unknown numbers

The UK population of Feral Pigeons has never been systematically censused, but there are estimated to be around 450,000–650,000 pairs. They are spread widely across Britain and Ireland, with the highest densities in cities and towns. In urban and suburban gardens they can congregate in numbers large enough to become a nuisance, particularly where kitchen scraps, bread or bird seed containing cereal is scattered on the ground. Providing high-quality bird food (without cereal) in hanging feeders may discourage Feral Pigeons, or they can be excluded from a ground feeding area by surrounding it with a two-inch-gauge wire mesh. They are most likely to be seen in gardens in the late spring, the peak of their breeding season.

Changing times

Feral Pigeons demonstrate many of the qualities that make this species suitable for keeping in dovecotes: they are happy to nest communally and, if conditions are suitable, they may breed throughout the year, producing a large number of young. Despite their productivity, and historical success in urban areas, Breeding Bird Survey figures show that nationally Feral Pigeons are now in decline. This has coincided with an increase in Woodpigeons in urban areas, though the mechanisms for a link have not been investigated. Despite this overall population decline, Feral Pigeons appear to be increasing in gardens, with the average Garden BirdWatch reporting rate rising from around 10% in the 1990s to closer to 15% in recent years.

ROCK DOVES

Some Feral Pigeons look nearly identical to their ancestral wild Rock Doves, having reverted to type over successive generations. However, they can be told apart by behaviour and habitat. Original wild Rock Doves, which have never been domesticated, live on sheer sea cliffs on remote Scottish coasts, and any 'Rock Dove' seen in a garden far from these areas should be recorded as a Feral Pigeon.

Rock Dove, by Paul Sterry/NPL

Stock Dove, by Edmund Fellowes

Stock Dove
Columba oenas

Stock Doves are widely distributed throughout England, and patchily in Wales, Scotland and Ireland. They are largely sedentary birds, though a handful migrate from mainland Europe to winter here. The highest densities occur around arable farmland and open woodland but some birds visit larger rural gardens.

Amber-listed

Spotlight

Size 33 cm; Wingspan 66 cm; Weight 300 g

Food: Mostly plant material in the form of seeds, leaves and buds, but may take invertebrates.

Breeds: April to October

Clutch size: 2 eggs

Incubation: 16–18 days

Young fledge: 27–28 days

Number of broods: 2–3 per year

Population: 260,000 territories

Max lifespan: 9 years, 2 months

Typical lifespan: 3 years

Garden reporting rate: 3%

Stock Dove chicks, by Moss Taylor

An overlooked visitor

Due to their similarity to Woodpigeons and Feral Pigeons, Stock Doves often get overlooked. They are similar in size and shape to Feral Pigeon, and smaller than Woodpigeon. They have blue-grey plumage and both their under and upper wings are plain grey distinctly bordered with black. Their key defining feature, however, is their shiny green neck patch; Woodpigeons have a white neck collar. The song is a monotonous series of 'ooo-ue'.

Breeding behaviour

Stock Doves are cavity nesters, usually preferring tree holes. Traditionally they favoured elm trees, but have diversified with spread of Dutch elm disease. They have been known to nest in holes in quarries, old buildings, nest boxes and even rabbit burrows. The nest materials are collected by the male and assembled by the female. The nest consists of a platform of sticks, rootlets, other plant materials and feathers, though in tree holes with existing debris they will quite often just scrape out a hollow. The nests are used year after year and often for successive broods within a year as well. Usually they have two to three broods of two eggs. They will defend their tree hole vigorously, whether they have built the nest or not, and have been known to attack Jackdaws and even kill a Little Owl.

Long-term fortunes

Despite a small decline in the early 2000s, there was an overall increase of 18% in their population between 1987 and 2012. Their range appears to have contracted slightly, especially in western Ireland where mixed farming is becoming increasingly rare, but both their breeding productivity and overwinter survival have increased.

Turtle Dove, by Edmund Fellowes

Turtle Dove
Streptopelia turtur

Turtle Doves are summer migrants, and among the last to arrive in Britain from the Sahel in Africa. They typically reach Britain from late April, leaving again by the end of September. They are mostly found on the eastern side of England as far as Yorkshire, though can be found as far west as eastern Wales.

Red-listed

Spotlight

Size 27 cm; Wingspan 50 cm; Weight 140 g

Food: Cereal seed and the seeds of weeds, notably Fumitory.

Breeds: May to August

Clutch size: 2 eggs

Incubation: 13–14 days

Young fledge: c.21 days

Number of broods: 2 per year

Population: 14,000 territories

Max lifespan: 11 years, 2 months

Typical lifespan: 2 years

Garden reporting rate: <1%

Turtle Dove nest with eggs, by Moss Taylor

A bird in decline

Turtle Doves are one of the most threatened birds in Britain and are red-listed. They used to be found all over lowland Britain, but their population has been declining for many decades; the Breeding Bird Survey shows that, between 1995 and 2013, they underwent a 91% decline in their population. There are several theories as to the causes of these declines, including adverse conditions on their wintering grounds, such as periodic drought, hunting pressure on migration and agricultural intensification in their breeding grounds.

Breeding behaviour

These birds prefer to breed in open deciduous woodland or copses with thick undergrowth, and they are mostly found in agricultural areas in lowland England and Wales. Nests are usually found in bushes, hedges or small trees. The male collects the nesting material and the female builds the flimsy nest, which is made of fine twigs or stalks and lined with rootlets or grass. Turtle Doves are known for being monogamous but, while many pair bonds do last throughout their lifetime, they will occasionally take a different mate.

Identification

Turtle Doves are small, slim birds with a neck patch of black and white stripes. Their wing feathers have black centres and orange-brown edges and their black tail has a white border. Underneath they are pale pink with whitish bellies. Their heads are blue-grey and they have orange eyes surrounded by reddish bare skin. Juveniles are browner and duller, lacking the neck patch. Their unmistakeable song consists of a deep purring 'turr turr', repeated several times over.

Woodpigeon, by John Harding

Woodpigeon
Columba palumbus

The largest British pigeon, and one of our commonest birds, Woodpigeon is among our most noticeable garden visitors. They are bold and visible in their habits, and the UK's five million pairs can be seen in flight, on open ground and on conspicuous perches throughout town and country alike.

Green-listed

Spotlight

Size 41 cm; Wingspan 78 cm; Weight 450 g

Food: Seeds, leaves and fruit (especially Ivy berries), plus buds and various agricultural crops.

Woodpigeon nest with eggs, by Mike Toms

Breeds: April to October

Clutch size: 2 eggs

Incubation: 17 days

Young fledge: 29–35 days

Number of broods: 2–3 per year

Population: 5.3 million pairs

Max lifespan: 17 years, 9 months

Typical lifespan: 3 years

Garden reporting rate: 78%

A diet of plant material

Often seen as lumbering and clumsy, Woodpigeons are not always welcome visitors to gardens, due to their destructive habits and voracious appetite. They will take food from hanging feeders if they are able to balance on a suitable perch, but generally they prefer to pick up seed from the ground. Almost entirely vegetarian, their natural diet consists of seeds, leaves, fruit, buds and root crops, and they can damage garden plants by eating the young leaves, or by trampling them to reach seed on the ground. If required, Woodpigeons can be excluded from ground feeding areas by using a large mesh cage that allows access to smaller birds, and kitchen gardeners will need to protect edible plants and berries with netting.

Woodpigeons can take in so much food at a sitting because they are able to store it in their crop, a muscular pouch in the upper chest. The weight of food in a Woodpigeon's crop is often over 70 g, and weights of up to 155 g have been recorded, including crops containing 725 Ivy berries, 758 wheat grains, 30 cherries, and 38 acorns. Once all this food has been taken on board the bird has to sit and rest while digestion takes place; this is why Woodpigeons spend much time perched and inactive. During this time food passes from the crop to the gizzard, a muscular organ that grinds down plant material. Woodpigeons will swallow pieces of grit to help with this process, and there is some indication that they eat more grit when they are mainly feeding on hard seeds, and less when they are eating soft fruits or leaves.

Breeding season

Woodpigeons have a protracted breeding season, and recently fledged juveniles can be seen in gardens from March through to December. The nests, flimsy lattices of twigs in trees and shrubs, are often very obvious. They always lay just two eggs, which fit into the incubation patches on either side of the female's breast. Unlike most birds, Woodpigeons feed their young with 'crop milk', a substance similar to mammalian milk produced by special cells lining the crop. As the chicks grow older their parents feed them increasing amounts of vegetable matter, supplemented with occasional invertebrates such as snails.

An agricultural pest

Woodpigeons are not just a menace in the kitchen garden; their appetite for vegetable matter, combined with their large population, makes them a major agricultural pest. Nationally their numbers are increasing, and it's thought that the spread of intensive arable cultivation, especially oilseed rape and winter-sown cereal, has driven this increase by allowing more birds to survive through the winter. In the autumn Woodpigeons often switch to natural foods, such as berries, acorns and Beech mast, and they are least likely to be seen in gardens at this time – although this is all relative, as they are now recorded by around 80% of Garden BirdWatchers in every week of the year thanks to their increasing breeding population.

Identification

Both adult and juvenile Woodpigeons are grey overall, with a pinkish breast, black outer wings and a broad black band at the end of the tail. Males and females look alike, and adults can be told from other pigeons by the large white patches on the sides of the neck, below a smudge of iridescent green. In flight they show broad white stripes running front-to-back across each wing, and these can be seen on standing birds as a white edge to the folded wing.

Juvenile Woodpigeons lack the white neck patches and could be confused with Stock Doves, but they do not show the smaller bird's noticeably large dark eye. Their song is a simple, five-note cooing phrase, part of the normal background noise in most parts of the country throughout the spring.

Young Woodpigeon, by Moss Taylor

Collared Dove
Streptopelia decaocto

Collared Doves, by Jill Pakenham

Collared Doves are closely associated with humans and are found all over the country including in suburbs, parks, churchyards and farms. In Germany they are so associated with sitting on TV aerials that they have acquired a modern folk name 'Die Fernsehtaube' or 'television dove'!

Green-listed

Spotlight

Size 32 cm; Wingspan 51 cm; Weight 200 g

Food: Mostly cereal grain and weed seeds, but also takes shoots and invertebrates.

Breeds: March to September

Clutch size: 2 eggs

Incubation: 14–16 days

Young fledge: c.18 days

Number of broods: 2–3 per year

Population: 990,000 pairs

Max lifespan: 18 years

Typical lifespan: 3 years

Garden reporting rate: 75%

Collared Dove nest with eggs, by Richard Castell

A recent colonist

The Collared Dove bred for the first time in Britain in 1955. Before 1930 it was only found in Turkey and the Balkans in Europe, but in the following 20 years it swiftly expanded its range north-west. Once it reached England, it continued to spread rapidly, and by 1957 it was seen as far north as Scotland. Two years later it had colonised Ireland, and by 1970 there were an estimated 25,000 pairs in Britain and Ireland. Almost 40 years later, in 2009, there were an estimated 990,000 breeding pairs in the UK alone.

Now, across Britain and Ireland, the only areas they are not found are in the highlands and areas without trees, such as bogs. Although it is not entirely certain why their range expanded as it did, one theory is genetic mutation with young doves acquiring the ability to travel over 600 km away from where they were born. This tends to be in a north-westerly direction, reflecting the direction of range expansion. It is likely that their high reproductive potential has had an effect as well.

A dip in fortunes

Found in gardens year round, Collared Doves are among our most commonly reported birds. While historically their population has been increasing, since 2005 Garden BirdWatch data have revealed a decline, though for unknown reasons. One theory is that Woodpigeon numbers are increasing and outcompeting Collared Doves for resources. It has also been speculated that the disease trichomonosis may have played a part in the Collared Dove's changing fortunes, since pigeons and doves are known to be susceptible to infection, and the disease has been shown to cause declines in in other species. It is hoped that disease monitoring will help to inform us about what is behind the recent dip in fortunes of this bird.

Feeding and breeding

Thanks to their diet Collared Doves have adapted well to human environments, favouring cereal grain, weed seeds, shoots and invertebrates. In gardens you can encourage them by scattering seed on the ground.

If the weather is mild enough, Collared Doves can breed all year round, though their core breeding season is between February and October. The nest consists of a fragile platform of twigs, plant stems and rootlets when new, becoming more solid if the nest is used again. They usually nest on tree branches or in bushes, but they will also nest on buildings using ledges or, more precariously, the bracket of a security light or satellite dish. Surrounding the nest will be the male's small territory which is defended by keeping watch for other males and by display flights consisting of a steep climb, followed by a glide.

Noisy neighbour

Collared Doves have a mostly creamy-grey-buff plumage with a pinkish-buff breast. The black half-collar around the back of the neck gives the Collared Dove its name, though it is worth noting that juvenile birds lack this feature. The only bird that is likely to cause confusion in Britain and Ireland is Turtle Dove, but the latter is much rarer and can be told apart by its distinct chestnut and black upperparts.

The song of the Collared Dove is a persistent and clear three-note 'coo COO coo' which is remembered by some as 'u-nit-ed'. This differs from the five-note song of the Woodpigeon 'COO coo coo coo-coo'. They may also deliver a much harsher-sounding 'kwurr' call. The repetitive nature of the song is not always a favourite with householders, particularly when the bird is perched above a bedroom window at dawn.

Collared Dove, by John Harding

Tawny Owl
Strix aluco

Tawny Owl, by Moss Taylor

The Tawny Owl is the only owl likely to be seen or heard from most gardens, being our most common species and the one owl to have pushed into some of our more leafy suburbs. Active at night, Tawny Owls may descend to take earthworms from garden lawns on damp evenings.

Amber-listed

Spotlight

Size 38 cm; Wingspan 99 cm; Weight 420 g

Food: Small mammals (notably mice and voles), birds, amphibians, worms and large beetles.

Breeds: March to July

Clutch size: 2–3 eggs

Incubation: 28–30 days

Young fledge: 32–37 days

Number of broods: 1 per year

Population: 50,000 pairs

Max lifespan: 21 years, 11 months

Typical lifespan: 4 years

Garden reporting rate: 4%

Tawny Owl nest with eggs, by Herbert & Howells

Nocturnal noises

Tawny Owls are generally only active at night, but roosting birds can occasionally be seen during the day by following the attention of alarmed smaller birds. They are by far the most common owl in the UK, with an estimated 50,000 breeding pairs, and are the only large owl likely to be found in gardens. The territorial call of the male Tawny Owl is a drawn out, wavering 'hooo – hu – oohoohooo', and both sexes make a 'ke-wick' call; these are occasionally heard together as a call-and-response between two different birds, thought to be the source of the popular belief that owls say 'to-whit-to-woo'.

A range of habitats

While their favoured habitat is broad-leaved woodland, Tawny Owls are widely distributed and can be found in conifer plantations, tree-dotted farmland, parks and large gardens. They are recorded in up to 5% of Garden BirdWatch gardens during the autumn and winter; less frequently in the spring and summer when they are less vocal.

They normally nest in tree cavities, but will take to secluded nest boxes in large gardens with mature trees. This gives a great opportunity to see the grey owlets 'branching' – sitting openly on tree branches around the nest site, and being fed by their parents, prior to fledging. Once the young leave the nest they will probably not travel very far at all, as this is one of our most sedentary species, rarely moving more than a few kilometres from where they were hatched. As well as being sedentary they are strongly territorial, giving them the intimate knowledge of their home area necessary for nocturnal hunting. They are entirely absent from Ireland; most sightings there are assumed to be of escaped captive-bred birds.

Sharp-eyed and -eared

In woodland habitats Tawny Owls feed mainly on small mammals, but they are resourceful predators and take a very wide variety of other prey, and in some urban areas have been recorded as feeding mainly on small birds. More unusual prey items include frogs and goldfish!

They are a 'sit and wait' predator, dropping silently from a high vantage point. While they cannot see in total darkness, their night vision is extremely good and their hearing is acute. Their asymmetrical ear openings allow them to triangulate and pinpoint the source of a sound, meaning they can pounce on unseen prey with great accuracy. Measures to benefit Tawny Owls in gardens include leaving areas of rough grass to encourage small mammals, and avoiding the use of rodenticides; these can be harmful to birds of prey that feed on dying rodents. Tawny Owls swallow their prey whole, and later regurgitate the indigestible bones as pellets. An individual owl may produce one or two pellets each day and, if found, these can be soaked in water and dissected to investigate the owl's diet.

Assessing the population trends of nocturnal birds is difficult, but there are indications of a long-term decline in Tawny Owl numbers, and this species is now an amber-listed bird of conservation concern. BTO research has identified and tested survey techniques based on the playback of Tawny Owl calls. This approach can be used to assess how many of these owls remain in the UK and the habitats favoured for breeding.

LITTLE OWL

Little Owls are widespread in Europe, and were successfully introduced to Britain in the 19th century. There are now thought to be around 6,000 breeding pairs, mainly in England, and preferring open farmland, areas with scattered trees and some larger rural gardens.

This small owl is most active at dawn and dusk, though individuals may also be seen during the daytime, often perched on a tree or building. Little Owls feed on small mammals and large invertebrates and, like Tawny Owls, often hunt by dropping onto prey from a perch. They are quite nimble on their toes, and will take earthworms, earwigs and other invertebrates by making darting runs across the ground.

Its small size allows this species to use small cavities for nesting, such as those within a tree or a building. They may also use subterranean cavities, perhaps located among tree roots.

Little Owls are particularly vocal and make a wide range of calls, the most common of which is a sharp, repeated 'KEE-ew' phrase.

Little Owl, by John Harding

Swift, by Graham Catley

Swift
Apus apus

Swifts are summer visitors and are associated with human habitation ranging from large villages to cities, though they occasionally nest on inland crags and sea cliffs. They prefer to nest in older buildings that have suitable cavities between the roof and walls, which most modern houses lack.

Amber-listed

Spotlight

Size 16 cm; Wingspan 45 cm; Weight 44 g

Food: Wide variety of flying insects and spiders, caught on the wing.

Breeds: May to August

Clutch size: 2–3 eggs

Incubation: 19–20 days

Young fledge: 37–56 days

Number of broods: 1 per year

Population: 87,000 pairs

Max lifespan: 17 years, 11 months

Typical lifespan: 9 years

Garden reporting rate: 6%

Swift nest with eggs, by Richard Castell

A life on the wing

After a long journey from southern Africa, Swifts arrive in the UK in late April and stay for about 16 weeks, leaving in August. Data from tagged Swifts have shown that West Africa is an important refuelling region for them before their final leg to Britain, and that one individual took just five days to travel the 5,000 km between the two areas. Once they have arrived back in Africa they may travel through several countries.

Healthy Swifts will only ever land to nest and feed their chicks, spending the rest of their lives on the wing. They will even sleep on the wing, though nesting adults will sleep in the nest site. Once fledged, a chick is likely to remain on the wing for many months, probably until its first breeding season – Swifts often don't start breeding until their fourth year. They manage this remarkable feat by feeding on small aerial insects and spiders and drinking either from raindrops or by skimming the surface of waterbodies.

A species in decline

Like many of our migrant birds, the Swift population has declined. In under 20 years we have lost almost a third of the population. In 2009, there were an estimated 87,000 pairs with densities higher further south and east. The decline is partly thought to be due to the designs of modern buildings, which lack suitable nesting space, and the refurbishment of old buildings, though this can be reversed by providing nest boxes. The establishment of new colonies is also a slow process as young birds are cautious when investigating potential nesting sites. Even if they do find one, they are unlikely to nest there until a year or two later. Other possible reasons for these declines include reduced numbers of aerial invertebrates for the birds to feed on during the breeding season, and problems encountered during migration.

Swifts are hard to study, their lifestyle making it difficult to collect even some of the more basic information on their ecology and behaviour. Much of our knowledge comes from nest box studies, most famously that operated at the Oxford University Museum of Natural History.

Identification

Often seen in parties flying rapidly around, Swifts live up to their name. They could be confused for Swallows or House Martins, but are larger and lack the pale breasts and bellies. Swifts are dark overall except for a small white patch on their throat. They also have narrower wings, which are scythe-shaped, and a small forked tail. The call is a shrill, monotone scream. Swifts tend to feed higher up than Swallows or House Martins and at night can fly up to 10,000 feet when sleeping. It's thought that Swifts can shut down half of their brain, but continually correct for wind drift so that they wake up roughly where they fell asleep!

Boxing clever

Specially designed nest boxes may be used for Swifts and these should be positioned high up, as this gives Swifts the opportunity to gain the momentum they need to get airborne. The nests of Swifts are formed of a shallow cup of grass, leaves and feathers cemented together with saliva. As they nest colonially, you will usually find several nests scattered along the same street, the birds favouring older properties with gaps under the roof tiles.

Swifts will pair for life and a pair may reuse the same nest site repeatedly. The number of eggs that they lay depends on how early they breed; if early enough they will lay three rather than two eggs. Successfully rearing their chicks will depend on the weather as this will affect the abundance of aerial invertebrates on which to feed the young. Should the weather turn foul, however, chicks can counteract the effects of not being fed by going into torpor for several days. This does mean that they can take between 37 and 56 days to fledge!

TRACKING SWIFTS TO AFRICA

Until relatively recently we didn't know where Swifts went when they migrated south for the winter; this was particularly worrying given their alarming population decline.

By using small geolocators attached to individual birds, the BTO have been able to track them and build up a better picture of Swift migration, identifying migration routes and important wintering areas for this species which could help to conserve them. For example, we now know that birds move quickly south along the west coast of Africa in August, on their way to the Congo Basin. Once they reach southern Africa, they regularly move and go as far east as Mozambique, presumably following the availability of their invertebrate prey.

It was also discovered that rather than slowly making their way to the UK, feeding on the wing, that they actually stopover in West Africa for a few days, refuelling for their final journey to the UK, which can take as little as five days.

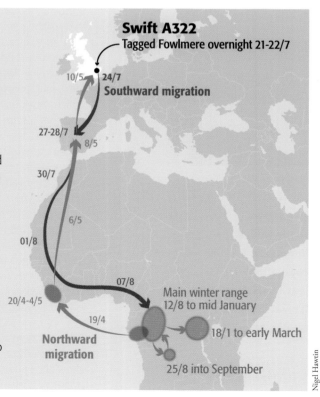

Swift A322
Tagged Fowlmere overnight 21-22/7

10/5   24/7
Southward migration

27-28/7
8/5

30/7

6/5

01/8

07/8

20/4-4/5

19/4

Main winter range
12/8 to mid January

18/1 to early March

Northward migration

25/8 into September

Nigel Hawtin

Juvenile Green Woodpecker, by Liz Cutting

Green Woodpecker
Picus viridis

The largest of our breeding woodpeckers, Green Woodpecker is a regular garden visitor, exploiting garden lawns for the ant nests they contain, and turning to windfall apples during the autumn and periods of cold winter weather.

Green-listed

Spotlight

Size 32 cm; Wingspan 41 cm; Weight 190 g

Food: Mostly ants taken from nests. Largely forages on ground.

Juvenile Green Woodpecker in nest cavity, by John Harding

Breeds: May to June

Clutch size: 5–7 eggs

Incubation: 17–18 days

Young fledge: 23–27 days

Number of broods: 1 per year

Population: 52,000 pairs

Max lifespan: 15 years

Typical lifespan: not known

Garden reporting rate: 3%

Large and noisy

Large, noisy and brightly coloured, Green Woodpeckers are hard to miss. In flight they can be recognised by their conspicuous yellow rump and strongly undulating flight path. Both males and females have a red cap and black surround to the eye, but given close views the sexes can be told apart by looking at the 'moustache', which is all black in females, and has a red centre in males. The juveniles have similar colouration to the adults, but are strongly spotted and streaked both above and below.

Green Woodpeckers are very vocal, and often make a piercing, fast 'kyu-kyu-kyu' call in flight. The territorial call of the male is a loud, laughing series of descending notes, known as 'yaffling', which provides the bird with one of its local names, 'yaffle'. They drum far less frequently than other woodpeckers; a short, soft roll.

An ant specialist

These birds specialise in eating ants and their larvae and eggs, which they gather with their extraordinarily long, mobile, sticky tongues, which are wide and flattened at the tip. They forage in open grassy areas including pasture, woodland glades, heathland and large gardens, frequently standing with head held high and bill angled upwards to look around, though they are often nervous and fly at the sight of humans. Like all woodpeckers they excavate holes in trees for nesting, and during the breeding season they favour lowland deciduous and mixed woodland with nearby areas of short grassland.

Liking it warm and dry

Green Woodpeckers are found across England, with the highest densities in the south and east, and are patchily distributed in Wales and in southern and central Scotland. Despite feeding on invertebrates that are hard to find in winter, Green Woodpeckers do not fly south for the winter, and in fact are extremely sedentary. Records of ringed birds moving more than 20 km are unusual, and out of the 10,000 that have been ringed in Britain not a single one has been recovered overseas. This aversion to crossing water means that Green Woodpeckers are entirely absent from Ireland.

Seasonality of garden use

Though they do not migrate, reports of this species nonetheless show seasonal patterns. During March and April the males become more vocal as they defend their nesting territories, though since they rarely nest in gardens this doesn't result in an increase in Garden BirdWatch records. They are also noticeable in July and August, when the juveniles disperse from wooded areas in favour of more open habitats. At this time they are seen in around 4% of Garden BirdWatch gardens, up from under 2% in the early part of the year. Even during this summer peak they are more likely to be seen in rural gardens with large lawns than in urban areas.

Patterns of change

The British Green Woodpecker population increased from the mid 1980s until around 2010, which coincided with their northward range expansion into Scotland, documented through *Bird Atlas 2007–11*. It has been suggested that this could be due to the generally milder winters in recent decades, reducing the number of frost and snow days during which they are unable to forage.

However, since then this species has disappeared from Pembrokeshire and Anglesey, and failed to consolidate its Scottish range. Since around 2010 numbers have shown a slight decrease. The declines in western areas are as yet unexplained, but given their very specific food requirements it seems likely that this is somehow related to the availability of ants. Management of grassland areas and fluctuations in rabbit populations can affect the amount of short grazed turf, which holds the highest densities of ant nests. Despite the recent slight decline, this species now has favourable conservation status across Europe and in 2015 was moved from the UK's amber list to the green list.

Female Green Woodpecker, by Allan Drewitt

Great Spotted Woodpecker
Dendrocopos major

Female Great Spotted Woodpecker, by Jill Pakenham

Great Spotted Woodpecker is a regular visitor to those gardens located close to areas of woodland. Visits peak during the summer months, when adult birds bring their youngsters to garden feeding stations to exploit the peanuts provided in hanging feeders.

Green-listed

Spotlight

Size 22 cm; Wingspan 36 cm; Weight 85 g

Food: Invertebrates, usually from under bark or in dead wood, but also tree seeds and birds' eggs.

Breeds: April to June

Clutch size: 5–6 eggs

Incubation: 10–13 days

Young fledge: 20–24 days

Number of broods: 1 per year

Population: 140,000 pairs

Max lifespan: 11 years, 1 month

Typical lifespan: not known

Garden reporting rate: 28%

Newly hatched Great Spotted Woodpecker chicks, by Ashley Jackson

Identification

Great Spotted Woodpecker is the more common of the two 'pied' woodpeckers in the UK, the other being Lesser Spotted Woodpecker. It has black-and-white plumage, with a red undertail and whitish belly. There is also a large, white oval patch on its shoulder. Telling the sex of the bird is very easy – males have a red patch on their napes and females have an all-black crown. Juveniles have a mostly red crown.

Great Spotted Woodpeckers have a short, sharp 'kek' call, which is sometimes repeated quickly when they are alarmed. In the spring, they produce far-carrying drum rolls by selecting a suitable piece of wood. They then strike the timber 10 to 40 times a second to make the wood resonate.

Where there are trees

Great Spotted Woodpeckers are usually found near areas of woodland, preferably mixed. They will also nest in parks, orchards and large gardens, however, providing there are sufficiently large trees present, but even here they are rarely far from a more substantial block of woodland. With their strong bills, these birds usually excavate a cavity for their nest in decaying wood. On occasion, Great Spotted Woodpeckers have been known to use deep nest boxes but they do not take to boxes as readily as other cavity nesting species.

Outside the breeding season, female and male Great Spotted Woodpeckers have separate feeding territories, but established males usually retain the same territory in subsequent years. These males tend to pair with a female for a single year; both parents tend to the eggs and the young, taking turns to incubate and feed them. The breeding territories are evident early in the year when birds can be seen calling and chasing one another.

Great Spotted Woodpecker diet mostly consists of invertebrates, found under bark or in dead wood, and conifer seeds. They will occasionally take other birds' eggs or nestlings if there is an opportunity. Sometimes they will try and break into nest boxes – this can be prevented by using a 'woodcrete' nest box. In gardens they mostly feed on suet and nuts.

On the up

The Great Spotted Woodpecker population has been increasing since the 1970s and has been fairly uniform across its British range. Before 2006 Great Spotted Woodpeckers had not bred in Ireland, so it was unexpected to find a pair in Northern Ireland that year. In the Republic of Ireland they were first reported breeding in 2009. Genetic studies indicate that Britain is likely to be the origin of these Irish woodpeckers. They still aren't found in the Northern Isles, Outer Hebrides and most of the Inner Hebrides, but they were confirmed breeding on the Isle of Man in 2010.

It is thought the success of the Great Spotted Woodpecker could be to do with the fact that competition with Starlings is decreasing, due to the latter's decline. This means that there is less competition for nest cavities. Another contributing factor could be the increased availability of garden feeders.

BTO Garden BirdWatch data show that numbers of Great Spotted Woodpecker have increased in gardens by almost 50% between 2003 and 2015. There is a peak in gardens at the beginning of the summer as adults bring their young to garden bird feeding stations. It is thought that the adults do this in order to show the chicks where they can find reliable sources of food, something that is likely to be important as the chicks gain independence.

LESSER SPOTTED WOODPECKER

Lesser Spotted Woodpeckers are very easily distinguished from Great Spotted Woodpeckers by the fact that they are a lot smaller, about the size of a sparrow. The male has a red crown patch, whereas the female's is black, and neither has a red undertail. The species is a rare visitor to garden feeding stations and has long been red-listed.

It is worth noting that juvenile Great Spotted Woodpeckers also sport a red cap, which lasts through until their first moult. Great Spotted Woodpeckers are much bigger, being Starling-sized or larger. Look for the red or pale red under-tail feathers, and solid white wing panel, in Great Spotted Woodpeckers; these are absent in Lesser Spotted Woodpeckers.

The decline of the Lesser Spotted Woodpecker has been significant, and this has now become a scarce or absent breeding species across much of its former British range. It is now most likely to be encountered in the south-east of England and in the English counties bordering southern Wales.

Lesser Spotted Woodpecker, by Steve Young/NPL

Ring-necked Parakeet, by Christine M Matthews

Ring-necked Parakeet
Psittacula krameri

Escaped aviary birds regularly turn up at garden bird feeders, but only Ring-necked Parakeets have established a sizeable wild-living population. Although this population is centred on London and north Kent, parakeets sometimes turn up elsewhere and new populations are becoming established.

Spotlight

Not listed

Size 40 cm; Wingspan 45 cm; Weight 130 g

Food: Seeds, fruit and flowers, though our population is more omnivorous, taking bird table fare.

Ring-necked Parakeet eggs, by Peter Castell

Breeds: March to June

Clutch size: 3–4 eggs

Incubation: 22–24 days

Young fledge: 40–50 days

Number of broods: 1 per year

Population: 8,600 pairs

Max lifespan: 8 years, 11 months

Typical lifespan: not known

Garden reporting rate: 1%

Origins

Escaped or released Ring-necked Parakeets were first confirmed breeding in the wild in Kent in 1971, and today they are common in parts of Greater London, Kent and Surrey, and present in smaller numbers across England and into Scotland and Wales, particularly in winter when they tend to range more widely. It may seem surprising that a tropical species can survive the British winters, but in their native range Ring-necked Parakeets are the most northerly parakeets in the world, inhabiting the foothills of the Himalayas. Genetic modelling has traced the origin of British breeding birds to the northerly parts of the native range in Pakistan and northern India.

These exotic, bright green parrots are around the size of a Collared Dove, but with a very long, pointed tail and a bright red bill. The males have a black and pink ring around the back of the head, which gives them their alternative name of Rose-ringed Parakeet. They are unlikely to be confused with any of our native species, and the combination of entirely green plumage and a red bill helps to distinguish them from other escaped parrots. In flight their long tail, pointed wings and rounded head gives them a distinctive outline, and they are most often detected by their noisy shrieks.

An adaptable lifestyle

Ring-necked Parakeets are adaptable generalists, feeding on a wide variety of fruit, berries, nuts, seeds and scraps. They favour parks and gardens in urban and suburban areas, and have learned to exploit garden bird feeders, often aggressively excluding the normal cast of garden birds. All parrots are intelligent birds with extremely strong beaks, and Ring-necked Parakeets have been known to prise open bird feeders to access the contents. They have taken to life in the UK so well that there has been a population explosion; numbers increased tenfold between 1995 and 2010, and this increase currently shows no sign of slowing. They are extremely gregarious, and gather together in spectacular numbers in nightly roosts, which may contain thousands of birds, drawn from a wide area, in just a few trees. Coordinated counts at roosts across their London breeding range have given an estimated post-breeding population of around 30,000 individuals.

A problem in the making?

This population explosion has caused concern, and not just among those who have to fill up or replace their bird feeders. While the British parakeet population is currently confined to urban and suburban areas, the species is a destructive agricultural pest in much of its African and Asian range, and could potentially cause serious damage if they expand into British farmland in large numbers. However,

while numbers have increased, these gregarious birds appear to be unwilling to move significant distances from urban centres, and their spread into other areas has so far been relatively slow.

It is also thought that parakeets could adversely affect our native bird species through competition for resources. Behavioural research has shown that the mere presence of the aggressive Ring-necked Parakeets caused other garden birds to become more wary and to spend less time feeding, thereby disrupting their normal foraging behaviour.

In addition, this species nests very early in the year, sometimes starting as early as January or February, and occupies tree holes that could otherwise be used by birds such as Nuthatch or Starling. In Belgium, where there is a large population of introduced parakeets, it has been suggested that competition for nest sites might be depressing Nuthatch numbers, though no such relationship has been found in Britain as yet.

Ring-necked Parakeet, by Richard Winston

UNKNOWN ORIGINS

Some say that our feral population of Ring-necked Parakeets is derived from birds that escaped from a film studio during the making of *The African Queen*. Others believe that Jimi Hendrix released them to 'bring some psychedelic colour to London's skyline'.

While both of these stories may be nothing more than urban myths, even if these events did occur they probably just added to a steady stream of escapes from the caged population; after all, these were popular pets.

Magpie, by John Harding

Magpie
Pica pica

Seen by some as a villain, the Magpie is a resourceful and opportunistic species that has been able to adapt to the opportunities that have been created through our activities. It is also one of our most striking and recognisable garden visitors.

Green-listed

Spotlight

Size 45 cm; Wingspan 56 cm; Weight 240 g

Food: Omnivorous, taking mostly invertebrates, fruit, seeds, carrion and scraps, plus small vertebrates.

Breeds: March to June

Clutch size: 4–6 eggs

Incubation: 21–22 days

Young fledge: 22–28 days

Number of broods: 1 per year

Population: 550,000 pairs

Max lifespan: 21 years, 9 months

Typical lifespan: 5 years

Garden reporting rate: 58%

Magpie nest with eggs, by Richard Castell

Blame the Magpie?

Magpies are often linked to declines in other bird species due to their predation of eggs and nestlings, but there is no scientific evidence to support this. Whilst the Magpie population has increased overall, and many other species have declined, these population changes have happened over different time periods and in different areas of the country. This suggests that the general patterns are a coincidence and not linked.

Instantly recognisable

Magpies are one of the most recognisable of our garden birds. They are large birds with striking black-and-white plumage and a long tail. While they may look black in some lights, their wings and tail are actually iridescent with purple, blue and green hues. Juveniles look similar but are duller and have a shorter tail. They have a loud, hoarse call which can be quite fast and staccato and sound like 'tsche-tsche'. They also have quieter, more conversational calls.

Habitat preferences

Magpies prefer to be in open country, though with plenty of trees and bushes around. This includes farmland with tall hedges, woodland edges that are relatively open, coastal scrub and moorland edges. They are also increasingly found in suburban parks and gardens.

They breed most commonly around farmland and in urban areas. Their nests are built in the tops of trees, or occasionally on top of pylons, and are made of two parts. The external frame of twigs and sticks forms a loose canopy to protect the inner nest which is a cup of mud, twigs and grass, to reduce the risk of predation. They can build their nests from as early as February, but they do not normally lay their eggs until April. Like many corvids, the eggs are hatched asynchronously, with the female incubating before all the eggs have been laid. This ensures that, if there is not enough food for all of the chicks, the older ones should survive.

Magpies have a catholic diet consisting of invertebrates, fruit, seed, carrion, scraps and small mammals. During the breeding season eggs and the young of other species are an important part of their diet as well. If not needed, they will cache food, some of which may be recovered within a few days.

One's for sorrow, two's for . . .

As well as caching food, Magpies are notorious for hoarding shiny objects. This, however, is more or less a myth and only really seen in captivity amongst hand-reared young. While wild birds may occasionally take shiny objects,

it seems to be more out of curiosity than anything else. These are intelligent, social birds though and it is most likely folklore, and their occasional taking of other birds' young, that has raised this suspicion around them. In western Europe they were thought to be bearers of bad omens and associated with the devil, which is why, to this day, some people still have a ritual to negate their perceived bad influence. It's not all bad though – in South Korea the Magpie is seen as a bird of good fortune.

One of the most interesting behaviours seen in Magpies is the communal gatherings of immature birds. These birds, which don't hold territories, form small flocks in the run up to the breeding season and target established pairs. The immature birds don't usually succeed in dislodging the territory holders but, if they do, then the dominant pair within the group will take the territory.

CHANGING TIMES

Until the late 1980s, the Magpie population steadily increased and then stabilised. These increases have mostly occurred in the central lowlands of Scotland and in parts of the south-east and are thought to potentially be due to lower levels of persecution of nests and individuals. However, since the beginning of the 21st century there has been a slight decrease in the population across the UK, echoing a widespread decrease across Europe. This is not reflected in gardens, where Magpies have been increasing since 2009, and this is partly due to the fact that they are flourishing in suburban areas and intensively farmed landscapes. Peaks in Garden BirdWatch gardens occur in the winter months and when Magpies have young in the nest, indicating their need for additional resources in challenging conditions.

Whilst they are found across Britain and Ireland, Magpies are localised in Scotland and are mostly absent from the north-west part of the country and its islands. However, they are continuing to spread, with increases seen in upland southern Scotland. They do only travel short distances though, as they are sedentary in nature. The highest densities of Magpies are found around urban areas where they benefit from the availability of food.

Magpie, by John Flowerday

Jay, by John Harding

Jay
Garrulus glandarius

Although predominantly a bird of deciduous woodland, the Jay is a regular visitor to rural and suburban gardens, particularly during late autumn. Often wary in their habits, Jays can be more approachable in gardens than they are in the wider countryside, providing an opportunity to take in their subtle but stylish plumage.

Green-listed

Spotlight

Size 34 cm; Wingspan 55 cm; Weight 170 g

Food: Invertebrates (especially beetles and caterpillars), fruit, acorns and other tree seeds.

Breeds: April to July

Clutch size: 4–6 eggs

Incubation: 16–17 days

Young fledge: 21–22 days

Number of broods: 1 per year

Population: 170,000 territories

Max lifespan: 16 years, 10 months

Typical lifespan: 4 years

Garden reporting rate: 14%

Jay nest with eggs, by Richard Castell

Identification

Jays are eye-catching birds, unusually colourful for members of the crow family. Standing, they appear mainly pinkish grey-brown, with a streaked head, heavy dark bill, thick black moustache, piercing pale eyes and black-and-white wings. In good light the finely striped blue and black covert feathers appear as a dazzling patch on the closed wing. In flight, the large white rump and white wing patches stand out against the dark tail and noticeably rounded wings. Their voice is a loud, hoarse screech, often uttered as a warning or alarm call.

An opportunist

While they mainly feed on acorns and other seeds in winter, at other times of year they will forage for invertebrates, and are also known to take small mammals, birds' eggs, bats and even fish. This generalist lifestyle, and a general decrease in persecution, has enabled them to expand from woodland habitats, where they are still most common, into more suburban areas. Jays breed across nearly the whole of Britain and Ireland, though they are patchily distributed in Northern Ireland and missing from northern Scotland. While numbers have generally fluctuated since the start of population monitoring in the 1960s, there was a sustained increase between the 1990s and 2015 which took numbers to their highest recorded levels.

The mighty oak

Jays are a resident species, but they are much more noticeable in autumn than in the spring and summer. At this time of year they collect acorns and store them for the winter, and to do this they will travel out of their home ranges to productive oak trees and spend hours every day ferrying acorns back and forth. Jays are able to carry several acorns at a time in their gullet, as well as a larger one in their bill, and they hide these in nooks and crannies in trees, under roots and moss and in the ground. They have even been known to dig holes and bury acorns in garden lawns. Caching food in this manner is a behaviour seen in a number of our bird species and tends to be associated with the availability of a seasonal glut in foods that do not go off rapidly, such as acorns.

It has been calculated that a single Jay can stash away 5,000 acorns in a few weeks during this autumn harvest, and with a British population of 170,000 pairs it's no wonder they are very visible at this time of year. Over the course of the winter the birds will revisit their many hiding places and eat the acorns, but a proportion are never retrieved and may go on to germinate.

Between two years

Acorn crops can vary hugely from autumn to autumn, or even fail entirely, depending on weather conditions earlier in the year and pest levels. In years when reports of acorns in the countryside are low, more Jays are seen in gardens, demonstrating how birds can fall back on human-provided foods when their preferred natural foods are in short supply. Garden BirdWatch reports of Jays in October can be as high as 20% of gardens or as low as 10%, depending on the acorn crop. On average, Jays are seen in between 10% and 15% of gardens each week, with a peak in June when the juveniles are dispersing. They will make use of most bird foods provided in gardens, but they prefer peanuts, and may even up-end hanging peanut feeders to empty the contents onto the ground.

ON THE MOVE

Jays are by nature sedentary, but if they find that they won't have an acorn store to see them through the winter they can move long distances, and in large numbers. These 'eruptive' migrations are common in Scandinavia, where they are unlikely to survive without a winter larder, and in years of particularly poor acorn crops across Europe these movements may even be noticeable in Britain. One such year was 1983, when thousands of birds were observed migrating into and across Britain as far as Cornwall, where 800 Jays were seen together in a single field.

Jay, by John Flowerday

Jackdaw, by John Harding

Jackdaw
Corvus monedula

Jackdaws are found in many habitats, including open countryside, woodland and town centres. However, they occur in their greatest numbers in areas of mixed farming and pasture. Pairs tend to nest in suitably large cavities, such as those within mature trees, but they regularly make use of household chimneys.

Spotlight

Green-listed

Size 34 cm; Wingspan 70 cm; Weight 220 g

Food: Invertebrates, fruit, seeds, and carrion. Jackdaw nestlings are fed mostly on invertebrates.

Jackdaw nest with eggs, by Richard Castell

Breeds: April to June

Clutch size: 4–5 eggs

Incubation: 21–22 days

Young fledge: 22–28 days

Number of broods: 1 per year

Population: 1.3 million pairs

Max lifespan: 17 years, 1 month

Typical lifespan: 5 years

Garden reporting rate: 35%

Our smallest crow

Jackdaws are the smallest of the crow family in the UK, about two-thirds the size of a Rook or a Carrion Crow. They are mostly dark grey with a lighter grey nape, and have a shorter bill than other crows. Adults have greyish-white eyes, but those of juveniles start off blue-grey. The eyes then turn brown in their first winter and white when they get their full adult plumage. Until then, juveniles lack the distinctive grey nape. A very conversational bird, the Jackdaw has very short calls. The most common is the high-pitched friendly 'tchack', which the species is named after, but there are many variations.

Breeding behaviour

Jackdaws usually pair for life, and pairs will be seen together throughout the year. They fly around together and can usually be picked out, even in large flocks. Individuals work hard to rear their young, but in most years they struggle to find enough food to rear all of their chicks. While the female will lay four or five eggs, she actually starts incubating halfway through the clutch, which means that the eggs will hatch asynchronously and the young will be different ages. The smaller chicks, which are the last to hatch, are most likely to suffer if there is not enough food around. A reason suggested for such a strong pair bond, despite losing clutches, is the amount of work they put in finding food for their chicks.

The nest itself is usually located within some form of cavity, ranging from man-made ones like chimneys to hollow trees in parks and deciduous woodland. Their nests are untidy constructions made using twigs and lined with materials including wool, hair, bark and soil. Jackdaws are very social birds and nest in colonies, often close to Rooks, though sometimes their nests can be quite scattered. They are what ornithologists call 'semi-colonial.'

A typical crow

Like most corvids, Jackdaws are omnivores and will eat invertebrates, fruit, seeds, scraps and even nestlings and eggs. On occasion they have been known to catch flying ants, or steal fish from Puffins. In the breeding season they prefer the larvae of moths and flies for their chicks. You can easily encourage them into the garden with fat products, cereals and nuts.

In gardens, Jackdaws peak in the summer when they are feeding their young, suggesting that garden bird feeding stations provide an important food source during the breeding season. There is a dip in the autumn when there is more food available in the wider countryside, and they then start to increase again in the winter. They tend to approach garden feeding stations early in the morning, so many people may not even realise that they regularly get Jackdaws in their gardens.

A broad distribution

Jackdaws are found across Britain and Ireland, except in the Scottish highlands. They are mostly sedentary, resident birds, though upland breeding pairs may migrate south and west to lowland regions or to Ireland for the winter. The wintering population may be increased by immigrants from northern Europe, which arrive along the east coast in the autumn.

Overall, the population of Jackdaws is increasing, and Garden BirdWatch data reflect this. This long-term increase is thought to be due to improvements in breeding performance, thanks to increased availability of food at garden feeding stations and more generally around human habitats. Additionally, changes in land use, especially in arable and mixed farming areas, appear to be providing food all year round, which may help both overwinter survival and breeding success.

Jackdaw, by Edmund Fellowes

Rook
Corvus frugilegus

Rook, by Jeff & Allison Kew

The Rook is a bird of rural gardens and one that often visits largely unnoticed very early in the morning before the householders have drawn back the curtains. Like other members of the crow family, this is an intelligent bird and one that has learned how best to exploit hanging feeders at garden feeding stations.

Spotlight

Green-listed

Size 45 cm; Wingspan 90 cm; Weight 310 g

Food: Invertebrates, especially beetles and earthworms, cereal grain, small vertebrates and carrion.

Breeds: March to June

Clutch size: 4–5 eggs

Incubation: 16–19 days

Young fledge: 30–36 days

Number of broods: 1 per year

Population: 990,000 pairs

Max lifespan: 22 years, 11 months

Typical lifespan: 6 years

Garden reporting rate: 12%

Rook at the nest, by John Harding

Identification

While superficially similar to Carrion Crows, adult Rooks can be identified by the area of unfeathered pale skin around the base of the bill. Their forehead and crown feathers form more of a peak than Carrion Crows, and their bills are more pointed; these features combine to give Rooks a distinctive profile, which helps when they are seen in poor light or in silhouette. In bright sunlight, look out for the green and purple sheen to the feathers. On their underparts the feathering is often loose and shaggy, giving the appearance of 'trousers' concealing the upper legs. Juvenile Rooks lack the bare white face of the adults, and are therefore much harder to tell from Carrion Crows; the main difference is the shape of the upper bill, being curved in Carrion Crows and straight and pointed in Rooks. In flight it can be seen that Rooks have slightly longer central tail feathers, giving a more rounded shape to the tail. They are vocal birds, calling with nasal, noisy croaks.

A sociable bird

The most striking feature of Rooks is their sociable nature. While it's not strictly true to say that a bird seen alone must be a Carrion Crow, and birds seen in large groups are always Rooks, this is very often the case. They forage together, and arise to wheel in spectacular, noisy, playful flocks. They nest communally in highly visible rookeries, with tens or even hundreds of nests at the tops of tall trees. These may be found in woodland, or in smaller groups of trees in farmland, the grounds of large gardens, in villages or suburbs or on motorway embankments. Rookeries can be ancient, and the largest, with hundreds of nests, may be split into distinct groupings. The largest recorded rookery, in Aberdeenshire, was recorded as having 6,700 nests in 1957; it has since reduced in size, though is still the largest in the UK.

Within the rookery successful pairs stay together for several years, or for life, and often renovate and reuse the same nests. They start nesting very early in the year, and are known to steal sticks from their neighbours' nests if they are unguarded. Nesting activity can sometimes be seen in late autumn, but that very early building appears to be generally for display purposes, with birds sometimes carrying items such as stones and pinecones that aren't actually used in nest construction. Generally during the winter months Rooks abandon their rookeries, and gather in huge overnight roosts, often together with Jackdaws. Birds from vast areas gather together, thought to fly over 20 miles to roosts, and the sight of thousands of Rooks coming together at dusk is an impressive spectacle.

Farmland associations

Rooks are strongly associated with agricultural areas, and are widely distributed in the lowlands of the UK, with the notable exception of urban areas. While they always need trees to nest in, they are essentially a species of open grassland, requiring accessible soil in which they probe for invertebrates with their sharp bills. Although soil invertebrates are their staple food, they also eat grain, bringing them into conflict with farmers. The long tradition of scarecrows in the British countryside is a testament to the efforts that are put into keeping Rooks away from crops.

Opportunistic garden visitor

Though they are primarily farmland birds, Rooks are recorded in over 10% of Garden BirdWatch gardens in April, though this percentage drops below 5% by the end of the summer. They are most likely to be seen in rural or village gardens, and have learned to take advantage of the food available from garden bird feeders. Rooks are extremely intelligent, and Garden BirdWatchers have observed them standing on branches and pulling up feeders hanging by string, or un-hooking feeders so they fall to the ground, spilling the contents. Given their social nature, it's not surprising elements of cooperation can be seen in their feeding habits, with individuals observed pushing feeders towards other birds, which are then able to access the food.

Periodic surveys of rookeries indicate that Rook populations have been increasing since the 1970s, perhaps due to additional foraging opportunities provided by new outdoor pig farms and landfill sites, increased roadside carrion, and higher stocking rates on grassland. Some rookeries have become fragmented as a result of persecution, leading to smaller rookeries becoming established over a much wider area.

Rooks, by Anne Carrington-Cotton

Carrion Crow, by John Harding

Carrion Crow
Corvus corone

Carrion Crows are widely distributed throughout England, Wales, southern and eastern Scotland and the Channel Islands. Where they overlap with Hooded Crows in the Scottish 'hybrid zone' they do interbreed and can produce fertile young.

Green-listed

Spotlight

Size 46 cm; Wingspan 98 cm; Weight 510 g

Food: Invertebrates (particularly during the breeding season), plus eggs, carrion, scraps and cereal grain.

Breeds: April to July

Clutch size: 4–5 eggs

Incubation: 18–19 days

Young fledge: 28–35 days

Number of broods: 1 per year

Population: 1 million territories

Max lifespan: 17 years, 1 month

Typical lifespan: 4 years

Garden reporting rate: 32%

Carrion Crow nest with eggs, by Richard Castell

Identification

Carrion Crows are the largest species of crow after Ravens, and are are entirely black with a faint metallic green-blue gloss to their plumage. They have broad short wings and a rounded edge to the tail. As well as the size difference, tail shape can help separate them from Ravens, which have a wedge-shaped tail. They could also be confused with juvenile Rooks but have thicker, blunter bills with a more curved tip, as well as a less steep forehead. Juveniles have greyish eyes, rather than the brown eyes of the adults, and duller, browner plumage.

Carrion Crows have very noisy calls that sound hard and croaking. The most common is 'kraa kraa' which is stronger sounding than that of the more softly-voiced Rook.

Nest sites and nests

Carrion Crows prefer to nest high up. They usually nest in the tops of tall trees, favouring open woodland, tree clumps in farming areas and larger town parks. They will also use man-made structures, such as pylons, but in the absence of trees they will nest on the ground. The nest is made of a bulky foundation of sticks and moss held together using mud. The inner cup uses finer twigs and plant material, and is lined with wool and hair. They will have one clutch of four to five eggs, which is laid any time from mid March.

A broad diet

They are omnivorous birds and will take almost any type of food if the opportunity arises. In spring and summer, insects and other invertebrates make up the bulk of their diet. During the breeding season, carrion and other scavenged food is important for feeding chicks. By winter, grain becomes a crucial part of their diet, and they will also eat berries. They will take mammals as large as hares or birds as large as Woodpigeons if the opportunity arises and, like other crows, also take chicks and eggs of other birds. Gardens may be visited for scraps and seed on bird tables or the ground, though some enterprising birds have also learned to use hanging feeders.

Populations and food availability

Overall the population increased by 47% between 1987 and 2012 as levels of persecution by gamekeepers, due to the Carrion Crow's diet including eggs and young birds, decreased. They were also occasionally targeted by sheep farmers due to the misconception that they regularly killed lambs. However, the population increase could also potentially be thanks to increased productivity. Ecological reasons for this could include increases in food availability and the expansion of Carrion Crows into urban areas. Densities of Carrion Crows are highest in lowland areas, especially those with mixed and pastoral farmland habitats.

Habitats and social interactions

Carrion Crows will visit a range of garden types throughout Britain whereas Hooded Crows are more likely to be seen in rural gardens. They are territorial and most gardens that are visited receive their local breeding pair consistently throughout the year. In the summer numbers may increase as the adults feed their fledglings. In the autumn a dip in the mean count may occur, indicating that there are good feeding opportunities elsewhere. If food resources in a territory become more abundant (whether temporarily or for an extended period of time) resident Carrion Crows will share them without too much squabbling.

At any time of year small flocks may also be seen – these are non-breeding birds that are less territorial. In the autumn and winter, these birds may join with breeding pairs and sometimes other species of crow to form large communal roosts in woodland areas. Such roosts can involve many hundreds or even thousands of individual birds, drawn from over a wide area and delivering a truly amazing wildlife spectacle.

HOODED CROW

While Carrion Crows are common across most of Britain, in north-west Scotland and Ireland you are more likely to encounter Hooded Crows. Until recently Hooded and Carrion Crows were thought to be different geographical races of the same species, but in 2002 they were separated. In areas where they overlap, the two species may interbreed and produce hybrid offspring with mixed plumage. Hooded Crows have bicoloured plumage with a grey body, black wings, a black head and a black tail.

Hooded Crow, by Ron Marshall

Goldcrest, by John Dunn

Goldcrest
Regulus regulus

The tiny Goldcrest can be hard to see, as they often forage high and concealed within tree canopies. However, on occasion they will move closer, often seemingly unconcerned by human observers, and then close views will reveal their delicate features.

Green-listed

Spotlight

Size 9 cm; Wingspan 14 cm; Weight 6 g

Food: Invertebrates, especially aphids, caterpillars, springtails and spiders, mostly from tree canopy.

Breeds: April to July

Clutch size: 7–12 eggs

Incubation: 14–17 days

Young fledge: 16–21 days

Number of broods: 2 per year

Population: 520,000 territories

Max lifespan: 4 years, 3 months

Typical lifespan: 2 years

Garden reporting rate: 6%

Goldcrest nest with eggs, by Richard Castell

A tiny visitor

The overall impression is of a diminutive, greenish bird, with paler wing bars and a short tail. The head is distinctively pattered, with a wide yellow central crown stripe flanked with black, though this can be hard to see when watching the bird from below. Their dark eyes are ringed with white, and appear relatively large, round and distinct in an otherwise plain face; this distinguishes them from the closely related but much rarer Firecrests, which have strongly black-and-white-striped faces.

While at rest, both male and female Goldcrests have a narrow yellow crown stripe. However, the under-feathers of the male's crest are bright orange, and these are brilliantly displayed when the bird spreads its crown, due to agitation or a territorial dispute. Juvenile Goldcrests lack any head pattern except an indistinct white eye ring, though they acquire the yellow and black crests by their first autumn. Their call is a thin, very high pitched, reedy 'zree-zree-zree', and their song is a cyclical refrain, likened to a tiny squeaky wheel, that ends with a flourish.

A diet of insects and spiders

Goldcrests are insectivores, feeding on tiny invertebrates found at the very ends of branches, and as such are rarely seen on bird feeders. Though they are resident in Britain year round, during the summer months they are seen by only around 3% of Garden BirdWatchers. However, they are seen in around 8% of gardens in the winter, when they accompany winter feeding flocks of Blue and Great Tits through a broad range of habitats, and may also take fat from bird feeders during periods of very harsh weather.

In the breeding season Goldcrests are strongly associated with conifers, though they do not require a large area of woodland, and can be found nesting in solitary Yew trees or other evergreens in churchyards or gardens. They are very widely distributed throughout Britain and Ireland, absent only from treeless landscapes in the uplands and the Fens.

An incredible journey

Goldcrest numbers are swelled in autumn by arrivals from northern Europe, including Scandinavia and even Russia, astounding though it is that such a fragile bird, weighing just 6 g, can make an autumn sea crossing. In the past some people did not believe that they could migrate at all, and observations of Goldcrests arriving on our eastern shores in the company of larger migrants led to the somewhat far-fetched belief that they hitched a lift in the feathers of Woodcocks or Short-eared Owls. Some of the birds that arrive in winter move further south to overwinter in France, but many remain and contribute to the peak seen in gardens during the winter months.

The challenge of winter

Though this country provides a more hospitable winter environment than Scandinavia, Goldcrests are still severely affected by harsh conditions, and in some winters very few individuals survive to breed the following year. Populations were severely affected by the bitter winters of the 1960s, but increased to an all-time high in the 1970s; since then numbers have shown dramatic fluctuations but the long-term pattern appears to be stable. These large year-to-year changes, with numbers bouncing back after crashes, reflect the high breeding potential of this species. Goldcrests can lay up to 13 eggs in a clutch, though 9–11 is more common, and nest twice during the breeding season. A clutch of eggs, though individually barely larger than peas, can represent one and a half times the bodyweight of the female – a huge reproductive effort.

Goldcrest, by Graham Catley

Blue Tit
Cyanistes caeruleus

Blue Tit, by John Harding

Blue Tits are among our most familiar garden birds, reported from nearly 100% of Garden BirdWatch gardens all year round. They are opportunistic and adaptable, and will exploit most kinds of bird food that we provide, but they are particularly attracted to peanut feeders, meaning that they have a long history as a garden bird.

Green-listed

Spotlight

Size 12 cm; Wingspan 18 cm; Weight 11 g

Food: Insects and spiders, will also take fruit and seeds in winter, and a regular at garden bird feeders.

Breeds: April to June

Clutch size: 8–10 eggs

Incubation: 12–16 days

Young fledge: 16–22 days

Number of broods: 1 per year

Population: 3.4 million territories

Max lifespan: 10 years, 3 months

Typical lifespan: 3 years

Garden reporting rate: 94%

Blue Tit nest with eggs, by Moss Taylor

A familiar bird

The diminutive Blue Tit is the member of the tit family that is most familiar to us all. Instantly recognisable by its small blue cap, white head and black eye-stripe, it also has yellow underparts and a bluish back, becoming brighter blue at the wings. Females and males look similar but juveniles are duller in appearance, with no blue cap or white cheeks.

Blue Tits have a range of calls which are thin but clear. The main song is a couple of drawn-out notes followed by a trill 'tsee-tsee-tsu-hu' and their alarm calls are scolding but recognisable by the churring notes uttered at the end.

Woodland origins

Traditionally a woodland bird, Blue Tits are now found in a variety of habitats and will readily breed in parks and gardens. While they originally nested in tree cavities, Blue Tit nests can also be found in a range of other places, including nest boxes, pipes and post boxes. Their nest is built on a base of moss and other plant materials, and consists of a deep cup lined with finer grasses, hair and wool. They rarely have more than one brood and normally lay 8–10 eggs.

Nests in garden nest boxes are usually less successful than those in deciduous woodland due to the number of caterpillars that are required by their growing young. Caterpillars are vital for raising Blue Tit chicks, but gardens have few in comparison to woodland. However, there is increasing evidence that garden Blue Tits survive better overall than those in the wider countryside, thanks to the food provided at feeding stations. They can also take advantage of nest boxes to roost in over the winter, as they shelter them from the cold nights and the energetic demands of keeping warm when temperatures fall below freezing.

In addition to caterpillars, Blue Tits readily take other invertebrates, seeds and nuts. In the spring they may supplement their diet with nectar and sap, and in the autumn they will take berries. They happily come to bird feeders for sunflower hearts and peanuts.

Stay-at-home birds
Our native Blue Tits are generally sedentary, rarely moving far, though they move around locally in the winter months, joining mixed flocks with other tit species, Goldcrests and wintering Chiffchaffs. Occasionally, but increasingly rarely, Scandinavian populations will move south-west in the winter, and some may join our resident birds, though such long-distance movements are the exception rather than the rule.

Blue Tits are widespread, absent only from high ground in Scotland and some Scottish islands. The highest densities can be found in central and south-east England, and lower-lying areas of Wales where there is plenty of deciduous woodland. There are also high densities found in urban areas, which could be due to high availability of nest boxes and supplementary food.

Supporting woodland populations
The UK Blue Tit population has increased overall (growing by 37% between 1967 and 2010) but there are large fluctuations from one year to the next. These occur either when many are killed off by cold winters, or when there is a poor breeding season, the latter happening when the availability of caterpillars is low. However, good breeding seasons mean that they can bounce back quickly, and in 2009 it was estimated that there were 3.4 million breeding territories in the UK.

In gardens, Blue Tit numbers peak in the winter when birds from woodland areas may move greater distances to find food. While you may be seeing no more than five or six birds at any one time at your garden feeding station, the reality is that many more individuals may move through during a typical winter's day. In fact, you could easily have 50 or 60 individuals making use of your hanging feeders during a single day. Throughout the year, Blue Tit is regularly one of the top three birds seen in Garden BirdWatch gardens, with up to a 98% reporting rate from across all gardens. This underlines just how common this species is within gardens and the built environment.

Juvenile Blue Tit, by John Harding

Great Tit

Parus major

Great Tit, by John Harding

This familiar visitor is one of a number of woodland species to have adapted well to gardens, making use of both the food and nest boxes that we provide. Garden populations are, however, less productive than those living within mature deciduous woodland, which reflects the lower numbers of favoured caterpillars available to Great Tits living in gardens.

Green-listed

Spotlight

Size 14 cm; Wingspan 24 cm; Weight 18 g

Food: Invertebrates (esp. caterpillars) and spiders; in winter seeds and fruit also taken.

Breeds: April to June

Clutch size: 6–9 eggs

Incubation: c.14 days

Young fledge: c.19 days

Number of broods: 1 (2) per year

Population: 2.5 million pairs

Max lifespan: 13 years, 11 months

Typical lifespan: 3 years

Garden reporting rate: 80%

Great Tit nest with eggs, by Richard Castell

Identification

Familiarity may not breed contempt, but some of our commonest garden birds perhaps don't get the appreciation their spectacular colours should attract. Great Tits would not be out of place in a tropical rainforest, with bright white cheek patches standing out against a black head, bright yellow belly, and blue and green upperparts with creamy wing bars. They are much larger than Blue Tits and Coal Tits, and can be told from both smaller species by the combination of an all-black crown and yellow underparts.

Juveniles have a yellow 'wash' over all their plumage; the cheeks are yellow rather than white, the blue of the wings is greenish. Adult males and females can be told apart by the width of the black stripe that runs down the centre of the chest; in females this tapers off towards the belly, while in males it broadens to a wide black patch between the legs. Research into Great Tit societies has shown that the width of the black chest stripe is a status symbol; males with wider stripes are likely to be dominant over other males, and to be preferred by females. In territorial disputes males often adopt a 'head up' pose, in order to most effectively display their chest stripe.

Song and calls

Their song is simple and familiar, a repeated, see-saw, 'teacher, teacher, teacher!', similar to Coal Tit but lower pitched. However, they have a very rich vocal repertoire, including a wide range of chattering and piping calls; it is said that an unfamiliar call heard in woodland is likely to be a Great Tit! While the song is generally recognisable, individual birds will put their own spin on the basic refrain, adding syllables or changing the rhythm. This variation involves an element of individual learning, with older males showing greater variety in their songs.

Bold and resourceful

Originally a bird of broad-leaved woodland, Great Tits are now entirely at home in urbanised areas, and a large proportion of the UK's estimated 2.5 million pairs are found in our gardens and parks. Their natural diet includes nuts and seeds, and they are among the most common visitors to peanut and seed feeders, though fewer Great Tits are seen in gardens in years with a good Beech mast crop. They are bold and resourceful, quick to learn and to take advantage of new opportunities. Research into Great Tit behaviour shows that individuals have distinct personalities, with some birds being consistently bolder, faster to explore new situations and more likely to take risks. Birds appear to inherit these traits from their parents, and they are not just due to age, sex or overall condition.

Nesting habits

Great Tits are very likely to take to nest boxes; being bigger than Blue Tits, they prefer cavities that are larger, with wider entrance holes, though they will nest in a very wide range of natural and artificial holes. They fill up the base of the cavity with moss, and construct a hair-lined cup for the eggs in the top layer. Males and females often conspicuously inspect holes together as part of pair-bonding behaviour. It's safe to look inside nest boxes, when the correct guidelines are followed, and counts of eggs and chicks are extremely valuable for research into bird populations. Results from the BTO Nest Record Scheme have shown that Great Tits now start laying their eggs 11 days earlier than in the 1960s, and this has been linked to warming spring temperatures.

Great Tits generally produce a single large brood each year, timed to coincide with the May burst of young leaves in broad-leaved woodland, and the resulting peak in caterpillar numbers. The parent birds need to collect 10,000 caterpillars to raise a brood of Great Tits, which they manage by working 18-hour days for two to three weeks! Most garden environments don't contain as many caterpillars as woodland, so brood sizes tend to be smaller. By early June the young birds will emerge, leading to a peak in Great Tit numbers which can be seen in Garden BirdWatch weekly counts.

AVIAN POX

In recent years an increasing number of Great Tits with large, tumour-like swellings have been reported; this has been shown to be a new strain of avian pox, thought to have arrived from the Continent via an infected mosquito. It seems unlikely that this new disease will affect Great Tit populations overall, but individual infected birds are likely to have reduced survival. The virus that causes the pox can survive on bird feeders, so it's particularly important to maintain good feeder hygiene if your garden Great Tits show signs of the disease.

Great Tit with avian pox, by Hazel Rothwell

Coal Tit, by Edmund Fellowes

Coal Tit
Periparus ater

The small size of the Coal Tit means that it loses out to our larger species when attempting to feed from bird tables and hanging feeders. This may explain why Coal Tits tend to visit a feeder, take a seed and eat it elsewhere, rather than remain on the perch. They also lose out to larger species in the competition for nest cavities, tending to end up using those located lower down.

Green-listed

Spotlight

Size 12 cm; Wingspan 19 cm; Weight 9 g

Food: Insects and spiders, with seeds also taken in winter, mostly from outer branches of conifers.

Breeds: April to June

Clutch size: 8–10 eggs

Incubation: 14–16 days

Young fledge: 18–20 days

Number of broods: 1–2 per year

Population: 680,000 territories

Max lifespan: 9 years, 3 months

Typical lifespan: 2 years

Garden reporting rate: 58%

Coal Tit nest with eggs, by Richard Castell

A shy garden visitor

The Coal Tit is slightly smaller than a Blue Tit, with buff underparts and a bluish-grey back. While it can be confused with Willow and Marsh Tit, it has a characteristic head pattern with a black bib, white cheeks and a black cap running down to the base of the neck at the sides. However, it is from behind that the Coal Tit is readily identified as there is a rectangular white patch running from the top of the head down to the neck. Occasionally, when agitated, it can raise a small crest on the hind crown.

The calls of the Coal Tit are either single fine, clear notes, or a few together like a weedy, higher-pitched version of the Great Tit; a thin-sounding 'tsee-tsee-tsee'. Their song, often delivered from the top of a tall tree, is a fast series of high-voiced 'teachoo-teachoo-teachoo', repeated several times.

A conifer specialist

Coal Tits mainly breed in conifer woodland, though in some areas they will take to mixed forests. They tend to nest in cavities in or near the ground, including old burrows of voles and mice. However, in conifer woodlands, they will also take to nest boxes. The nest consists of a small cup on a base of moss, lined with soft materials including hair, fur and wool. Due to their specific nesting requirements they rarely nest in gardens but will occasionally use parks and cemeteries, especially if there are ornamental conifer trees present.

During the spring and summer, Coal Tits will spend much of their time foraging in the tops of trees, or on outer branches, searching out insects and spiders. However, during the autumn, when invertebrates become more scarce, they take seeds, with Sitka Spruce one of their preferred foods. This is when you are most likely to see them in gardens, but blink and you will miss them. Due to being the lowest on the feeder 'pecking order', Coal Tits dart in to grab a seed, and then disappear to shelter. In addition to seeds, they are able to supplement their diets with the occasional hibernating insect, thanks to being light and nimble enough to peck at the undersides of branches.

Coal Tits will cache food to retrieve later, so it is worth watching them between June and December to see what they do with the seeds they take from feeders. When caching, they tend to regularly dart back and forth to the feeder over a short period of time. This is because their beaks are so small that they can only carry one seed at a time, as well as the fact that they take each food item to a separate location, which is known as scatter hoarding.

Marching on

Coal Tits are largely sedentary birds, though populations in the far north of Europe move south in the winter. They are mostly faithful to specific sites, found in heavily forested areas in Scotland and Wales, and localised pockets in England, though they may move when there are severe food shortages. Areas where they are generally absent include those with few trees, such as some islands and the Fens in East Anglia. However, with the spread of commercial softwood plantations, and the popularity of exotic evergreen trees in more built up areas, the Coal Tit's range has expanded, especially in northern Scotland and eastern England.

Boom and bust

The Coal Tit population increased rapidly until the mid 1970s, since when it has remained more-or-less stable. There have been population increases along with the range expansion, and it is thought that the increase in supplementary feeding in the winter has helped. Their ability to survive cold winters relies heavily on the crops of conifer trees, especially that of Sitka Spruce. Research using Garden BirdWatch data has shown that in years where the Sitka Spruce seed crop is poor, the use of gardens by Coal Tits increases, a similar pattern to that seen in Siskins which also rely on conifer seed. However, whether it is a poor or good seed crop, Coal Tit numbers peak in gardens during the winter months.

Coal Tit, by Jill Pakenham

Marsh Tit, by Richard Winston

Marsh Tit
Poecile palustris

More likely to be seen in woodland than in gardens, Marsh Tits can present an interesting identification challenge when they turn up at bird feeders. With Willow Tit, it is one of a pair of woodland birds seriously affected by habitat changes.

Red-listed

Spotlight

Size 12 cm; Wingspan 19 cm; Weight 12 g

Food: Insects and spiders form the bulk of the summer diet, but seeds, nuts and berries are taken in winter.

Breeds: April to June

Clutch size: 7–9 eggs

Incubation: 13–15 days

Young fledge: c.19 days

Number of broods: 1 per year

Population: 41,000 pairs

Max lifespan: 10 years, 5 months

Typical lifespan: 2 years

Garden reporting rate: 1%

Marsh Tit nest with eggs, by Richard Castell

Territorial behaviour

Like other tit species, Marsh Tits do not generally move large distances, and their distributions in winter and summer are very similar. They are mainly a bird of broad-leaved woodland, and while they are often found in areas near streams and rivers they are not confined to marshy areas, as their name might indicate. They hold larger territories than other tit species, up to three times larger than Great Tit territories. Established pairs remain on territory all year round, while first years will join in with mixed flocks and roam slightly further afield.

It is during these winter wanderings that Marsh Tits are most likely to be seen in gardens. They have feeding habits similar to other tits, often seen on peanut feeders. They are known to cache food, like Coal Tits, though this habit appears to be less common in the UK than in continental Europe. They are less likely to be seen in gardens during the breeding season and, though they are cavity nesters, they do not generally take to garden nest boxes.

Identification

At first glance Marsh Tits could be confused with Coal Tits, but they are plainer in appearance, lacking the white dotted wing bars and white patch on the back of the head. Marsh and Willow Tits look extremely similar, and familiarity with both is required for confident separation. Marsh Tits generally do not show a paler patch on the folded wing, have a smaller black bib and the white cheeks are duller, but both species show variation in all of these features. The best way to be sure of identifying Marsh Tits is by their characteristic call, an explosive, spirited, whip crack: 'pi-CHAY', which Willow Tits do not make. Their most common song involves repetition of a single note, though the pitch and speed of delivery is variable.

Willow Tit
Poecile montana

Willow Tit, by Edmund Fellowes

These two 'black-capped' tits were not identified as separate species until the 1890s. Britain has seen substantial decreases in numbers of both over recent decades. Willow Tit is much the rarer of the two and is less likely to be encountered in a garden than its close relative.

Red-listed

Spotlight

Size 12 cm; Wingspan 19 cm; Weight 12 g

Food: Insects and spiders form the bulk of the summer diet, but seeds are taken in winter.

Breeds: April to June

Clutch size: 6–9 eggs

Incubation: c.14 days

Young fledge: 17–20 days

Number of broods: 1 per year

Population: 3,400 pairs

Max lifespan: 10 years, 5 months

Typical lifespan: 3 years

Garden reporting rate: <1%

Willow Tit eggs, by Peter Castell

Distribution

Willow Tits are much less common than Marsh Tits, with only 3,400 pairs in the country, compared to over 40,000 pairs of Marsh Tits. Their calls and songs are variable, but with practice this is the best way to tell them from Marsh Tits (see Marsh Tit account). They are found in Wales and the Midlands, with patchy distributions in northern England and southern Scotland. Like Marsh Tits they are absent from Ireland.

Habitat preferences

Found in wet woodland, they are unusual in excavating their own nest cavities; their beaks are not strong enough to dig into solid wood, so they need plenty of standing rotten wood in which they can dig out their nest holes. While they are occasionally seen in gardens they are generally very unlikely to be seen at bird feeders.

A bird in trouble

Until relatively recently Willow Tits were also found across southern and eastern England, but their numbers have declined dramatically and now they are almost absent from these areas. Both Willow and Marsh Tits are red-listed birds of conservation concern due to their declines, though the losses of Willow Tits have been more severe.

Investigations into these declines indicate that they are probably due to changes in management of our woodlands; most broad-leaved woodlands are no longer managed for timber, which means the canopy grows thicker and shades out the undergrowth that these birds need. Increasing numbers of deer, which also reduce the amount of undergrowth in woodlands, have also contributed to this habitat change, something that is known to impact other breeding bird populations.

Swallow
Hirundo rustica

Swallow, by John Harding

While one Swallow may not make a summer, there can be little doubt that this long-distance migrant is seen by many as the archetypal summer bird. Unlike Swifts and House Martins, which can be truly urban in their habits, Swallows tend to be recorded only from larger rural gardens, often those with suitable outbuildings provided for horses or other livestock. Some pairs make use of car ports.

Green-listed

Spotlight

Size 18 cm; Wingspan 34 cm; Weight 19 g

Food: Flying insects, especially small flies, caught on the wing by aerial pursuit.

Breeds: May to September

Clutch size: 4–5 eggs

Incubation: 14–16 days

Young fledge: 19–25 days

Number of broods: 2 (3) per year

Population: 760,000 territories

Max lifespan: 11 years, 1 month

Typical lifespan: 2 years

Garden reporting rate: 6%

Swallow chicks at the nest, by John Harding

Identification

Swallows have a familiar shape, with long pointed wings and a distinctive forked tail that ends with very thin, elongated streamers. Their backs are glossy blue, and they have creamy underparts, with a bluish-black breast, and a red throat and forehead. Swallows could be confused with House Martins, especially in flight when the red colouring is harder to see, but they have much deeper forks in their tails, and lack the white rump of the House Martin. Males and females are alike, though the longer the tail streamers, the more likely the bird is to be a male. Juveniles have much shorter, blunter tail streamers and a buffy-white or brownish forehead and throat.

A bird of the countryside

Unlike Swifts and House Martins, which prefer to nest in and around villages and towns, Swallows prefer open country. They like to breed in areas of pasture, with access to the interior of buildings including open sheds, garages, derelict buildings, smallholdings and industrial sites. They are mostly found in rural areas, but will sometimes nest in suburban gardens that border farmland.

Swallows are migratory and usually arrive in the UK from early April, departing again in October. They start to nest from late April or early May and will have two or three clutches. The nest of the Swallow is a shallow half-cup made up of mud pellets or dung mixed with straw and grasses, and lined with grass and feathers. They tend to build their nests on rough-textured vertical surfaces inside a building, often placed on a high beam, rafter, narrow ledge or recess, and nearly always close to the top of the building. Existing nests are often reused from year to year. They are gregarious birds, and may nest semi-colonially, with individuals returning to the same site in subsequent years.

Aerial feeders

Their diet consists of flying insects, especially flies, and they usually hunt low over the ground in a swooping flight. Due to this, they are most likely to be seen above gardens, either feeding or perched on telephone wires. Unlike other small migratory birds, Swallows tend to do most of their migration during the day, stopping frequently to refuel on their several-thousand-kilometre journeys to and from southern Africa.

Before they cross major barriers, including deserts or large expanses of water, they will feed up for several days to ensure that they have enough fat reserves to complete the crossing. Studies show that the amount of fat laid down is closely correlated with the size of the barrier that they have to cross, as carrying more fat than needed can impair their flight. During this migration, and when on their wintering grounds, Swallows will gather in large roosts in reed beds or crop fields at night, making the most of safety in numbers.

Populations and distribution

Swallows are found throughout Britain and Ireland, and have the most extensive distribution of any summer migrant. The only places they are missing are some parts of northern Scotland and in central London. They are found in low densities in upland areas, and in arable areas in eastern England, probably due to the lack of cattle grazing and with that a low abundance of flying insects.

The population of Swallows has been increasing since the mid to late 1990s, especially in northern Britain. However, in south-east England, local populations have decreased for unknown reasons. This pattern is similar to that seen for other long-distance migrants. The amount of rain in the western Sahel prior to the birds' spring migration back to their breeding grounds has been shown to affect populations, but no correlation has been found with cattle numbers or nest availability in the UK, suggesting that it is factors on their migration routes or on their wintering grounds that are causing localised population declines. While Europe has also seen more widespread declines, our Swallow – the Barn Swallow – is still the most abundant and widely distributed swallow species in the world.

Warmer weather in the winter seems to be affecting Swallows as well, with a growing number departing later, and increasing attempts to overwinter. While they traditionally arrive in April and leave by mid October, an average of 1.4% of BirdTrack lists have been recording them in November.

Death and divorce

Males unpaired by midsummer may go to extreme lengths to produce offspring of their own. Their best chance of pairing up with a female is if her mate is dead or if an existing nest fails, as Swallow pairs often divorce afterwards. As it is easier to ensure a nest fails than to kill another male, unpaired males will often kill an entire brood of chicks in an unattended nest. If the pair then split up, the unpaired male will take his chance to mate with the female. This rather unpleasant behaviour may explain occasional reports from BTO Garden BirdWatchers of dead Swallow chicks found underneath a nest.

Swallow at nest, by John Harding

House Martin, by John W Walton

House Martin
Delichon urbicum

House Martins are the creators of probably the most visible nests of any British bird, the familiar mud cups nestled under the eaves of houses. While they live closely alongside us in the summer, they winter in tropical Africa, and face all the challenges associated with long-distance migration.

Amber-listed

Spotlight

Size 12 cm; Wingspan 28 cm; Weight 19 g

Food: Flying insects, especially small flies, aphids also taken during the summer months.

Breeds: May to September

Clutch size: 4–5 eggs

Incubation: 14–16 days

Young fledge: 19–25 days

Number of broods: 2 (3) per year

Population: 510,000 pairs

Max lifespan: 7 years, 2 months

Typical lifespan: 2 years

Garden reporting rate: 5%

House Martin chicks, by John Harding

An urban migrant

Long-distance migrants, House Martins arrive with us for the breeding season in the second half of April or early May. They would naturally nest on exposed rocks or cliff faces, but now the vast majority nest on buildings, or other structures such as bridges, and are found in villages, rural habitation and small towns in lowland areas. They feed on airborne invertebrates, concentrating on a different part of the airspace to Swallows and Swifts, and are generally absent from large urban centres, presumably due to the lack of a suitable food supply. They will forage in the airspace above gardens, particularly around large ponds, and will land to collect mud for their nests from ponds and puddles.

Mud, glorious mud

House Martin nests, typically constructed under overhangs high up on vertical walls, are built from 1,000 or more beak-sized mud pellets. They are reinforced with plant fibres, and lined with grass and feathers, and are often found in small groupings, with several plastered alongside each other. Nests are sometimes taken over by House Sparrows, which enlarge the entrance hole and construct their own nest inside, often leaving messy strands of grass protruding from the entrance. House Martins generally raise two broods in the same nest during the season and chicks from the first brood may help out with feeding their younger siblings. Adults usually reuse the same nest year after year, often with some repairs, though they will occasionally reduce their workload by making use of artificial nests where these are provided. The ground under nests does become soiled with droppings, and if this is in an inconvenient area it may be worth installing a shelf below the nest – though this should be constructed so that other pairs are not able to attach their own nests under the shelf!

Difficult to monitor

Their colonial nesting habits mean that it is difficult to assess breeding numbers accurately, but the House Martin population appears to have declined, and the species is now on the amber list of birds of conservation concern. We know surprisingly little about where House Martins spend the winter, beyond that they travel to tropical areas of Africa such as the Congo Basin. We do, however, know that many of the bird species that migrate to central Africa are showing similar declines, presumably due to habitat degradation in the wintering areas and at their stopover sites. Research has shown that more birds survive the winter in years with good rainfall in their tropical African wintering grounds, indicating that winter food supplies may limit their numbers. Securing information on the wintering sites used by our House Martins will be an important first step in understanding the threats that they face. This information could then be used to support conservation efforts in Africa and, potentially, at sites along their migration routes.

Identification

House Martins look similar to Swallows and Sand Martins, to which they are closely related. They have shorter tails than Swallows, and from below they can be identified by their all-white undersides, from chin to tail, unlike Swallows, which have dark heads and upper breasts, and Sand Martins – rarely seen around gardens – which have an indistinct dark breast band. Their most distinctive feature is the large white patch on the lower back, above the tail, which is particularly noticeable when watching flying birds against a dark background. At close range it can be seen that the dark areas of the back and head are in fact a glossy blue, and that the gleaming white plumage of the underside extends all the way down to the unusual feathered feet. Despite their similar habits they are not closely related to Swifts, which appear all-dark above and below. The juveniles look like the adults, but with duller, duskier plumage. They make a continuous, pleasant, dry chattering sound, interspersed with somewhat insect-like 'prrrit' calls.

House Martin, by David Hutton

Long-tailed Tit
Aegithalos caudatus

Long-tailed Tit, by Liz Cutting

In gardens, Long-tailed Tits can be seen all year round, often in groups. Numbers increase in the winter as family parties pass through, often attracted to suet products or peanut feeders, and fall during the spring when birds are presumably splitting into their pairs and nesting nearby.

Green-listed

Spotlight

Size 14 cm; Wingspan 18 cm; Weight 9 g

Food: Mostly arthropods, especially small bugs and insect eggs, plus the larvae of moths.

Breeds: March to June

Clutch size: 6–9 eggs

Incubation: 14–16 days

Young fledge: 14–17 days

Number of broods: 1 per year

Population: 330,000 territories

Max lifespan: 8 years, 11 months

Typical lifespan: 2 years

Garden reporting rate: 35%

Long-tailed Tit nest in gorse, by Mike Toms

A widespread species

Long-tailed Tits can be found throughout Britain and Ireland, though they are largely absent from upland areas and some of the Scottish islands. Due to their preference for nesting in deciduous woodland, they occur in higher densities in wooded lowland areas. As they struggle to survive through very cold winters, their numbers can vary from year to year and in severe winters can fall quite dramatically. For example in the winters of 1917, 1947 and 1963 the Long-tailed Tit population was reduced by as much as 80%. However, between 1967 and 2012, their population increased overall by 98%, probably due to progressively mild winters boosting overwinter survival and leading to better breeding success, with earlier laying dates and more fledglings being produced.

Not a tit at all

Long-tailed Tits are not 'true' tits but they are a member of the same larger group that also includes warblers and swallows. They have very small, rounded bodies with long tails that make up more than half their length. The head is white and there is a wide black band that runs from the side of the forehead back along the crown, giving them the appearance of having eyebrows. The throat and breast are also white and they have a light pinkish belly and flanks. The upperparts are black with pink on the shoulders, and the long narrow tail is black with white edges. They have orange or pink bare skin above their eyes.

Juveniles are duller in appearance than the adults, with a dark forehead and side of head, and brown on their bodies, lacking the pink altogether. Soon after leaving the nest, however, they undergo a full moult of their entire plumage, making them indistinguishable from adult birds.

Family ties

During the spring, Long-tailed Tits are often seen only in pairs, but some breeding pairs do receive help raising their young from one or more close relatives. These 'helpers' may be birds whose own breeding attempts have failed. Up to eight helpers have been recorded feeding a single brood, strongly increasing the chances of the young fledging successfully.

Once the young have fledged, Long-tailed Tits come together in extended family parties, numbering several dozen individuals. This is especially advantageous in the winter as they are extremely susceptible to cold weather and so will huddle together in roosts during the night, very occasionally using nest boxes or commercially available roosting pouches.

Long-tailed Tits communicate with clicking calls that sound like they are chatting, along with a loud sharp 'srih srih srih' call. These calls can often alert you to the approach of a foraging party. They may also make a loud drawn-out trill when alarmed.

A thorny issue

Long-tailed Tits prefer to nest in areas of deciduous woodland that have dense undergrowth, though they seem equally happy in scrub or hedgerow habitats. Bramble bushes, Gorse and Blackthorn are all well used. If suitable vegetation is present they will nest in large suburban parks and gardens, but they only rarely penetrate more urban areas.

The nest is usually found attached to the outer twigs of a bush, especially one with thorns, but they will nest in climbing plants and in trees, often placing the nest up against the trunk, and within a fork. Built by both the male and the female, the nest is a dense ball of moss that is bound together with cobwebs and hair, and covered with grey lichen. The entrance is near the top, and the inside is thickly lined with hundreds of feathers. The pair take their time building the nest and it can be up to three weeks before they complete it. Once complete, the nest may be left for several days before egg-laying begins. This may reassure the pair that the nest-building activities have not attracted the unwelcome attentions of a nest predator. Certainly, Long-

tailed Tits can be fairly conspicuous when nest building, particularly when taking feathers to the nest. The birds rear one large brood from late March onwards. As the chicks grow, the nest stretches so that there is enough room for them all.

Rare visitors

Long-tailed Tits used to be rare visitors to gardens, but Garden BirdWatch results have shown an increase in the use of garden resources, including supplementary food. They will take fat products, small seeds, finely grated mild cheese and bread crumbs from both bird tables and hanging feeders. They are most likely to be seen at feeders during winter, when invertebrates are scarce. There are several different races of Long-tailed Tit in Europe and some look distinctly different from those found in Britain and Ireland. Occasional birds migrate here from northern Europe, mostly turning up in the east of England, and these individuals can be told by their entirely white heads.

Long-tailed Tit, by Ric Jackson

Chiffchaff, by John W Proudlock

Chiffchaff
Phylloscopus collybita

Generally associated with woodlands and other natural habitats, Chiffchaffs may also be found in large rural gardens, and can turn up nearly anywhere during their autumn migration. As well as spending the breeding season with us, many of these tiny warblers now overwinter in the UK, particularly in the south-west, where the climate tends to be more favourable.

Spotlight

Green-listed

Size 10 cm; Wingspan 18 cm; Weight 9 g

Food: Insects and other small invertebrates; some fruit taken in autumn and winter.

Breeds: April to July
Clutch size: 5–6 eggs
Incubation: 12–14 days
Young fledge: 12–17 days
Number of broods: 2 per year
Population: 1.1 million territories
Max lifespan: 7 years, 8 months
Typical lifespan: 2 years
Garden reporting rate: 4%

Chiffchaff nest, by Mike Toms

Identification

Chiffchaffs are small, delicate warblers with fine, sharp bills adapted to their diet of insects. They generally appear grey-brown with a greenish tinge, and have a pale underside and an indistinct yellow eye-stripe. Their legs are dark, which helps to distinguish them from the very similar Willow Warblers, and they are quick and lively, flitting around among small twigs, with a characteristic habit of pumping their tails up and down when foraging.

They are one of the first migrants to arrive in the spring, and their simple, distinctive 'chiff-chaff' song is often heard before the end of March. It is this refrain, of course, that gave them their name, and not just in English – they're called 'Zilpzalp' in German, 'Tjiftjaf' in Dutch, and 'Siff-siaff' in Welsh. Even the scientific name *collybita* is derived from a Greek word meaning money-changer, because the song was thought to sound like coins clinking together. Their call is a gentle, rising 'hueet'.

Distribution

Chiffchaffs breed throughout much of Britain and Ireland, though they are most common in the south and west. Their preferred habitats are woodland and scrub, where they construct their domed nests in vegetation near to the ground, but they also nest in more open areas as long as there are tall trees nearby to use as song posts. Their breeding numbers are increasing, and they are spreading northwards, becoming more common in Scotland and northern England.

Wintering habits

Many British breeders winter around the Mediterranean, while others will cross the Sahara and winter in the region of Senegal. They are most likely to be seen in gardens in autumn, when young birds are dispersing from their parents' territories, and both the adults and juveniles are beginning their autumn migration. At this time of year they will join mixed feeding flocks of tits, and will accompany these groupings into gardens, but as insectivores they are unlikely to be attracted to bird feeders.

It's thought that one of the reasons why breeding numbers are increasing is that the conditions encountered on their short-distance migration are currently favourable, leading to good overwinter survival. Some individuals are choosing to migrate an even shorter distance, staying in the UK all winter, and numbers of overwintering birds have increased markedly over the last 40 years, presumably linked to milder conditions. Unlike Blackcaps, which are also spending the winter with us more often than in the past, wintering Chiffchaffs are not often seen at garden bird feeders. They generally remain in the wider countryside, most commonly in the warmer south-west of England, and often near wetland sites where invertebrates can be found all year round. Chiffchaffs seen at this time of year may be British breeders, but we are also joined in winter by birds from Scandinavia and even further east.

WILLOW WARBLER

Willow Warblers look very similar to Chiffchaffs but, depending on the time of year, they may appear brighter yellow, with a more distinct eye-stripe, as well as paler legs. However, without familiarity with both species they cannot reliably be told apart by eye. In the breeding season they can most easily be identified by their song; Willow Warbler song is a sweet series of descending notes, quite different from the up-and-down Chiffchaff refrain. However, despite this distinctive difference they were once thought to be the same species, together with Wood Warbler, and it was Gilbert White, in his Natural History of Selborne in 1789, who told us that there was not just one, but three species of 'willow-wren'.

In contrast to Chiffchaffs, Willow Warblers are much more common in Scotland and northern England than further south, and they are our commonest warbler. Their breeding populations in Scotland and Ireland are holding up, but they have suffered severe declines in England. These declines are thought to be linked to conditions on their wintering grounds, south of the Sahara in tropical Africa.

Willow Warbler, by Edmund Fellowes

Blackcap
Sylvia atricapilla

Blackcap, by Edmund Fellowes

The Blackcap has evolved a surprising migration strategy that now sees this summer migrant turn up at garden feeding stations during the winter months. The reasons for the evolution of this piece of behaviour have been explained thanks to the efforts of BTO Garden BirdWatchers.

Green-listed

Spotlight

Size 13 cm; Wingspan 22 cm; Weight 21 g

Food: Insects and other invertebrates dominate in summer, with fruit in autumn and winter.

Breeds: April to July

Clutch size: 4–5 eggs

Incubation: 11–12 days

Young fledge: 11–12 days

Number of broods: 2 per year

Population: 1.1 million territories

Max lifespan: 10 years, 8 months

Typical lifespan: 2 years

Garden reporting rate: 13%

Blackcap nest in Bramble, by Mike Toms

Evolution in action

Traditionally Blackcaps were summer visitors, migrating here from the Mediterranean to breed. As with several other summer migrants, their arrival dates have been getting earlier, and this could be a reflection of climate change. During the summer they are most commonly found in lowland areas of southern England and Wales though their range stretches into the lowland areas of Scotland and across Ireland. In 2009 it was estimated that there were 1.1 million breeding territories in the UK and the Breeding Bird Survey shows that the summer population has increased by 143% since 1995.

Since the 1960s the wintering population of Blackcaps has also rapidly increased. During the 1940s and 1950s an average of 22 individuals were recorded wintering, mostly found in the south-west. By the 1970s this had increased to 380 and now they are regular visitors, especially in the south and west of Britain. These are not birds from our breeding population, but have come from central Europe. Generally these birds head south for the winter, but from time to time some individuals, due to genetic mutations, flew in the wrong direction and arrived in the UK. Historically they would have perished in cold winters, but today's milder conditions allow them to survive. The birds that winter in the UK have been shown to arrive back at their breeding grounds earlier than those individuals that still head south for the winter, which might offer a competitive advantage and allow them to raise more young. In addition to a warmer climate, it has also been shown that the provision of supplementary bird food, especially in suburban gardens, has also helped Blackcaps to evolve this successful new migration strategy. Wintering birds could arrive in the UK as early as October to take advantage of natural foods in the wider countryside before moving into gardens from late November.

Breeding behaviour

During the breeding season, Blackcaps are usually found in areas with low, dense vegetation including in woodland, copses and dense hedgerows that have mature trees. While they are rarely seen in gardens during the summer, they have been recorded nesting in overgrown hedges and scrub within urban parks and larger gardens. Their nests are usually quite near the ground in Brambles, or the low branches of a hedge that is surrounded by tall vegetation. The male builds a number of flimsy 'cock nests' and shows them off to the female. If she decides to stay she will finish her chosen nest, which turns into a neat cup of grass and moss woven around supporting stems; the whole nest is strengthened with spiders' webs, and the lining is made up of finer grasses and hair. They usually have two clutches of four to five eggs from about mid April.

During the summer, Blackcaps primarily feed on insects and therefore rarely need to visit gardens. They come into gardens during the winter to take advantage of fruits including windfall apples, *Viburnum* and Ivy berries. When visiting garden bird feeding stations, especially during the winter, their preferred foods seem to be fat products and sunflower hearts. A study that looked at Blackcaps using Garden BirdWatch data found that gardens where food is provided regularly in winter are more likely to be visited by Blackcaps. These birds have a reputation for being quite aggressive at bird feeders and this could be because garden bird foods are important to their survival.

Identification

Blackcaps are stocky birds with grey upperparts and light grey plumage below. The male's small black cap gives the species its name, whereas females and juveniles have a reddish-brown cap.

The call of the Blackcap is a clicking 'teck', sounding like two pebbles being tapped together, which is repeated when they're uneasy. As they often sing from dense cover, their song can easily be confused with that of the Garden Warbler, a related species. It takes practice to separate the two species; you may find that the BTO YouTube video guide is a good place to start.

Juvenile Blackcap, by Liz Cutting

Waxwing
Bombycilla garrulus

Waxwings, by Jeff Baker

Charismatic winter nomads, Waxwings are one of our most exotic garden visitors. They are similar in size and shape to Starlings, but their shorter bills and thicker necks give them a large-headed appearance. Dependent upon berries, these birds can travel long distances in search of food, turning up in gardens and supermarket car parks to feed on *Cotoneaster* and other amenity shrubs.

Green-listed

Spotlight

Size 18 cm; Wingspan 34 cm; Weight 63 g

Food: Winter diet is berries and tree buds; in summer insects are important, especially midges.

Breeds: from late May

Clutch size: 5–6 eggs

Incubation: 14–15 days

Young fledge: 14–15 days

Number of broods: 1 per year

Population: highly variable

Max lifespan: 3 years

Typical lifespan: not known

Garden reporting rate: <1%

Waxwing nest with eggs, by Richard Castell

On the move

In most years only very small numbers of Waxwings are seen in Garden BirdWatch gardens, one or two each winter. On average every three or four years we have a 'Waxwing winter', with flocks of up to several hundred individuals recorded by Garden BirdWatchers. To date the best week for Waxwing records in Garden BirdWatch was in November 2010, when groups of between 20 and 80 birds were recorded by a number of observers, giving a combined total of over 600 individuals just in GBW gardens. Waxwings are most attracted to berries, but if none are available they can be tempted into gardens by apples tied onto to branches; they rarely feed on the ground. For a relatively large and heavy bird they can be surprisingly agile, hanging upside-down to pluck berries from the outermost tip of a branch.

Then and now

It has been suggested that Waxwings are arriving here in greater numbers, and in more years, than they used to, though the variation in counts makes this kind of assessment difficult. It may be that the increasing regularity of Waxwing arrivals is related to the growing use of berry-bearing ornamental shrubs, such as Rowan, Guelder Rose and *Pyracantha*, planted to beautify urban developments. Waxwings can be remarkably unafraid of people, and these winter wanderers are frequently found in supermarket car parks and out-of-town industrial estates.

In the Waxwing winter of 2010/11 over 500 birds were marked with unique colour-ring combinations by bird ringers. Of these, nearly 100 were sighted elsewhere in Britain and Ireland the same winter. This high proportion of resightings goes to show just how visible and popular these birds are. During that winter, colour-ringed Waxwings from Scotland were recorded all the way down to the south coast of England, presumably searching for new food sources, and perhaps being moved on by competition from other berry-eaters such as thrushes. They are most likely to be seen in eastern areas of England and Scotland, though they can appear much further west in those years when large numbers reach our shores, as the *Bird Atlas 2007–11* map (opposite) reveals.

Readily recognised

Overall their plumage shades from grey to buff to brick red, with bright yellow markings on their black wing and tail feathers, as well as the unique, bright red tips to the wing feathers that give them their name. Another striking feature is the sweeping black 'bandit mask' beneath the large, dark buff crest, rendering them stunning and unmistakable when seen well. Males and females look broadly similar, though the females may have a blurred lower edge to the black bib and fewer red appendages on the wing.

Adult birds show white tips to the flight feathers that are visible as a 'ladder' down the folded wing, while juveniles have only the pale yellow edges to the flight feathers, appearing as a single line on a perched bird. In flight they look similar to Starlings, plump-bodied with triangular wings, often flying in tight formation. Their contact call is a ringing, bell-like trill.

From the north

While some birds have set migration routes, Waxwings are extremely unpredictable in their movements, making them true nomads. They breed in the northern taiga, with a circumpolar distribution that stretches across all of Scandinavia, Russia and North America. They nest in stunted conifers in mossy, lichen-rich terrain. After the breeding season Waxwings attempt to subsist on winter berries in the boreal forest, particularly Rowan, but this food source is unreliable and in lean years they resort to making irruptive movements to the south, seeking out areas where the berry crop has been more successful. This may seem to be a risky strategy but it seems to work and Garden BirdWatchers certainly benefit, receiving such a stunning visitor.

Waxwing, by Liz Cutting

A DIET OF BERRIES

In the winter Waxwings are specialist fruit eaters, capable of consuming two to three times their body weight in fruit in a single day; one bird was observed consuming over 600 *Cotoneaster* berries in a day.

Their preferred foods are reported to be the fruits of Rowan, hawthorn, Guelder Rose and *Cotoneaster*, but Waxwings will also take a very wide range of other fruit and berries. Despite their nomadic lifestyles, anecdotal reports suggest that they are able to remember the locations of good food sources, returning to the same berry-bearing bushes and shrubs year after year.

Nuthatch, by John Harding

Nuthatch
Sitta europaea

This striking bird is a regular visitor to those gardens located within its breeding range and close to areas of deciduous woodland. Early in the year its presence may be revealed by its piercing calls, including a series of sharp whistling notes delivered in rapid succession.

Green-listed

Spotlight

Size 14 cm; Wingspan 24 cm; Weight 24 g

Food: Invertebrates taken throughout the year, with seeds important in autumn and winter.

Breeds: April to June

Clutch size: 6–8 eggs

Incubation: 15–16 days

Young fledge: 23–25 days

Number of broods: 1 per year

Population: 220,000 territories

Max lifespan: 9 years, 9 months

Typical lifespan: 2 years

Garden reporting rate: 16%

Nuthatch nest with eggs, by Richard Castell

Identification

Nuthatches stand out at any garden feeding station. They have a long pointed bill and, unlike most small garden birds, appear to have no neck, giving them a large-headed appearance. Their upperparts are blue-grey and their underparts are a buff-orange, which in males becomes more chestnut on the flanks. They have a blue-grey crown and nape, a black eye stripe and white on the rest of the face. The more intense chestnut flanks of the male are evident also in juveniles and even in nestlings. Nuthatches could be confused for Treecreepers as they both have the ability to walk up a tree trunk, but Treecreepers are a much browner bird.

The Nuthatch call most often heard is a sharp 'zit' when foraging, and the song is a rapid selection of whistling notes: 'viiu viiu viiu'. They have a large selection of loud calls and songs but call less frequently once breeding is under way.

Mud and wood

Due to their preference for nesting in holes in deciduous trees, Nuthatches are most likely to be found in mature woodland, parks and gardens near woodland or hedgerows with tall trees. They usually nest in knot holes, preferring those of the oaks, Beech and Ash, or holes made by woodpeckers. They will also use nest boxes, and often use the same nesting site from year to year. If their selected nesting place has an entrance hole that is too large, they make it smaller using mud to guard against predation. Sometimes the hole is made as small as just 3 cm so that the female can just fit through it. If using a nest box, they may also cement the lid shut, or stick the box to the tree with mud. The female builds the nest, which is completed with a loose lining of bark or dead leaves. They have one clutch of 6–8 eggs from early April onwards.

Aggressive interactions

Nuthatches are very territorial birds, defending their space as a pair all year round. This allows them to know where the best nesting and feeding opportunities are in their area. The male may start singing in December, and the pair select their nest hole fairly early in the year in order to defend it. Young birds are driven from their parents' territory soon after fledging and must find their own elsewhere. Research has shown that the older the female, the earlier she tends to lay, giving her young the opportunity to find the best vacant territories first.

Where there's woodland

Historically, Nuthatches were known as a southern English woodland bird, but now they are found across Wales, most of England and southern Scotland, though they are absent from areas lacking deciduous woodland such as the Fens in East Anglia. The Nuthatch population has increased in England and Wales, which is thought to be due to increasing availability of nesting sites, increased provision of supplementary food and milder winters. They do not occur in Ireland and, given their sedentary nature, are unlikely to cross the sea.

The main diet of Nuthatch consists of invertebrates taken from the bark of trees but in autumn and winter seeds and nuts become important, especially those of Beech, oak and Hazel. Larger nuts are wedged into cracks in trees, where the bird smashes them open with its bill. Nuthatches visit bird feeders for nuts, seeds and suet-based products and can be very aggressive, chasing the other birds away. They often cache their food in preparation for harder times.

The route north

Nuthatch populations have been expanding into Scotland since the late 1980s, with breeding first proved in the Borders in 1989 and northward range extension still continuing. In fact in 1995, when Garden BirdWatch started, southern Scotland provided no records of Nuthatches. By 2013, this had risen to 10% of gardens.

In gardens Nuthatch numbers peak first in the summer after breeding, and then again in the autumn if food availability is low. In years where there is a poor crop of Beech mast, the numbers of gardens reporting Nuthatches increases sharply as birds roam around looking for food.

Nuthatch, by Liz Cutting

Treecreeper, by Paul Newton

Treecreeper
Certhia familiaris

The glimpse of a small brown bird working its way up a vertical tree trunk in your garden can only mean one thing, the presence of a Treecreeper. Although seemingly indifferent to our presence, these small birds can have an unhelpful habit of moving around the trunk and out of sight when viewed.

Green-listed

Spotlight

Size 12 cm; Wingspan 19 cm; Weight 10 g

Food: Insects and spiders taken from crevices in bark; also pine and spruce seeds in winter.

Breeds: April to June

Clutch size: 5–6 eggs

Incubation: 14–15 days

Young fledge: 14–16 days

Number of broods: 2 per year

Population: 180,000 territories

Max lifespan: 8 years

Typical lifespan: 2 years

Garden reporting rate: 2%

Treecreeper nest with eggs, by Richard Castell

A tree-trunk specialist

Treecreepers may sometimes be hard to see, but their behaviour is instantly recognisable. They are frequently seen running mouse-like up tree trunks, and even upside-down along the underside of branches, clinging on using strong claws and steadied by unusually stiff, pointed tail feathers. When they reach the top of the trunk they will fly down to the base of the next tree; unlike Nuthatches, they don't like going down head-first. If they know they have been spotted they sometimes freeze, or creep round to the opposite side of the trunk from the observer. They are rarely seen on small twigs, preferring to forage along the bark of tree trunks and larger branches.

The tree mouse

While at a distance they may resemble small mice, up close intricate black-and-brown patterning can be seen, including the step in the wing markings that distinguishes this species from the closely related Short-toed Treecreeper, which is common on the Continent but not found in Britain and Ireland. Their white chins and bellies contrast strongly with their darker upperparts, and they have relatively long, thin, slightly curved bills. Like Goldcrests they have very fine, high-pitched voices, often making a repeated 'see-see-see' call. Their song is of the same high pitch, a short descending phrase ending with a slight flourish. Both the song and the bird itself are easily overlooked.

As well as foraging in bark, Treecreepers can even sleep in holes excavated in tree bark. The introduced conifer *Wellingtonia* has unusually soft, spongy, insulating bark, unlike our native trees. In the early 20th century Treecreepers were first observed excavating small depressions in the bark of *Wellingtonia* trees and huddling down within them to roost overnight. This behaviour has now spread through the Treecreeper population, and is now a common occurrence where these introduced soft-barked trees are present.

Distribution

Treecreepers are widely distributed across the whole of Britain and Ireland, and are found in all areas where trees grow, feeding on small insects all year round. They are absent only from the Northern and Western Isles, the highest peaks of Scotland and the treeless fenland areas around the Wash, and are most common in Wales and in southern England.

This is one of our most sedentary species, making no significant movements, but they are less likely to be recorded in gardens in the breeding season, when they will remain close to their woodland nesting site, which is often behind a flap of bark. While they may be present in gardens at any time of year, as insectivores they are unlikely to visit feeders, and often stay high in trees hidden behind foliage, so may not be detected.

Winter weather

Treecreepers are much more likely to be seen in gardens during the winter months, when they often accompany roaming feeding flocks of Blue and Great Tits and, additionally, become more visible on the leafless trees. During the winter they may investigate peanut feeders, especially during particularly harsh winters. One way of attracting Treecreepers is to rub fat or suet into the bark of trees, since their normal feeding method is probing the bark for insects.

Being so small, Treecreepers are susceptible to bad weather, and analyses of ringing data has shown that winter mortality is higher in those years with low temperatures or heavy rainfall. It could be that winter rain freezes to tree trunks, making it impossible for birds to feed, or that their plumage becomes damp and bedraggled through contact with wet bark, leaving the birds susceptible to chilling. The combination of small size, which means high energetic needs to maintain their body temperature, and an insectivorous diet certainly makes winter a challenging time for the Treecreeper.

Responding to climate change

Overall, Treecreeper numbers have remained generally stable since the 1980s, quickly bouncing back after harsh winters. Despite high winter mortality, they can be surprisingly robust; a Treecreeper ringed in Hampshire in 1979 was caught again, alive and well, at the same site in 1987, the longest recorded lifespan for this species. As for many other birds, BTO Nest Record Scheme data show that Treecreepers now nest earlier than they used to, as a response to a warming climate.

Treecreeper, by John Harding

Wren, by Dennis Atherton

Wren
Troglodytes troglodytes

Despite its tiny size, the Wren is a very powerful songster. Its piercing song is often heard in gardens, even though the bird itself is easily overlooked. Wrens usually forage in areas with good cover, which may be another reason why they can be hard to spot. It is, however, one of our most common and widespread breeding species.

Green-listed

Spotlight

Size 10 cm; Wingspan 15 cm; Weight 10 g

Food: Insects (especially small beetles) and spiders, typically taken from on or close to the ground.

Breeds: April to August

Clutch size: 5–6 eggs

Incubation: 13–18 days

Young fledge: 14–19 days

Number of broods: 2 per year

Population: 7.7 million territories

Max lifespan: 7 years, 3 months

Typical lifespan: 2 years

Garden reporting rate: 41%

Wren nest in Ivy, by Mike Toms

The 'cave dweller'
The scientific name of the Wren – *Troglodytes* – means 'cave dweller' and possibly refers to the fact that they will happily nest wherever there are small holes. This means that they are found in a wide range of habitats, including gardens. As well as small holes in trees and walls, Wrens may use old nests of other birds and occasionally nest boxes. The male, however, builds a number of different nests, known as 'cock nests', from which the female chooses the one she likes best. The average number of nests found in a male Wren's territory is more than six! The male constructs the nest, which is dome-shaped, out of dry leaves, moss, grass and other plant material. Once selected, the chosen nest will be lined with feathers by the female.

Playing the field
Most pairs will have two medium-sized broods each year, beginning in early April. Male Wrens are sometimes polygynous, mating with more than one female. As the male builds several nests (up to 12), he may as well try and attract more than one female to use them. However, the original female is likely to get most of the help in raising her brood, as both male and female feed the young. Wrens are primarily insectivores, eating insects and spiders. In the winter they may venture out to take small scraps from the ground or low bird tables, including small seeds, mealworms and fat products.

The challenge of winter
During the winter Wrens are vulnerable to cold nights. To cope with this they often gather in communal roosts at night, a contrast to their usual solitary existence. These roosts will occur in anything from nest boxes to roof eaves. Depending on how small the

space is, birds will often pile on top of one another. The largest roost on record was over 60 birds, found in Norfolk in a nest box!

Population change

Their vulnerability to very cold winters means that our Wren population is prone to large fluctuations. Overall their population has increased since the 1980s, perhaps due to winters generally being milder, but severe weather does hinder the population growth. Following the winter of 1962/63, for example, it was estimated that the British population declined by 80%. Thankfully they bounce back from these declines quickly due to the fact they can produce more than one large brood of chicks every year.

Interesting Breeding Bird Survey results indicate that between the mid 1990s and late 2000s there was a strong population increase in northern Wales, northern England and mainland Scotland, and a minor decrease in areas in southern England. Overall, they are a very common bird, but they may not appear so thanks to their solitary lifestyle and furtive habits.

A sedentary bird

In Britain and Ireland Wrens are mostly sedentary. In the winter, some that breed in upland areas may move to lower altitudes. Scottish island populations, however, can remain where they are, thought to be because the tide lines around the islands provide good numbers of invertebrates all year round. Populations on mainland Europe are more mobile, and every autumn birds do migrate across to Britain to spend the winter. While Wrens use gardens in all seasons, they are more likely to be seen during the winter when invertebrates are harder to find and the birds forage more widely.

The Wren in folklore

The Wren features in some British and Irish folk tales and country customs, notably 'the Wren hunt' that was, until relatively recently, common across parts of Ireland. This involved the capture of a Wren by a group of boys, who would then parade it around their village with a great deal of ceremony, in return for rewards of cake or money.

Identification

Wrens are tiny birds, weighing no more than a pound coin, with brown upperparts and brownish-buff plumage underneath. They have a small tail that is often held vertically and a pale line above the eye. The bill is quite long for the size of the bird, pointed and slightly curved down. Its call is a hard clicking 'teck' or 'zerrrr' and its song is typically fast with a high trilling phrase. Both calls and song are surprisingly loud for such a small bird.

ISLAND RACES

There are actually six different subspecies of Wren in Britain, four of which occur on islands. *Zetlandicus* is found on Shetland, *fridariensis* is found on Fair Isle, *hebridensis* lives on the Outer Hebrides and *hirtensis* is from St Kilda. Two other subspecies are found on the mainland: *troglodytes* in southern and central England and *indigenus* throughout mainland Britain and in Ireland. The island forms are usually darker and have more heavily barred plumage.

Shetland Wren, by Jill Pakenham

Starling, by John Harding

Starling
Sturnus vulgaris

Loved by many but disliked by some, the Starling is a bird that can split opinion. They can be boisterous, and their large winter flocks can leave a considerable mess, but there can be little doubt that the iridescent adults are stunning, and the wheeling aerobatics of their winter pre-roost flocks are breathtaking to watch.

Red-listed

Spotlight

Size 22 cm; Wingspan 40 cm; Weight 78 g

Food: Mostly insects (especially the larvae of crane-flies), but also fruit, seeds and fat products.

Breeds: April to June

Clutch size: 4–5 eggs

Incubation: c.12 days

Young fledge: c.21 days

Number of broods: 1 (2) per year

Population: 1.8 million pairs

Max lifespan: 17 years, 8 months

Typical lifespan: 5 years

Garden reporting rate: 69%

Starling nest, by John W Proudlock

Identification

Boisterous and gregarious, Starlings are familiar garden visitors. Adults appear dark overall, though smart pale dots and spectacular green, blue and purple iridescence are visible in good light. In the breeding season, males have an unspotted breast, and close observation may reveal a blue-grey base to their yellow bills. Adult females also have yellow bills in the breeding season, but theirs have a pale pinkish-white base. The bills of both males and females are dark in winter. Juveniles are the same shape as the adults, with short tails, long, strong beaks and streamlined heads, but they are a uniform pale grey-brown colour, which can make them look quite different to their parents. During their first moult, in the autumn of their first year, they can show a confusing patchwork of brown juvenile plumage mixed with blacker adult feathers.

Starlings have a very variable vocal repertoire; the male's song, often heard from gutters or chimney pots in suburban areas, is a mix of soft whistles, knocking sounds and descending trills, interlaced with skilful mimicry of other birds. A common call made by both adults and begging youngsters is a buzzing 'churr'.

An opportunist

In the countryside, where they were once extremely common, Starlings nest in tree holes, stone walls or farm buildings, and feed by probing in the soil for invertebrates. However, they have also long been a familiar urban species, and in towns and cities they nest in building cavities, mainly under eaves and in loft spaces, and also take to nest boxes. They are opportunistic and generalist feeders, and are often quick to take advantage of scraps left out on garden lawns and on bird tables. Despite being adapted to feeding on soil invertebrates, they have learned to exploit hanging bird feeders, and will cling to suspended fat balls or peanut feeders with their powerful feet and dig away with strong beaks.

Winter wonders

They are extremely gregarious, and on winter evenings they are known to form swirling flocks known as murmurations, some consisting of tens of thousands of birds, as they prepare to roost. The numbers in gardens are highest at this time of year, and large hungry groups often descend on garden feeding stations. As expected of a common urban breeder they are frequently recorded in gardens throughout the breeding season, and while they remain more social than many other birds, counts of individuals reported to Garden BirdWatch drop through March and April as breeding birds spread themselves out into separate territories. In May and June numbers in gardens shoot up again as the juveniles mix with the adults at bird feeders, but into the autumn counts start to decline again as birds gather into larger flocks.

Status and distribution

Starlings are widely distributed throughout Britain and Ireland during the breeding season, with the lowest concentrations in Wales, the south-west of England and the uplands of Scotland, and the highest in Ireland, low-lying farmland in eastern England and large urban areas. In winter they are joined by large numbers of migrants from northern Europe, especially Scandinavia, and Russia, swelling the national population and increasing the numbers seen in gardens. At this time of year they are still found across the whole of Britain and Ireland, but with the highest counts in western areas.

A decline in fortunes

While they are still one of the most numerous birds in the UK, numbers have fallen precipitously since the 1960s, and this is now a red-listed species of conservation concern. The core farmland population appears to have declined more on pastoral than arable farmland, and there is evidence that the intensification of grassland management has affected the soil invertebrates that they feed on. The causes of declines in urban areas are less well understood, but several studies of Starlings have indicated that their numbers generally seem to be limited by food availability in the non-breeding season.

Juvenile Starling, by John W Proudlock

Blackbird, by John Harding

Blackbird
Turdus merula

One of our most familiar birds, the Blackbird is a species that has adapted particularly well to the garden enviroment. Part of this success stems from the fact that the Blackbird is a bird of woodland edges, a habitat which our gardens resemble in many of their key features – such as scattered trees and bushes, and areas of lawn.

Green-listed

Spotlight

Size 24 cm; Wingspan 36 cm; Weight 100 g

Food: Invertebrates, especially earthworms. Fruit taken in autumn and winter.

Breeds: March to July

Clutch size: 3–4 eggs

Incubation: 13–14 days

Young fledge: 12–15 days

Number of broods: 2–3 per year

Population: 4.9 million pairs

Max lifespan: 14 years, 9 months

Typical lifespan: 3 years

Garden reporting rate: 98%

Blackbird nest and eggs, by Herbert & Howells

A garden success

Originally a woodland bird, from the 19th century Blackbirds shifted into gardens and farmland, with a large proportion of their population now found in urban and suburban habitats. Garden BirdWatch data show that Blackbirds use gardens seasonally, with a marked reduction in numbers in autumn due to secrecy during their moult, and then the search for autumn fruit and seeds in the wider countryside. The rest of the year their diet mainly consists of insects and earthworms but they have also been known to eat newts and fish from ponds.

Breeding behaviour

Blackbirds build their untidy cup nests most often in trees and bushes but will also use a variety of other situations including ledges, log piles and even open-fronted nest boxes. Nests are usually positioned within some cover to reduce the risk of predation and the impact of adverse weather. Birds nesting in towns and villages are more productive than those in woodland and appear to begin their breeding season somewhat earlier. It is thought that the increased productivity in urban areas is due to the lower rate of nest predation in gardens (50%) compared to woodland (80%). They will have two to three broods a year to increase their overall breeding output.

Both sexes are territorial during the breeding season. They usually defend their territory through display and calls, but occasionally short, violent fights will occur. Birds from different pairs may be seen together in feeding areas outside breeding territories but even here there can be some degree of tension between individuals. In the winter, however, Blackbirds are more gregarious, often feeding together in small flocks and associating with other thrush species, such as Redwing and Fieldfare.

Ecology

According to BTO data, UK Blackbird abundance underwent a long-term decline from the mid 1970s to the mid 1990s, probably due to reduced survival. This was followed by a strong, partial recovery and now the Blackbird is green-listed on the Birds of Conservation Concern list. In 2009, there were an estimated 4.9 million breeding pairs.

Found across Europe and Asia, they are partial migrants, and while many are sedentary, in the autumn some British individuals migrate west and south-west within the country, or to mainland Europe. As local birds move out, others from Fennoscandia and mainland Europe replace them, looking for a milder winter. Birds ringed in Britain have been found as far as Iberia and Italy.

Many people think that the Blackbirds in their garden are the same ones all the time. However, in one BTO RAS (Retrapping Adults for Survival) colour-ringing project in Norfolk, the greatest number of individuals recorded on one day was 74, showing that birds are constantly moving locally in search of food.

Description

Adult male Blackbirds are instantly recognisable with black plumage and, during the breeding season, an orange yellow eye-ring and bill. An adult male with a dull bill and no eye-ring at the beginning of the breeding season will probably be a winter visitor. Females are brown, often with a paler throat patch. Juveniles are a warm brown with spotted plumage. When moulting through to adult plumage, male juveniles gain black body feathers but retain their brown wings until their first full moult a year later. Blackbirds have a rich, varied and fluty song in the breeding season and, especially around street lighting, will even sing at night. Their calls are often very loud and include a warning call sounding a little like 'chook' and their alarm call which is a loud rattle.

Blackbirds may be seen with white feathers and this is usually due to 'leucism', a form of abnormal plumage in which white feathers replace dark ones due to an inherited absence of pigment cells. Leucisim is especially obvious in birds where the plumage is normally dark.

Female Blackbird, by John Harding

Fieldfare, by Jonathan Tyler

Fieldfare
Turdus pilaris

This winter visitor to gardens is most often encountered during cold weather, when poor feeding conditions in other habitats force individuals to turn to gardens, particularly to those where windfall apples and berries are available. The large size and characteristic plumage should make the species readily identifiable.

Spotlight

Red-listed

Size 26 cm; Wingspan 40 cm; Weight 100 g

Food: Invertebrates, fruit and berries, the last two of particular importance during the winter.

Fieldfare nest with eggs, by Richard Castell

Breeds: May to July

Clutch size: 4–6 eggs

Incubation: 13–14 days

Young fledge: c.14 days

Number of broods: 1–2 per year

Population: a handful of pairs

Max lifespan: 14 years, 9 months

Typical lifespan: 2 years

Garden reporting rate: 6%

A winter visitor

Fieldfares start arriving for the winter in October, with peak numbers reported from the countryside in November. They slowly move out of the country in early spring, and all but a very few stragglers have left by May. There are estimated to be slightly more Fieldfares than Redwings in the UK in winter, around 700,000, but is extremely difficult to assess population sizes of mobile wintering species, and numbers arriving each year vary dramatically, depending on food supplies and weather conditions. They are seen in gardens less often than Redwings, on average being seen by around 6% of Garden BirdWatchers in December and January, but this midwinter peak can vary between 2% and 20%, depending on the severity of the winter. During long periods of freezing conditions and snow cover birds are unable to forage in the fields, and they will start to search out windfall fruit and bird seed in gardens if berries are hard to come by.

Origins

Fieldfare breeding grounds stretch across much of northern Europe and Russia. Nesting in small treetop colonies, they are known for the vigorous defence of their nests against crows, attacking the intruders and even bombarding them with excrement. While this tactic might be seen just as an irritation, Fieldfares working together have been known to ground or even kill potential predators. Although the breeding populations in remote areas are not well monitored, their global population is believed to be secure. Since the 1960s a very small number of Fieldfares have been recorded breeding sporadically in Britain, mostly in Scotland and northern England. It was once thought that this was the start of a colonisation, but numbers of confirmed nests have never reached double figures.

A robust bird

Fieldfares are large, stocky thrushes, similar in size and their upright posture to Mistle Thrushes, and larger than both Song Thrushes and Redwings. They have a grey head with black markings, and their pale grey rump stands out against their dark tail, chestnut wings and shoulders, especially in flight. They are strongly marked below with black spots and streaks against an ochre breast, which in good light can appear strongly yellow. In flight the underwings are bright white; Mistle Thrushes also have white underwings, but they are more uniformly spotted below, while Fieldfares have a white belly and dark-streaked chest. As in other thrushes, first-winter birds have pale spots in a line across the folded wing, formed by the paler tips of the greater coverts. They have a rattling 'chack chack chack' call which sounds similar to Mistle Thrush but very different from the thin 'tseep' made by Redwings; this is a useful way of telling apart groups of thrushes flying overhead in dull light.

Winter distribution

This species is widely distributed across Britain and Ireland in winter, with the densest gatherings in central and eastern England. They prefer low-lying farmland and woodland, and are often seen in large flocks foraging for soil invertebrates in open fields, as benefits the meaning of their name, 'traveller of the fields'. They will also feed in orchards and on berries in hedgerows, particularly Holly, hawthorn and Dog Rose. They are less likely than Redwings to be seen in urbanised areas during the winter, though on their breeding grounds in northern Europe they will readily nest in city parks.

The large numbers of Fieldfares that arrive with us in winter were once exploited as a food supply. Birds were shot, or trapped and fattened up for the table; fig-fattened Fieldfares were once regarded as a delicacy. Shot thrushes, including Fieldfares, were still being sold in markets in England in the early 20th century, and were relished baked in pies with hard-boiled eggs and bacon.

Fieldfare, by John Harding

Song Thrush, by Jill Pakenham

Song Thrush
Turdus philomelos

This familiar songster is a bird whose fortunes have dipped, with populations declining by more than 50% in just a few decades. In some parts of the country the species is now far more common in gardens than it is in the wider countryside. The Song Thrush is seen more regularly in gardens than its larger cousin, the Mistle Thrush.

Red-listed

Spotlight

Size 23 cm; Wingspan 34 cm; Weight 83 g

Food: Invertebrates, especially earthworms. Fruit taken in autumn and winter.

Breeds: March to September

Clutch size: 4 eggs

Incubation: 13–14 days

Young fledge: 13 days

Number of broods: 2–4 each year

Population: 1.1 million pairs

Max lifespan: 11 years

Typical lifespan: 3 years

Garden reporting rate: 31%

Song Thrush nest with eggs, by Herbert & Howells

Gardens are important

Song Thrushes prefer to breed in woodland, parks and gardens with plenty of thick vegetation, as they like a well-developed shrub layer. In some areas, gardens are a very important habitat for Song Thrushes. A study showed that in Essex, for example, Song Thrushes used gardens to breed in more than any other habitat, suggesting that there was more food available than in the surrounding farmland.

They usually nest in bushes or trees, though will use trailing creepers and natural or man-made ledges. The female builds the nest, which is a neat cup made of grass, moss, dead leaves and other plant material, on a foundation of small twigs. Inside the cup is hard and resembles chipboard, being made of mud mixed with rotten wood, dung or peat and cemented with saliva. Song Thrushes usually begin breeding from late March in urban areas, but appear to nest later in rural localities.

A snail hunter?

The preferred food of Song Thrushes is soil invertebrates, especially earthworms, though in autumn and winter they supplement their diet with fruit. When food is particularly scarce Song Thrushes will use garden feeding stations that provide mealworms and fat products.

The classic image of a Song Thrush smashing a snail against a stone is achieved by grabbing the lip of the shell and transporting it to a favoured 'anvil'. By smashing the snail against the anvil, the Song Thrush breaks open its shell and can remove the soft body. The thrush then usually wipes the snail's body on the ground, potentially to decrease the amount of slime, before eating it. Snails are only really important for Song Thrushes during late summer, when other foods are hard to find.

A winter boost

A widespread bird throughout the year, Song Thrush is only really absent from parts of the Scottish Highlands and other upland areas during the winter. Our breeding population is mostly resident, though some birds do migrate south to spend the winter in France, Spain or Portugal. Others may move if forced by severe weather, especially if food is hard to find.

Most common in gardens between January and June, they are likely to be seen alone or in pairs. Our winter population is boosted by birds migrating here from the Low Countries. Chances to see Song Thrushes increase in the winter when they feed alongside other thrush species including Blackbirds and Redwings. When seen in such company, their neat and compact appearance become more obvious. Some individuals may be heard singing very early in the year, especially on bright mornings.

In decline

During the early part of the 20th century, Song Thrushes appear to have been more common than Blackbirds! Now, however, they are a red-listed bird of conservation concern because of the dramatic population decline of 54% seen between 1970 and 2010. In recent years the population has been showing positive trends.

The historical declines were thought to be due to reduced survival of first-year birds linked to changes in agricultural practices, drainage of land and increased pesticide use, all reducing the amount of invertebrate prey available. The decline has been particularly bad in eastern England. The species also struggles to survive during periods of long drought or cold weather when they find it hard to access enough food. There is still a sizeable breeding population but is has become increasingly apparent that the species has been lost from former haunts.

IDENTIFICATION

Separating Song Thrush from its larger cousin Mistle Thrush can be tricky, particularly when you can't see the bird very well. Song Thrush is smaller with warmer tones to its plumage and the spots on the breast differ from those of Mistle Thrush, being inverted 'arrowheads'. In Mistle Thrush the spots are more rounded and coalesce to form dark patches at the fold of the wing. Song Thrush is more compact with a fairly short tail. A yellowish-brown tone may be evident on the flanks near the wing edge.

As its name suggests, the Song Thrush is known for its vocal abilities, with its characteristic song formed of frequent repetitions, many of which may be repeated three times over. Loud, clear and striking, it can include many different phrases, drawn from other bird calls. The call note is a soft 'tic'; the Mistle Thrush call is a harsh-sounding rattle.

Song Thrush, by Peter Howlett

Redwing, by John Harding

Redwing
Turdus iliacus

These small thrushes are winter visitors to gardens, arriving in varying numbers depending upon the severity of the winter weather and the availability of their favoured invertebrate and berry foods. They may be seen in the company of other thrushes and their dark tones, size and the prominent stripe above the eye all help to separate them from other birds.

Red-listed

Spotlight

Size 21 cm; Wingspan 34 cm; Weight 63 g

Food: Invertebrates. Berries and windfall fruit taken in autumn and winter.

Breeds: April to August

Clutch size: 5–6 eggs

Incubation: c.13 days

Young fledge: 12–14 days

Number of broods: 2 per year

Population: a handful of pairs

Max lifespan: 11 years, 10 months

Typical lifespan: 2 years

Garden reporting rate: 8%

Redwing nest with eggs, by Richard Castell

Identification

Attractive winter visitors, Redwings are closely related to the slightly larger Song Thrushes, but can be recognised by their boldly striped heads, and rusty red (rather than orange) flanks and underwings. Their backs are a greyish brown, and the spots on their front are dusky and often indistinct. First-years show some pale white spots on the closed wing, but otherwise resemble fully adult birds, and all ages show a yellow base to their dark beak. Redwings normally migrate under cover of darkness, and their contact call is often heard overhead on clear autumn nights; a drawn-out, penetrating, whistling 'tseep'. Their alarm call is a rattling chatter.

Birds of a feather

These are social birds, and are often seen in groups with Fieldfares and other thrushes, sometimes in spectacular winter flocks. They generally start arriving in September but most reach Britain and Ireland in November, and leave in March. Hundreds of thousands of Redwings are distributed across Britain and Ireland in winter, most densely in central and south-west England and in Ireland. They are common in fields, woodland edges, orchards and parks, and though they are generally wary of humans they are most likely to visit garden bird feeders during particularly cold, snowy conditions, especially in January and February. On average they are reported by around 8% of Garden BirdWatchers in midwinter, but during especially harsh weather they can be seen in over a fifth of gardens. In the winter they are nomadic, and will move on to areas further south if the weather gets too cold.

During the breeding season they feed on insects, but in the winter they take berries and fruit, including hawthorn, Elder, Yew and Holly, as well as foraging for earthworms and other invertebrates on the ground. In gardens they are most likely to feed on windfall apples or other fresh or dried fruit.

Origins

Most of the world population breeds in Iceland, Scandinavia, north-east Europe and Russia, building their nests in birch scrub or on the ground. In their Russian breeding range they are poorly studied, but breeding numbers in Europe have shown moderate declines, and it is suspected that populations outside Europe have also declined. They have therefore been given a global conservation status of Near Threatened. A handful of pairs breeds in the Scottish Highlands each year, but this tiny breeding population also appears to be declining, perhaps due to a changing climate and its wider effects.

Their main breeding range is almost entirely abandoned in winter when much of the population moves to Europe, meaning that birds that breed in Siberia have to migrate at least 6,500 km to reach their wintering areas. Ring recoveries suggest that that many of the birds that winter with us are Scandinavian breeders, though they are rarely faithful to winter territories, and birds that are with us one winter might be in Spain, Italy or even Azerbaijan the following year. In one case, two Redwings that were ringed in the same nest in Finland were both reported in the February of their first winter, one from Wales and the other in south-east France.

The race of Redwings from Iceland and the Faroe Islands, known as *coburni*, averages larger and darker than the *iliacus* birds that originate from Scandinavia and Russia. These bulkier Icelandic birds are more likely to be seen in Ireland and western Scotland during winter, while the smaller *iliacus* race winters more extensively throughout Britain, with fewer individuals wintering in western Scotland and in Ireland.

Redwing, by Liz Cutting

Mistle Thrush, by Howard Stockdale

Mistle Thrush
Turdus viscivorus

Mistle Thrushes are most common in gardens during late winter, when berries start to run out in the wider countryside. Due to their sedentary behaviour, they tend to be reported from the same areas each year. Mistle Thrushes may travel in family parties of around five or six birds. During the autumn, however, the young disperse and therefore most gardens will be visited only by one or two birds.

Red-listed

Spotlight

Size 27 cm; Wingspan 45 cm; Weight 130 g

Food: Predominantly invertebrates, but also takes berries during autumn and winter.

Mistle Thrush egg and chicks, by Herbert & Howells

Breeds: March to June

Clutch size: 4 eggs

Incubation: 13–14 days

Young fledge: 14–16 days

Number of broods: 2 (3) per year

Population: 160,000 territories

Max lifespan: 11 years, 4 months

Typical lifespan: 3 years

Garden reporting rate: 7%

An early breeder

Mistle Thrushes tend to nest in open woodland areas with tall trees located close to short grass for feeding. They will also breed in parks, orchards, scrubby habitats and large gardens, including in urban areas, as long as there are suitable trees present. The nest, built by the female, is usually found at the base of a branch, placed against the trunk, or in a horizontal fork. They may, however, also build on ledges or inside buildings (especially in ruins) and have even been known to build on objects like traffic lights. The nest is a cup of grass and other plant material, strengthened with earth and lined thickly with fine grasses. Mistle Thrushes are one of our earliest breeding birds and, if the weather is mild, can lay eggs as early as February. Pairs can have up to three broods so nesting activity may continue well into June.

What's in a name?

During the spring and summer Mistle Thrushes eat a range of invertebrates, but during the autumn and winter they depend on berries. Their name is based on their long-standing relationship on mainland Europe with Mistletoe. In the UK they will feed on Mistletoe berries but they are more commonly associated with Holly and hawthorn berries. Once they have found a richly laden tree of berries, especially one that is quite isolated, Mistle Thrushes will defend it vigorously, sometimes for the whole winter. Holly bushes are particular favourites as the berries can remain for many months without deteriorating. First the bird will give a vocal warning, and then make swooping attacks against any bird that approaches for berries. Occasionally breeding pairs will stick together to defend feeding resources throughout the winter. They won't feed from just that bush but will make the most of any other unguarded bushes nearby – making sure that their supply lasts. This aggressive behaviour is also seen when they protect their nests, and they have been known to chase off much larger birds including Sparrowhawks and Buzzards.

Movements

Apart from local movements from high upland areas during the winter, Mistle Thrushes in Britain and Ireland are mostly sedentary. Elsewhere, however, they are a migratory bird, with north-easternmost birds in Europe moving south during the winter months. Occasionally, small numbers of migrant Mistle Thrushes are recorded arriving in Britain in autumn and spring, but mostly our winter and breeding populations are the same birds.

The Mistle Thrush population has been declining in England since the 1970s, falling by a third between 1995 and 2010. The Scottish population was increasing until the mid 2000s but since then has also been declining. It is thought that this could be due to reductions in survival rates among juveniles, possibly linked to agricultural intensification.

Identification

Despite looking similar to the Song Thrush with a brown back and speckled breast, Mistle Thrushes are actually quite easy to distinguish. They are larger birds and often adopt an upright, alert position when standing, unlike the Song Thrushes which remain low to the ground. Mistle Thrushes are paler overall in their plumage tones, with light brownish-grey sides to the head and neck, greyer wing feathers with pale edges and more rounded black spots on their breast and belly (unlike the arrow-shaped spots of the Song Thrush). They have white underwings which are visible when the bird is seen in flight.

The Mistle Thrush call is a dry rattle 'zer-r-r-r' and is often compared to the noise made by old-fashioned football rattles. Their song is similar to that of the Blackbird but with much shorter phrases, delivered in a clear and loud voice. They often sing from the highest branches of tall trees, even in wet and windy weather, which has earned them the nickname 'stormcock'.

Mistle Thrush, by Peter Howlett

Spotted Flycatcher
Muscicapa striata

Spotted Flycatcher, by Vic Froome

This species is one of the last migrants to arrive in the spring, with the first birds not seen until the end of April, and continuing to arrive until late May. Despite this late appearance, pairs may be able to raise two broods of chicks before departing in August. During the migration times of May and August Spotted Flycatchers may turn up in unexpected places, so it's always worth keeping an eye out.

Spotlight

Red-listed

Size 14 cm; Wingspan 24 cm; Weight 17 g

Food: Mainly flying insects (especially small flies and wasps), hunted from a perch.

Spotted Flycatcher at the nest with young, by John W. Proudlock

Breeds: May to August

Clutch size: 4–5 eggs

Incubation: 12–14 days

Young fledge: c.13 days

Number of broods: 1 (2) per year

Population: 33,000 territories

Max lifespan: 8 years

Typical lifespan: 2 years

Garden reporting rate: <1%

Summer visitor

Spotted Flycatchers are long-distance migrants that spend the winter in the humid zone south of the Sahara; like many other migrants they are in decline. In the case of Spotted Flycatcher the declines have been rapid and consistent since standardised monitoring began, and the total UK breeding population is now less than a fifth of what it was in the 1960s, though they are still widely distributed across Britain and Ireland.

Since so many other long-distance migrants show similar population changes, it's assumed that habitat deterioration on the wintering grounds and at stopover sites has mainly driven the declines, but there could be other factors at play. It's known that many nests are lost to predators, though nests in gardens are to some extent protected from these losses, and are more likely to be successful than those in the wider countryside. However, demographic analysis has shown that declines are probably driven by lower survival of first-year birds, rather than lower breeding success. Populations of many moths, butterflies and other insects are lower than in the past, presumably due to habitat degradation and use of pesticides, and this may have affected Spotted Flycatcher food supplies.

Identification

Spotted Flycatchers may appear drab and unremarkable at first sight, but their distinctive posture and behaviour makes them unmistakable. Only the recently fledged juveniles are spotted; adult birds, despite the name, are mainly plain grey and white, with subtle streaking across the wings, breast and head. They often sit out on a prominent perch in an upright position, paying close attention to their surroundings through round dark eyes set in a large head, their wide bills frequently angled slightly upwards.

Their lack of distinguishing plumage features could cause confusion with several warbler species, or even female House Sparrows, but the head shape and posture, along with the fine streaks on the breast and head, should clinch the identification. Their calls are high-pitched and easily overlooked, and the song is a quiet, unstructured series of well-spaced squeaky and scratchy notes.

Behaviour

Originally birds of sparse woodland and forest edges, Spotted Flycatchers can be found in parkland, churchyards, and large gardens with mature trees. They feed on aerial insects, including large flies, bees, butterflies and moths, and often forage from a favoured open perch. With a flick of their wings they fly out to intercept their prey, sometimes hovering mid-air, before returning to their spot with their prize. In quiet conditions the 'snap' of their bills can be heard mid-flight.

When nesting in gardens they will often choose a ledge on a wall or in an outbuilding, or against the trunk of a tree concealed in the leaves of a climber. They may nest in an open nest box, or other man-made object, and the sitting female, who likes to see out of the nest, is often visible from a distance. Their reliance on flying insects as a food source means they are unlikely to visit bird feeders, but a diverse garden flora should encourage the invertebrates on which they depend.

Winter quarters

Spotted Flycatchers start leaving the UK in August, and due to their foraging methods are thought to be opportunistic feeders while on migration, stopping to eat little and often, rather than fattening up through intensive feeding then making non-stop flights.

On their African wintering grounds they favour the same kinds of 'edge' habitats with scattered perches that they use for breeding in this country. They avoid dense forest, and can be found in cultivated land, disturbed areas and secondary forest in the humid zone, stretching from Sierra Leone in West Africa all the way down to South Africa. It's not clear exactly where British-breeding Spotted

Flycatchers winter; ring recoveries suggest that many winter in coastal West Africa, but others continue south, and there have been small numbers of recoveries from the Congo Basin. In the longest journey recorded by a British-ringed Spotted Flycatcher, a juvenile ringed in Wales during August (which could have been on passage from a breeding area outside Britain) was recovered in South Africa the following March.

Spotted Flycatchers start their return journey northwards in March, and the most southerly wintering grounds are vacated by April. Records from birdwatchers, collected through BirdTrack, show that the first birds do not appear in the Britain until the very end of April, with the main arrival not taking place until May.

Spotted Flycatcher feeding young, by John Harding

Robin, by Edmund Fellowes

Robin
Erithacus rubecula

Our most familiar garden bird and also one of the best studied, the Robin is a firm favourite with Garden BirdWatchers. It is a bird that is instantly recognisable to the wider public, featuring on Christmas cards, and was recently voted Britain's national bird.

Green-listed

Spotlight

Size 14 cm; Wingspan 21 cm; Weight 18 g

Food: Insects, especially small beetles, and spiders, but also takes fruit and seeds during the winter.

Breeds: March to July

Clutch size: 4–5 eggs

Incubation: 13–14 days

Young fledge: 13–14 days

Number of broods: 2 per year

Population: 6 million territories

Max lifespan: 8 years, 5 months

Typical lifespan: 2 years

Garden reporting rate: 93%

Robin nest with eggs, by Herbert & Howells

From woodland edge to garden home

Robins will happily breed in and along the edge of deciduous woodland, in gardens and in parks. They have a wide range of places where they will nest, leading to some seemingly odd choices. Usually they will go for a hole or recess sheltered by thick vegetation in a wall, tree trunk or stump. In addition, they will nest on ledges, use open-fronted nest boxes or even nest on the ground, perhaps within a tussock of grass.

Thanks to their preference for holes, they will also use a wide range of abandoned objects, ranging from plant pots to kettles. If it's still there, they will often use the same site from year to year. The nest is built by the female and is made to suit the size of the hole. The foundation is made of dead leaves, followed by a cup of moss, grass and dead leaves and lined with finer plant fibres and hair. These are wary birds around the nest and if they think they are being watched then they may drop what they are carrying, or even make a 'false visit' to somewhere other than the nest site.

A lack of tolerance

Robins defend their territories throughout the year and their red breast feathering plays an important role in deterring rival Robins. For this reason juveniles do not start to attain their adult plumage until some weeks after they have left the nest. Watch Robins in the garden and you may see aggressive encounters between neighbouring pairs, during which the birds position themselves to best display their red breasts. If this posturing fails, Robins will resort to fighting, sometimes to the death. Due to the fact that they are territorial throughout the year, they sing all year round too, and will often sing at night if their territory is close to street lighting. However their song is slightly less convincing in the winter, as it is used to defend only a feeding territory.

Diet and ecology

The main part of a Robin's diet consists of invertebrates, including insects, snails and worms. In the winter, they will also eat berries and seeds. They readily visit garden feeding stations, preferring to feed on fat products and mealworms on the ground or bird tables, but increasing numbers are taking to using hanging seed and fat feeders.

Found almost everywhere across Britain and Ireland, Robins are notably absent from exposed uplands and some Scottish islands, though they are increasing in the latter due to more trees being planted. The population has increased since the mid 1980s, but started to drop again from the late 2000s, perhaps in response to cold winters. The overall increase has been attributed to lower rates of nest failure, higher survival rates and earlier breeding in those years when winters have been milder. Due to their sedentary nature, Robin numbers vary little in gardens throughout the year. There is a slight dip in the summer when birds are breeding, and in cold winters numbers may increase.

Identification

Adult Robins need no description; they are unmistakable birds, and in gardens they can be very confiding, approaching particularly closely

Juvenile Robin, by Christine M Matthews

to anyone digging the soil who might turn up a morsel. Males and females look the same, but juveniles lack the red breast for their first few months. Instead, their whole plumage is brown and finely spotted. You might mistake a juvenile Robin for one of the other brown birds that frequent the garden, but they still have the look of a Robin in the way they stand and move. Their call is a short sharp 'tick' which can be repeated quite rapidly. The song is easy to recognise, starting with a few high long notes, but then speeding up with a series of clear notes. Robins rarely sing the same verse twice.

MOVEMENTS

Robins are generally sedentary in Britain and Ireland with most not moving more than 5 km. Colour-ringing studies have shown that once a male Robin has established its territory it is generally non-migratory for the rest of its life, excluding the odd shift locally as territories expand and contract. However, some Robins, mostly female, will cross over to mainland Europe or even North Africa to spend their winters. In addition to this, migrants from Scandinavia, continental Europe and Russia pass through Britain and Ireland.

Robin, by John Harding

Dunnock, by Adrian Dancy

Dunnock
Prunella modularis

Many gardens will hold a pair or 'threesome' of breeding Dunnocks, but the species is easily overlooked because of its unobtrusive nature and rather plain plumage. You will almost certainly hear the song and calls of Dunnocks from your garden but again, these often go unnoticed or unidentified.

Amber-listed

Spotlight

Size 14 cm; Wingspan 20 cm; Weight 21 g

Food: Mostly insects and spiders, taken from the ground, but will also take small seeds in winter.

Dunnock nest with a Cuckoo egg, by Mike Toms

Breeds: April to July

Clutch size: 4–5 eggs

Incubation: 11–12 days

Young fledge: c.12 days

Number of broods: 2 (3) per year

Population: 2.3 million territories

Max lifespan: 11 years, 3 months

Typical lifespan: 2 years

Garden reporting rate: 82%

The hedge 'sparrow'

Sometimes known as Hedge Sparrow or Hedge Accentor – it isn't a sparrow but it is an accentor – the Dunnock is a very common garden resident. Streaked black and brown above and below, with a lead-grey head, the overall impression is of a nondescript, dark, 'little brown bird'. Dunnocks have fine, dark bills, which help to tell them apart from the stout-billed House Sparrows. For their first few weeks young juvenile Dunnocks have pale bills and light speckled feathers, but they soon develop into their adult features.

Dunnock song consists of a series of undistinguished rushed phrases, less melodious than a Robin. Their alarm call is a single, flat, piping note. They forage for invertebrates and small seeds on the ground and in undergrowth, and are generally unlikely to be seen on hanging bird feeders, though they may visit raised bird tables.

Widespread but in decline

Dunnocks are common in both winter and the breeding season throughout Britain and Ireland, and are found in all habitats with low, thick growth, including woodland, farmland, scrubland and gardens. Despite the abundance of this species in built-up areas, Dunnock is an amber-listed bird of conservation concern due to significant population decline in the 1970s, possibly due to changes in woodland management and increased deer browsing reducing the amount of undergrowth available for nesting, from which the species has not recovered.

The Dunnock's nest is one of the most beautiful of all garden birds, with bright blue eggs in a neat moss-covered cup. Some, however, contain more than just Dunnock eggs, as this species is one of the main hosts of the Cuckoo (see photograph). Female Cuckoos that target Meadow Pipit or Reed Warbler nests produce eggs that look very similar to their host species, but the lineage of Cuckoos that lay their eggs in Dunnock nests has not developed any such strategy; the speckled Cuckoo egg is immediately obvious beside the small blue eggs of the parent Dunnocks. The Cuckoo egg shown in the photograph was laid by a bird specialising on Reed Warblers – the Dunnock nest was next to a reed bed and the Reed Warblers were late arriving to breed that year.

It is thought that Cuckoos started laying their eggs in Dunnock nests only relatively recently, in evolutionary terms, and the Dunnocks are not yet capable of recognising and ejecting 'impostor' eggs.

A complex lifestyle

Breeding Dunnocks have one of the most complex social systems of all British birds, discovered through research in Cambridge Botanic Garden in the 1980s. Pairs may be monogamous, but it is also common for two males to mate with one female, or one female with two males, and occasionally two or more males might simultaneously partner two or more females. If a female shares a territory with two males, the dominant male will spend most of his time guarding the female in order to secure exclusive mating rights, but she will aim to shake him off to mate with the subordinate male. If she succeeds, both males will supply her chicks with food. If she fails, the subordinate male may attempt to destroy the nest and eggs. Despite this uneasy relationship, the males will work with each other to defend the territory from intruders. A single male holding a territory with two females will mate with both of them, but the females will also attempt to mate with subordinate males from other territories.

While it's not easy to tell the difference between individual Dunnocks in a garden, the presence of a complex social system can be inferred by watching their behaviour. A small group of Dunnocks engaged in wing-flicking display is probably an aggressive interaction between males from neighbouring territories, often involving both dominant and subordinate males. Another often-observed behaviour is 'cloaca pecking', where a male who is about to mate with a female will peck her cloaca in order to displace the sperm from a previous mating, in an attempt to fertilise as many of her eggs as possible.

EASILY OVERLOOKED

The habit of feeding on the ground and often under bushes and shrubs, coupled with a superficial resemblance to a sparrow, means that the Dunnock is easy to overlook.

Confronted with a small brown bird in your garden, start by looking at the bill. Insectivorous birds, like the Dunnock, have fine pointed bills, while sparrows, finches and buntings have larger more robust bills, adapted for feeding on larger seeds and grains.

Dunnock, by John Flowerday

House Sparrow, by Les Foster

House Sparrow
Passer domesticus

The decline in UK House Sparrow populations came as a surprise to ornithologists, the species having been so common that its future seemed secure. Now, with a population substantially smaller than in the 1970s, research efforts are being directed to halt the decline and improve the fortunes of this familiar garden bird.

Spotlight

Red-listed

Size 14 cm; Wingspan 24 cm; Weight 34 g

Food: Mainly seeds, but also shoots, berries and scraps. Nestlings are fed on invertebrates.

Breeds: April to August

Clutch size: 4–5 eggs

Incubation: c.12 days

Young fledge: 14–15 days

Number of broods: 2–3 per year

Population: 5.1 million pairs

Max lifespan: 12 years

Typical lifespan: 3 years

Garden reporting rate: 78%

House Sparrow nest with eggs, by Richard Castell

A close neighbour

As their name suggests, House Sparrows breed in and around human habitation. They will nest in almost any type of building as long as there is a hole or a crevice, and will readily take to nest boxes, use old House Martin nests or even build untidy nests within dense vegetation. The nest is usually large and domed with a side entrance and made of straw, grass and moss. It is often lined with feathers, hair and other soft materials. In smaller cavities, though, it may just be a lined cup. House Sparrows often lay two to three clutches of four or five eggs from late March onwards.

House Sparrows are predominantly seed-eaters, though will also eat berries and kitchen scraps. They feed their chicks mostly on insects, but seeds and green plant material are also given, especially if invertebrates are scarce. They can be attracted into gardens with mixed seed, sunflower seed and peanuts, though they are most likely to use feeders where several birds can feed at once, and that are in easy reach of cover.

Identification

House Sparrows are often heard before they are seen, chirping and chattering away in hedges and on rooftops. They are fairly bulky-looking birds, with stout heads and thick bills. Males are easily told by their black bib, black face mask and chestnut-brown head with grey crown. They also have a broad white wing-bar. Female and juvenile House Sparrows appear dusky brown with greyish-white undersides and dull-brown but streaked backs. They lack the black bib of the male, and have pale brown crowns and a buff line above the eye. They can be confused with Dunnocks but the latter have much thinner beaks and a grey head and breast. Tree Sparrows are another possible source of confusion;

both females and males of this species are distinguishable by their red-brown crowns and a small black cheek patch.

Stay-at-home birds

They are mostly sedentary birds, though they will move short distances to find food, especially just after the breeding season. Though they are still widely distributed throughout Britain and Ireland, House Sparrows have undergone a rapid decline since the 1970s, with a population reduction of approximately 70% between 1977 and 2010. This has led them to be red-listed as a bird of conservation concern. Numbers appear to have started to stabilise, however, especially in gardens. The decline was more severe in urban areas, with London and eastern England greatly affected. In contrast some areas, including Wales, Northern Ireland and Scotland, have seen recent increases in local populations.

Local fortunes

It is thought that different factors are behind the declines in rural and urban areas. In rural areas, agricultural intensification may have been important, mostly due to reduction in food availability through the loss of winter stubbles and there being less spilt grain around. In urban areas, a more complex mix of influences is believed to be behind the declines seen. These include the loss of feeding grounds as green space is lost to development and, for example, to people paving over their front gardens to create off-road parking. Lack of insect food for chicks, in both rural and urban areas, has been shown to be a problem; a study published in 2014 showed that supplying mealworms in gardens can substantially improve breeding success.

BTO research also suggests that the loss of nest sites has also been a major issue, with plastic fascias and soffits replacing wooden ones, and modern roof tiles lacking the space underneath where House Sparrows would traditionally have nested. Increased levels of pollution, predation by cats and a recovering Sparrowhawk population, and competition for food with pigeon species have also been suggested as potential problems.

This multitude of issues is thought to be one of the reasons that the decline has been occurring for so long. Garden BirdWatch data will continue to play an important role in supporting research into the species. Where House Sparrows still occur, their numbers increase from March and peak in late summer, as young birds enter the population.

SPARROW SOCIETY

Due to their sociable nature, House Sparrows nest in colonies, though male House Sparrows do have very small territories consisting of their nesting hole and the area around it. How vigorously the male defends this nest hole will partly determine whether a female will mate with him. The other decisive factor will be the size of the black bib on his chest. The importance of this feature has been shown through experiment – male House Sparrows that had larger black bibs painted on their chests acted more boldly than they did usually.

House Sparrow, by John Harding

Tree Sparrow
Passer montanus

Tree Sparrow, by John Harding

Tree Sparrows are very social, more often seen in groups than as singletons, and their chirping contact calls are similar to House Sparrows, although slightly higher pitched with a more musical sound. A less common garden visitor than its cousin, the Tree Sparrow is a farmland bird that uses some rural gardens.

Red-listed

Spotlight

Size 14 cm; Wingspan 21 cm; Weight 24 g

Food: Mostly seeds as an adult but nestlings are fed on a diet of insects and spiders.

Tree Sparrow nest with eggs, by Peter Castell

Breeds: April to August

Clutch size: 5–6 eggs

Incubation: 11–14 days

Young fledge: 15–20 days

Number of broods: 2 (3) per year

Population: 180,000 territories

Max lifespan: 10 years, 11 months

Typical lifespan: 2 years

Garden reporting rate: 5%

Identification

Smaller, trimmer cousins of House Sparrows, Tree Sparrows can be distinguished by the black spots that stand out from the centre of their white cheeks. The plumage on their bodies is similar to House Sparrows, being buff-grey below and streaked chestnut, black and white above, but the whole top of the head is rich chestnut brown, and they have a white collar which is broken only at the back of the neck. Males and females look the same, while in juveniles the white cheeks and collar are smudged with grey. Male House Sparrows can be mistaken for Tree Sparrows, particularly when strong light makes their grey cheeks stand out brightly against the chestnut sides to the head. However, male House Sparrows are always grey on top of the head, and often have a black bib that spreads further down the chest than the small neat bib shown by Tree Sparrows.

Distribution and habitat

They are mainly found in low-lying farmland in central and northern England, eastern Scotland, the Welsh Marches and parts of eastern Ireland, with the highest densities along the east coast of Scotland, Lincolnshire and Yorkshire. Here they are sedentary, and the breeding and wintering distributions are similar. They generally nest in cavities in old trees or buildings, though they will build a domed nest in thick vegetation, and have also been known to nest in old Sand Martin holes, or in the bases of the stick nests of much larger birds, such as Grey Herons.

Though they are primarily a farmland bird, they are also found in rural and suburban gardens, and will take to nest boxes. They are recorded by around 5% of Garden BirdWatchers throughout the year, though they are absent from many gardens in August and September, when birds disperse after breeding. A social bird, they are often seen in large groups in gardens in January and February, sometimes in flocks of 50 or more, when seed supplies in the winter countryside run low. Like House Sparrows, they are comfortable feeding on the ground or from hanging feeders.

Agricultural change

While their populations were always known to fluctuate, numbers of Tree Sparrows declined dramatically in the UK between the late 1970s and the early 1990s, and they are now a red-listed bird of conservation concern. In the 1960s they were widespread across southern and eastern England, but they are now almost entirely absent from those areas. The loss of Tree Sparrows has been attributed to agricultural intensification, as they are known to congregate in places where seed food is available in winter, such as cereal stubble fields and weedy brassica fodder crops, and these areas of food-rich habitat are now much reduced, meaning that Tree Sparrows are less able to survive through the winter. It has also been suggested that today's farmland does not include enough wetland patches to support the invertebrates that Tree Sparrows, and other farmland birds, once fed to their chicks. Since 2000 the population has started to increase, though this upturn is negligible in comparison with the previous declines. Despite these widespread declines, Tree Sparrows have increased their range in Ireland and north-east Scotland.

Something else

Tree Sparrows are very closely related to House Sparrows, and the two species are similar enough in appearance and habits that mixed-species pairs have been known to breed successfully, raising hybrid chicks. Hybrids show a mixture of features of the two parents, with some grey in the crown, like House Sparrows, but also the Tree Sparrow's black cheek patch. It's thought that hybrids are more likely to occur in areas where one species is rare but another is abundant, as members of the rare species have trouble finding a mate of their own kind and are more likely to pair with the more common species.

GOING GLOBAL

Ireland is at the western end of the Tree Sparrow's world range, which spreads east to Japan and Indonesia. In the UK this is a farmland species, and the 'urban sparrow' is the House Sparrow, but further east Tree Sparrows are more often found in towns and cities, and in the far east they replace House Sparrow as the common urban sparrow. House Sparrows are not found in China, and here Tree Sparrows have been extremely abundant across both farmland and urban areas. In fact, Tree Sparrows were once seen as a serious agricultural pest in China and Chairman Mao Zedong mobilised millions of people to kill them in 'The Great Sparrow Campaign'.

Tree Sparrows, by John Harding

Female Pied Wagtail adult and youngster, by Liz Cutting

Pied Wagtail
Motacilla alba

As a garden bird, the Pied Wagtail will be familiar to those lucky enough to have an expanse of lawn, this being their preferred foraging habitat. Usually seen singly or in pairs, it is only during the winter months that Pied Wagtails come together in larger flocks.

Green-listed

Spotlight

Size 18 cm; Wingspan 28 cm; Weight 21 g

Food: Small insects and spiders, either taken from the ground or by flycatching from a perch.

Breeds: April to August

Clutch size: 5 eggs

Incubation: 12–14 days

Young fledge: 13–16 days

Number of broods: 2 (3) per year

Population: 460,000 pairs

Max lifespan: 11 years, 4 months

Typical lifespan: 2 years

Garden reporting rate: 13%

Pied Wagtail nest with eggs, by Richard Castell

In the neighbourhood

The Pied Wagtail is a distinctive subspecies of the White Wagtail, which is found throughout Europe, Asia and northern Africa. Pied Wagtails are normally found in areas of open ground with short vegetation which makes it easier for them to see and catch their prey. They are usually seen close to water and often associated with human activities, in and around farmyards, industrial sites, ruins and urban areas. When using gardens, they prefer those with large lawns and a pond.

When looking for a nest site, Pied Wagtails prefer to use fairly open holes or recesses. Their nest consists of a cup of stems, twigs and leaves lined with wool and hair, and can be found in natural sites such as tree hollows, but are also often found in man-made sites, including log piles, buildings, sheds and walls. They will use open-fronted nest boxes on occasion.

On the menu

Primarily insectivores, you will regularly see Pied Wagtails feeding along roads and pavements where it is easy to catch stray invertebrates. They have adapted well to human activities and will on occasion pick off insects from car radiator grilles. In the winter, when invertebrates are scarce, they will come into gardens to feed on seeds and bread. Due to this shortage of resources, males establish winter territories – though, in years with a lot of food, they tolerate females and first-winter males feeding in their patch.

Pied Wagtails form communal roosts in winter and, while many roost in reed beds, where they are safer from predators, birds may also congregate in urban areas. Here they favour trees located in car parks and city centres, or buildings. Roosts can be as large as 4,000 individuals and urban birds benefit from the additional warmth that escapes from factories and other buildings.

On the move

Whilst generally a resident bird, Pied Wagtails in upland and northern areas leave their territories, some migrating as far south as north Africa. In Britain in the winter, valleys, floodplains and the south coast have the highest densities.

Between 1995 and 2010, there was an 11% decline but overall the UK population seems to be stable with around 460,000 pairs. Declines seem to occur more along rivers and canals, but there may also be a link with decreasing insect populations.

Identification

As its name suggests, the plumage of the Pied Wagtail is black, white and grey. It has black wing feathers with white edges, a mostly white head and its long tail, which constantly wags up and down, is black and white.

The breeding plumage of the male includes black on the throat, chest and upperparts. The

Male Pied Wagtail, by Morris Rendall

breeding female is similar to the male but has dark grey shoulders and back. Juveniles are mostly brownish-grey, with a yellow wash on the face.

Their call is a loud 'tsli-vit' or a hard 'chissick' in flight. Their song is a plain, rambling medley interspersed with call notes.

GREY WAGTAIL

Another wagtail that may be found in gardens is the Grey Wagtail. Mostly associated with fast-flowing streams, it is a rare visitor but in the winter months it may come in search of food. Grey Wagtails look very different to Pied Wagtails, with slate grey upperparts and lemon-yellow underside. In first-year birds the yellow is restricted to just under the tail.

A third wagtail species, the Yellow Wagtail, also breeds in Britain but this is a summer visitor, wintering in Africa, and one that does not make use of gardens. A wagtail with yellow colouring in a garden is much more likely to be Grey than a Yellow Wagtail.

Male Grey Wagtail, by Ron Marshall

Male Brambling, by John Harding

Brambling
Fringilla montifringilla

This winter visitor is closely related to the more familiar Chaffinch and it may go unnoticed when feeding alongside its relative in winter flocks. Slightly larger, and more robust, the Bramblings using our gardens arrive in varying numbers, depending upon the size of the Beech seed crop.

Green-listed

Spotlight

Size 14 cm; Wingspan 26 cm; Weight 24 g

Food: Winter diet of seeds and some berries; summer diet of invertebrates.

Breeds: May to July

Clutch size: 5–7 eggs

Incubation: 11–12 days

Young fledge: c.14 days

Number of broods: 1 per year

Population: Occasional pairs

Max lifespan: 8 years, 8 months

Typical lifespan: 3 years

Garden reporting rate: 4%

Brambling nest with eggs, by Richard Castell

Identification

Bramblings resemble the closely related Chaffinches in size, shape, general pattern and habits. The most immediate identifying feature of these winter visitors is the light orange colour of the breast and shoulder, present in both sexes but somewhat more vivid in males. Both males and females have white bellies with dark-spotted flanks, and a tortoiseshell mixture of orange and black on the upperparts, which once gave rise to the local name of 'tartan back'. When flitting between perches they can be easily separated from Chaffinches by the bright white rump that stretches up onto the lower back, most noticeable in flight when it contrasts with the dark wings and tail.

In the breeding season the males have solid black heads and upper backs, and black beaks. However, when they replace their feathers in their annual autumn moult these black feathers have pale fringes, which overlay and conceal the dark areas. Over the course of the winter the fringes wear off, and by the time the birds are back on their breeding grounds the inner glossy black feathers of the head and back are revealed. When they are with us in the winter we never see them in their full glory, but males can still be distinguished by the indistinct shadow of the black 'executioner's hood' under the pale grey feather tips, while females have solid pale grey heads with darker stripes along the sides of the crown. In the winter both sexes have yellow bills, with a small black tip. The call is a nasal, croaking 'ehp', heard both in flight and when perched.

A winter visitor

Though a very small number of Bramblings have bred in the UK, they generally arrive for the winter in October and stay until April, and during these months they are present throughout the whole of Britain and Ireland except parts of central Ireland and western Scotland. Numbers in gardens tend to build throughout the winter, peaking in February or March, though numbers vary markedly from year to year. In winter they are highly social, often associating with Chaffinches, and, though the majority of Garden BirdWatch records are of single birds, garden flocks of fifty or more have been recorded. Like Chaffinches they prefer to feed on the ground, though they will also visit hanging seed feeders.

The importance of Beech
Their preferred natural food is the seeds of Beech trees ('mast'), but crops are unpredictable, varying between years and between different regions. Highly migratory birds, Bramblings entirely vacate their breeding grounds in Fennoscandia and Russia in winter, moving south-west towards southern Europe in search of suitable Beech crops. They have a tendency to remain as far north-east as food supplies will allow, stopping when they reach a good source of Beech mast. Where food is plentiful, extremely large numbers of birds can build up, resulting in mass onward movements if the Beech mast then becomes inaccessible later in the winter due to snow cover. These habits mean that enormous concentrations of birds can be seen in central Europe; flocks in the tens of millions were recorded in Beech woods in Switzerland in one winter in the 1950s. In years where the Beech crop is poor Bramblings are more likely to migrate as far as the UK, and more likely to visit garden bird feeders once they are here, demonstrating how the conditions in the wider countryside affect the birds we see in our gardens. In total, between 50,000 and two million Bramblings are estimated to winter in the UK every year.

Making the journey
In their European wintering areas, adult males remain closest to the breeding grounds, while females and juveniles are likely to travel further to the south-west, possibly due to competition for food. However, individuals do not have set wintering grounds, and ring recoveries have shown that the same bird might spend different winters in Britain and Croatia, or Belgium and Italy. Bramblings have been recorded making short-distance 'reverse migrations' in Sweden, where birds backtrack 10 or 20 miles from the Baltic coast to farmland areas to spend some time feeding; it's thought these are individuals with low fat reserves, not sufficient for a sea crossing.

FROM RUSSIA
Bramblings breed mainly in the far northern birch forests, from Scandinavia across Russia to Siberia. Breeding birds in these areas are not well surveyed, and it is difficult to assess population status from the mobile wintering flocks, so we know very little about their population trends. However, to the best of our knowledge the breeding population does not appear to be of conservation concern.

Female Brambling, by John Harding

Male Chaffinch, by John W Proudlock

Chaffinch
Fringilla coelebs

Chaffinches are common visitors to garden feeding stations, where they typically feed from the ground or a bird table. The use of hanging feeders appears to vary depending upon the type of perch available. Chaffinches appear to favour perches that allow them to face the feeder opening, and overall are more comfortable on the ground.

Green-listed

Spotlight

Size 14 cm; Wingspan 26 cm; Weight 24 g

Food: Insects and spiders dominate in the summer, with seeds important at other times of the year.

Breeds: April to July

Clutch size: 4–5 eggs

Incubation: 11–13 days

Young fledge: c.14 days

Number of broods: 1 (2) per year

Population: 5.8 million territories

Max lifespan: 14 years

Typical lifespan: 3 years

Garden reporting rate: 80%

Chaffinch nest, by Mike Toms

Setting up home

Chaffinches were originally woodland birds, and are still found in the highest density in deciduous or mixed woodland – oak woodland has been identified as being particularly important for them. However, they have now also adapted to conifer woodland, farmland and human habitats. They will nest in gardens where there are suitable trees or shrubs for nesting.

Breeding behaviour will start as early as February, when males start to defend their territory, but nest building not until late April. The nest is built by the female, usually low down in the fork of a tree or bush. It is a neat deep cup with a bulging edge and is mostly made of moss with grass and fibres woven in. It is lined with hair, feathers, wool or other soft material and has the appearance of a half-finished Long-tailed Tit nest.

Food and feeding

Their diet mostly consists of seeds, especially in the autumn and winter when Chaffinches are often seen feeding on the ground. Beech mast is particularly important to them, but they will feed on a variety of different seed types, and will come into gardens to feed on seed spilt on the ground. In the summer, Chaffinches will move on to eating invertebrates, including small flies, caterpillars and spiders, which are particularly important for their chicks.

During the winter you may see them in large flocks which are usually swelled by birds that have migrated to the UK from continental Europe. When in mixed flocks with Bramblings they avoid competition by going for different sized seeds – Bramblings can take larger seeds thanks to their bigger beaks. The use of gardens increases during the winter, and has been shown to reflect the size of the Beech mast crop; in years where this is poor, they increase their use of garden resources.

A common bird

Chaffinches are one of the most common birds in Britain and Ireland. Given their preference for deciduous or mixed woodland, they are found in their highest breeding densities in southern and eastern England and on the upland edges of northern Britain. Their densities are quite low in the centre of large urban areas and anywhere else with few trees.

Their population increased by 8% between 1987 and 2012, but recently has taken a downturn – possibly due to the effects of the disease trichomonosis that emerged in 2005. Most increases occurred in western Scotland and central and eastern England. The overall increase could be due to their adaptability and their use of gardens, as well as their ability to maintain populations in highly fragmented woodland and hedgerows.

In the winter, the Chaffinch population is joined by migrants visiting from Fennoscandia, as well as from further east. Most of these birds stay in southern and eastern Britain, but some make it further west. The British resident birds are highly sedentary, though there may be some movement away from areas where there is less food available in the winter, especially further north.

Identification

About the size of a House Sparrow, the main feature of both female and male Chaffinches is their double white wing bar. Male Chaffinches are striking birds throughout the year, though their plumage is brighter in the summer than in the winter. They have a grey-blue crown and nape, a chestnut back, an olive-green rump and pink-buff cheeks, throat and chest. Females and young birds, on the other hand, are duller. They have an olive-brown back and grey-brown underparts. The female also has a greenish rump. Chaffinches could be mistaken for Bramblings in the winter and they do form mixed flocks, making the confusion easier. However, Brambling has a diagnostic white rump and all-black tail, whereas Chaffinch has white outer tail feathers. The main call that Chaffinches make is a clear 'pink pink'. The song starts with two to three repeated notes followed by a 'whee-oo' ending.

Female Chaffinch, by D Waistell

Bullfinch, by John Harding

Bullfinch
Pyrrhula pyrrhula

Easily overlooked in the wider countryside, the Bullfinch is a species that seems to have increased its use of garden feeding stations. Favoured gardens tend to be those well connected to the countryside and often close to woodland or scrubby habitats.

Amber-listed

Spotlight

Size 16 cm; Wingspan 26 cm; Weight 21 g

Food: Feeds on the seeds of fleshy fruits (e.g. cherries), plus buds and shoots; young fed on invertebrates.

Breeds: May to August

Clutch size: 4–5 eggs

Incubation: 12–14 days

Young fledge: 14–16 days

Number of broods: 2 (3) per year

Population: 190,000 territories

Max lifespan: 9 years, 2 months

Typical lifespan: 2 years

Garden reporting rate: 13%

Bullfinch nest, by Mike Toms

Identification
Primarily birds of woodland and scrub, these large beautiful finches are a treat when seen in gardens. The cheeks and underparts of the male are a striking bright pinkish-red, fading to frosty white under the tail, contrasting with a striking black cap and dark midnight-blue wings and tail. Females show the same overall pattern, but where the males are pink the females are grey-buff. Their shape is distinctive, being plump and bull-necked, accentuated by the very short, rounded black bill which merges with the black face. In flight, the large white rump is obvious on both males and females. Juvenile Bullfinches have dark wings and tails like the adults, but they are otherwise grey-brown, without the black cap of the adults. This gives them a very different appearance, showing an obvious dark eye in a plain face, but they can be recognised by their round-headed shape and short bills.

Food and feeding
They feed mainly on seeds of fleshy fruit and plants, flower buds, and shoots, though they will also take invertebrates, particularly to provision young in the nest. They can consume flower buds at a rate of 30 or more per minute, and were once a major pest in fruit-growing areas, severely affecting crops of plum, cherry and apple orchards in particular. Back in the 1960s licences were issued to destroy Bullfinches that were damaging crops, and many thousands were killed on some farms.

Being adapted to feeding on hanging fruit and flowers, in gardens they favour hanging seed feeders. They can be shy, and tend to stay near thick cover, so are most likely to be seen in gardens that can be accessed via hedges or undergrowth. Throughout most of the year they are reported by around 10–15% of Garden BirdWatchers, though are seen in fewer gardens in autumn, when fruits and seeds are abundant in the wider countryside. By midwinter these food supplies are running low, and there is a small peak of Bullfinches in gardens during the lean months of January and February. Later in the year sightings peak again in June, when adults bring their offspring to visit bird feeders.

Distribution

This species is widely distributed throughout Britain and Ireland, with the highest densities in lowland wooded landscapes. They breed in woodland, scrubland, hedgerows, thickets in farmland and large gardens, constructing a distinctive platform of twigs supporting a shallow cup of rootlets. The eggs are particularly beautiful, being a pale blue scrawled and spotted with lilac brown. While British breeding Bullfinches are mainly sedentary, we can be joined in winter by a few migrants from northern Europe, Scandinavia and Russia, which can appear noticeably larger.

In decline

Although once common enough to be considered an agricultural pest, Bullfinch numbers declined significantly in the 1970s, and as a result this species was red-listed as a bird of conservation concern. This severe decline was thought to be mainly due to agricultural intensification, particularly the loss of hedgerows and scrubby areas which this species needs for nesting. In addition, it's thought that their core woodland habitats became less suitable, with less understorey and fewer flowering plants, possibly due to increased grazing pressure from rising deer numbers. Numbers started to rise at the start of the 21st century, and as a result they moved from the red list to the amber list, though the increases have been mainly seen in north-east England and eastern Scotland, with ongoing declines evident in southern and eastern areas of England.

A CLOSE BOND

Bullfinches have a strong and persistent pair bond, and males and females are likely to be seen together for much of the year. They frequently call to each other, a soft and piping 'phew', but they are not particularly territorial, and the quiet, whistling song of the male is seldom heard. Both adults and young are sedentary in their habits, and if they find a good food source they will remain nearby for weeks at a time.

Bullfinch, by John Harding

Greenfinch, by John W Proudlock

Greenfinch
Chloris chloris

The impact of trichomonosis saw a change in fortunes for the familiar Greenfinch and it was lost from many gardens as populations fell by nearly a third in the years following 2005. Evidence from BTO Garden BirdWatch was central to revealing the impact of this emerging disease, underlining the power of simple weekly observations by a community of citizen scientists.

Green-listed

Spotlight

Size 15 cm; Wingspan 26 cm; Weight 28 g

Food: Mostly large seeds but with some invertebrates; nestlings are fed exclusively on invertebrates.

Breeds: April to July

Clutch size: 4–5 eggs

Incubation: c.13 days

Young fledge: 13–16 days

Number of broods: 2 (3) per year

Population: 1.7 million pairs

Max lifespan: 12 years, 9 months

Typical lifespan: 2 years

Garden reporting rate: 74%

Greenfinch nest, by Herbert & Howells

Identification

Greenfinches are one of the larger finches found in gardens and are stocky birds with stout bodies and heads. Males have a yellowish-green breast, greyish-green upperparts, greyish sides to their heads and a light grey wing panel. Females are dull greyish-green all over, tinged with brown. Both have yellow edges to primaries forming a yellow panel on the folded wing, though this is duller in the female. Juveniles show similar colours to the female, but are streaked all over. The main call of the Greenfinch is a short 'chupp', though males utter a characteristic nasal 'dzwee'. Their song is also very wheezy; however, they do have a version that is more musical, consisting of trills, whistles and twitters.

Behaviour

Greenfinches tend to breed in wooded areas, whether along a woodland edge, in wooded pasture or in bushy areas in parks and gardens. The latter preference makes them a common breeding bird in villages and towns. The nest is usually built just inside the canopy of the bush or tree, either in a fork or against the trunk. It is built by the female and consists of a bulky cup of moss and plant material built on a twig foundation. There may be wool found on the rim, and it is lined with soft plant material and hair. They usually have two broods of four to five each. Although the male can start singing as early as January, they usually do not pair until late February or early March.

A diet divided

Greenfinches are principally seed eaters and their large bill enables them to take a wider range of seed sizes than other finches. They seem, however, to have a preference for those seeds with fleshy fruit around them, such as rosehips. They will readily come to feeders for mixed seed and peanuts but overwhelmingly seem to prefer sunflower seeds. During the breeding season, the chicks will be fed invertebrates while the adult birds stick to a plant-based diet. Greenfinches form large feeding flocks during autumn and winter and, due to their size, can dominate garden feeding stations – though this is becoming a rarer sight.

Seasonal movements
While the Greenfinch breeding population in Britain is largely resident and sedentary, some of our birds do migrate longer distances to spend the winter in Ireland or continental Europe. Individual birds behave differently from year to year, suggesting that the movements may be made opportunistically, in response to high breeding densities or lack of feeding opportunities elsewhere. Our winter population is often added to by a small number of migrants from continental Europe, with many from Norway. It is thought that often these are birds that have drifted west from their usual migration route. The winter population is widely distributed throughout the country, though there appears to be some association with villages and towns, perhaps due to warmer temperatures. At all times of year the highest densities of Greenfinches are to be found in eastern and south-eastern England.

Ups and downs
While many seed-eating garden species seem to have been affected by agricultural intensification, Greenfinches are different. A century ago they were restricted to woodland edges and rarely seen in gardens, as is still the case in some parts of continental Europe today, but their range has expanded in the UK and, until 2005, Greenfinches were common throughout the country. Since 2005, however, their population has decreased by a third due to a parasitic disease, trichomonosis.

Historically known in pigeons, doves and birds of prey, the disease 'jumped' to smaller birds possibly at a garden bird feeding station. While the disease has been documented in other garden birds, such as House Sparrow, Goldfinch, Siskin, Bullfinch and Dunnock, the most frequently affected species are Chaffinch and Greenfinch, but only the latter has undergone such a dramatic decline in its breeding population.

DISEASE
Trichomonosis affects the back of the throat and gullet, affecting the ability of the bird to feed and breathe adequately. This leads to diseased birds appearing lethargic, with fluffed-up plumage and occasionally having food stuck to their bills and faces. These symptoms are also seen with other diseases and are considered generic.

They may also drool and have obvious difficulty in swallowing. It is thought that the parasite is transmitted via contaminated, regurgitated food or water, for example at garden bird feeding stations. The parasite is unable to survive for long periods outside of its host.

Greenfinch, by John Harding

Lesser Redpoll, by John W Proudlock

Lesser Redpoll
Acanthis cabaret

This small and often overlooked bird has made greater use of garden feeding stations over recent years, with individuals often appearing alongside Siskins during the second half of winter. The numbers using gardens are likely to reflect the availability of tree seeds, especially Birch, in the wider countryside.

Red-listed

Spotlight

Size 12 cm; Wingspan 22 cm; Weight 11 g

Food: Small seeds, especially Birch, but also some invertebrates. Feeds mainly within the trees.

Lesser Redpoll nest with eggs and chicks, by Richard Castell

Breeds: May to August

Clutch size: 4–5 eggs

Incubation: c.11 days

Young fledge: c.12 days

Number of broods: 2 per year

Population: 190,000 pairs

Max lifespan: 6 years, 1 month

Typical lifespan: 2 years

Garden reporting rate: <1%

Identification

Lesser Redpolls are small, brown, streaked finches. They show a buff bar across the closed wing, and their dark red crowns, dark eyes and small black bibs give an overall impression of a dark face around a small, triangular, yellow bill. Both males and females have a red crown (the 'red poll') but only adult males have a metallic red breast, though a few pink feathers can sometimes be seen on first-year males. They are sociable birds and are often seen in groups, sometimes associated with Siskins. Even a large flock of these tiny finches can be surprisingly hard to see when the birds are foraging in the treetops, seemingly as happy upside-down as they are the right way up, but they can be detected by their frequent, metallic, stuttering 'chett' calls.

The challenge of redpolls

The small, dark Lesser Redpolls are the species of redpoll most likely to be seen in gardens. However, variable numbers of the slightly larger and paler Common (or Mealy) Redpoll visit Britain and Ireland each winter from continental Europe. There are few definitive identification features, but look out for the paler rump, white streaking on the back, white wing bars and a thick-necked appearance. Elsewhere Lesser and Common Redpolls are commonly treated as different races of the same species.

Winter movements

In winter Lesser Redpolls are widely distributed across Britain and Ireland, and this is the time of year that they are most likely to be seen in gardens. In their natural woodland habitats they feed on tree seeds, mainly Birch and Alder, but they are becoming an increasingly common sight at garden bird feeders. They prefer hanging feeders, and are particularly attracted to nyger and mixes containing small seeds, but while in gardens they will sometimes gather seed from bird tables or the ground.

A red-listed bird

They mainly breed in Wales, Scotland, Ireland and northern England; in central and southern England they are more patchily distributed, and restricted to wooded areas. Favoured breeding habitats are young conifer plantations, scrub, and sometimes scattered trees in parks, moors and gardens, preferably with some understorey. Lesser Redpoll was once much more common as a breeding bird across England, perhaps due to the post-war boom in forestry, but breeding numbers have fallen since the 1970s, and this species is now on the red list of birds of conservation concern. This decline has been attributed to a reduction in the amount of suitable young forest growth. In recent years there has been a slight upturn in the breeding population, though this is insignificant compared to earlier declines.

Lesser Redpoll, by Chris Knights

Lesser Redpolls are partial migrants, and in winter breeding birds from northern or upland areas move southwards. In years with a poor Birch crop they may migrate in larger numbers and longer distances, with some individuals travelling as far as southern Europe.

LINNET

Mainly thought of as a farmland species, Linnets are generally seen in gardens only during harsh winter weather, and even then normally only in rural gardens near farmland or wild open areas. Like Lesser Redpolls, adult male Linnets have a red breast and crown, but can be recognised by their grey heads and chestnut backs. In behaviour they are quite different, with Linnets preferring open habitats with low bushes or hedges rather than wooded areas. Linnets feed on the seeds of weeds and crops, and are one of the few birds to supply their nestlings with seeds rather than invertebrates. Agricultural intensification has therefore affected Linnets in both the winter and the breeding season, and is thought to be the main cause of the severe decline of this red-listed bird.

Linnet, by Jill Pakenham

Goldfinch, by Edmund Fellowes

Goldfinch
Carduelis carduelis

Goldfinches are found in gardens throughout the year, but are least likely to be seen in autumn when there is a glut of natural food in the wider countryside. There is a small peak during the summer when adults bring their young to bird feeders.

Green-listed

Spotlight

Size 12 cm; Wingspan 24 cm; Weight 17 g

Food: Takes some invertebrates in the summer, but mostly small seeds (especially from daisy family).

Breeds: April to August

Clutch size: 4–5 eggs

Incubation: 12–13 days

Young fledge: 14–15 days

Number of broods: 2 per year

Population: 1.2 million pairs

Max lifespan: 8 years, 8 months

Typical lifespan: 2 years

Garden reporting rate: 47%

Goldfinch nest with eggs, by Richard Castell

A charming bird

Known as a charm of Goldfinches, flocks of these birds are welcome in any garden. Adults have black-and-white heads with red faces, a pointed narrow beak and jet-black wings with a broad yellow wing bar. They have relatively short black tails with white spots. The sexes are only distinguishable by small features on their faces. Males have red that extends above and beyond the eye and black nasal hairs; the red on the faces of the female often stops in front or level with the eye and their nasal hairs are partly buff. Juveniles, until late autumn, have the distinctive wings but lack the colourful heads; theirs are grey-brown and streaky. Goldfinches have a chatty trisyllabic call 'tic-ke-lit' and a twittering song consisting of trills, mewing notes and sequences involving the call note.

Behaviour

Goldfinches like to breed in amongst well-spaced trees, such as in deciduous woodland, pine plantations, orchards and occasionally gardens and parks. The nest is usually found in the outermost fork of a branch, typically in broad-leaved trees or bushes, and can be much higher than the nests of other finches. It is a compact cup of rootlets, grass, wool and cobwebs and lined with vegetable matter and wool. They typically have two broods from early April though they can still have young in the nest as late as September.

Outside the breeding season, Goldfinches are usually seen in flocks and are often found with other finches including Lesser Redpoll and Siskin. Their long, pointed beaks are perfectly adapted to accessing seeds that other species cannot obtain, such as those from burdock and thistle. They are the only finch that can extract seeds from teasels, even though it is harder for females as their bills are slightly shorter than those of the males.

On the increase

In the early 1990s, Goldfinches were rare in gardens but they have increased rapidly since then and, by 2015, a maximum of 70% of Garden BirdWatchers reported them in their gardens. It is thought that this extraordinary increase could be thanks to the introduction of small, supplementary, oil-rich seeds such as nyger and sunflower hearts at garden feeding stations. While their diet mainly consists of seeds, they feed their nestlings on a mixture of regurgitated seeds and insects. Early broods receive more insects than later ones, perhaps because there are more available early in the season.

The Goldfinch population declined sharply between the mid 1970s and the mid 1980s. It is thought that they were affected by factors that influenced many seed-eating species at the time, including agricultural intensification reducing the availability of weed seeds such as Teasel. Since then, however, the population has been growing, and between 1995 and 2010 there was a 91% increase in numbers. Their range has also expanded by almost a third since the early 1980s. This turn in fortune can almost completely be explained by improved annual survival and it is thought that this can be partly attributed to the provision of specialist seeds, such as nyger, in gardens.

Should I stay or should I go?

While many of our breeding Goldfinches are resident, some of them do migrate during the autumn to spend the winter further south, often in France or Spain. They don't seem to go to the same place every winter, however, but instead move around looking for the best feeding grounds. It has been shown that female Goldfinches are more likely to migrate south during the winter than males. Although this means that males may suffer more during the winter from cold weather and reduced feeding opportunities, it also means that they are more likely to claim a good breeding territory in the spring. This pattern is also seen in other finch species, such as Chaffinch. Even Goldfinches that stay with us will move around looking for food, with some crossing from Britain to Ireland.

A 'charm' of Goldfinches, by Graham Catley

Siskin
Spinus spinus

Male Siskin, by John W Proudlock

The Siskin is now a familiar visitor to many gardens during the winter months but this wasn't the case just a few decades ago. This bird of coniferous woodland has benefited from the establishment of conifer plantations and the seeds they provide, allowing the population to grow and expand.

Spotlight

Green-listed

Size 12 cm; Wingspan 22 cm; Weight 15 g

Food: Takes some invertebrates during the summer but mainly takes seeds of spruce, pine, Alder or Birch.

Breeds: April to August

Clutch size: 4–5 eggs

Incubation: 12–13 days

Young fledge: 13–15 days

Number of broods: 2 per year

Population: 410,000 pairs

Max lifespan: 8 years, 2 months

Typical lifespan: 2 years

Garden reporting rate: 19%

Siskin nest with eggs, by Richard Castell

From the forest

Siskins are a bird of northern coniferous forests, nesting high in the tops of pine trees. Until the 1950s the UK breeding population was mainly confined to the Scottish highlands, and while they moved to the lowlands in winter they kept to forested areas. It is only in recent years that wintering birds have developed a habit of using garden bird feeders, but they have quickly learned to exploit this new resource. It has been suggested that they were originally attracted to red mesh bags of peanuts because they resembled giant Alder cones! Today, however, they are rarely seen feeding on peanuts, preferring nyger seed and sunflower hearts. This exploitation of garden food supplies, combined with more lowland conifer forestry in England, may have contributed to the increase of the breeding population reported by the Breeding Bird Survey.

Identification

Siskins are small, acrobatic finches, often seen in flocks with other species. The overall impression is of yellow and black stripes, but the males have brighter yellow colours and solid black crowns, while females are duller with fine stripes on the head. Perched birds show a yellow stripe or bar running across the folded wing, which helps to distinguish them from the larger Greenfinches, which have a yellow stripe down the edge of the folded wing. In flight they show a broad yellow stripe through the wings, similar to the closely related Goldfinches, though their colour schemes are otherwise quite different.

Their trilling, twittering calls and songs are similar to other small finches, but are characterised by a squeaky, nasal wheezing tone, which with practice is easy to recognise. Their natural diet consists of tree seeds, particularly pine cones and Alder cones and Birch catkins, as well as some invertebrates during the breeding season.

They are particularly agile feeders, often dangling upside-down on thin twigs when feeding on catkins, and have small pointed bills suited to winkling out seeds.

Winter wanderings

In winter Siskins are widely distributed across the whole of Britain and Ireland, and this is when they are commonly seen in gardens, with a peak normally in February or March. In the breeding season they retreat to areas of extensive coniferous woodland, such as in Scotland, Wales and the south-west of England, as well as the New Forest in Hampshire and Thetford Forest in East Anglia. During this time they are much less common at garden bird feeders, normally reported by fewer than 5% of Garden BirdWatchers. However, their breeding range is expanding and they are rapidly colonising new areas, breeding in parks and gardens as well as woodlands, though still strongly associated with conifers.

The annual late-winter reporting peak can be as high as 30% of gardens and as low as 5%. Tree seed crops can vary significantly from year to year, and the large fluctuations in Siskin garden sightings are probably related to food availability, with birds eschewing bird feeders in years with bumper tree seed crops. It has also been shown that breeding performance is linked to seed crops, with birds breeding earlier and producing more young in good years.

Research using Garden BirdWatch data from Scotland has linked abundance of Siskins at feeders to the local Sitka Spruce crop, showing that birds turn to garden food supplies at times when their natural food is in short supply.

Partial migrant

Siskins are partial migrants, and in winter the British population is augmented by arrivals from the Continent. Occasionally these winter influxes are very large, normally linked to severe weather or poor availability of conifer crops in northern Europe. After these large-scale movements birds do not always return to their original breeding grounds, and it's thought that winter influxes may be behind the fluctuations of the British breeding population, as birds stay to breed. Ringing studies have confirmed that Siskins can settle to breed in completely different locations in different years; a female Siskin ringed in Thetford Forest as a juvenile in 2003 was caught in the same location as a breeding adult in 2004, but two years later was found to be breeding in Russia!

Female Siskin, by John W Proudlock

Male Yellowhammer, by John Harding

Yellowhammer
Emberiza citrinella

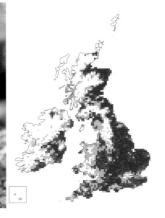

This farmland bird is an occasional visitor to garden feeding stations, most likely those located in rural areas. Influxes are reported in late winter, the period when the farmland seed supplies on which these birds feed are at their low point. Such gardens may be important for this declining farmland bird.

Red-listed

Spotlight

Size 16 cm; Wingspan 26 cm; Weight 31 g

Food: Grass seed and cereal grain; invertebrates taken in the summer and fed to young.

Breeds: May to August

Clutch size: 3–4 eggs

Incubation: 13 days

Young fledge: c.16 days

Number of broods: 2 (3) per year

Population: 700,000 pairs

Max lifespan: 11 years, 9 months

Typical lifespan: 3 years

Garden reporting rate: 4%

Yellowhammer nest, by Mike Toms

Identification

Despite their name, Yellowhammers are not all yellow. About the size of a sparrow, they have olive-brown backs that are streaked with black, chestnut-brown rumps, long notched tails and small bills. In the summer, males have an almost completely yellow head, a streaked yellow belly and a green-tinged breast. In the autumn, males lose some of the yellow on their heads and underparts, though it can still be seen on the head, under the bill and below the cheeks. Females look the same all year round, lacking the clean yellow on the head, with a dull brown streaked crown. Their underparts are yellow, but paler than that of the male, and they have greyish streaks on their breast and flanks. Juveniles are similar to females. In the garden, Yellowhammers may be confused with Greenfinches and Siskins, but these finches lack any warm brown tones.

Yellowhammers are known for their song of 5–8 rapid short notes 'sre sre sre sre sre sre sre siiisuuu' which is often remembered as the popular mnemonic 'a little bit of bread and no chee-ese'. They are one of only a few species to continue singing right through until late summer.

Behaviour

While Yellowhammers are associated with arable landscapes in the east of Britain, they tend to favour scrub elsewhere, especially in parts of south-west England, Wales and Scotland. However, they will breed in many different habitats including farmland, bushy scrub and woodland edges, as long as there are hedges, bushes or trees around. This is because they typically nest on or near the ground in vegetation growing around the base of these, usually under dead bracken or inside Brambles. There need to be taller shrubs, trees or other objects around from which they can sing. The nest is built by the female and consists of a loose, deep cup of grass, straw and plant stalks. It is lined with finer grasses and hair.

Diet

During the breeding season Yellowhammers eat mainly insects and other invertebrates. It is outside the breeding season that large grass seeds, including those of cereals, become most important and they can be seen on stubbles or game-cover strips with other seed-eaters. Once food becomes hard to find, due to either depletion or weather, Yellowhammers will move into gardens in rural areas in search of fallen seed on the ground, though they will also take wild fruits, leaves and grasses.

Ecology

Yellowhammers are mostly found in lowland areas of mainland Britain and in southern and eastern Ireland, with densities highest in the east of Britain, and are mostly sedentary. They can be found on some of the northern Scottish islands, but rarely breed there. Cereal farming is of great importance to them as they require a minimum abundance of seed to survive in a landscape, and their distribution reflects this. They are another of our declining farmland species, having shown a population decrease of 55% in the UK between 1970 and 2010. This is most likely due to changes in farming methods which have reduced winter seed availability and led to reduced overwinter survival. In addition to cereal farming, weed seeds are also important but, with a lot of grassland now intensively managed, fewer invertebrates and weeds are found in those habitats. Yellowhammers have also become very scarce in upland margin areas, where maturing plantations have caused the loss of nesting sites. There are now fewer than 700,000 pairs left and the species is red-listed. Numbers peak in gardens in late winter and early spring, This coincides with the time when food becomes scarce elsewhere in the countryside. In some areas, numbers may reach double figures in gardens, and they are often seen in flocks with Reed Buntings, Tree Sparrows and finches.

Female Yellowhammer, by John Harding

Reed Bunting, by Ric Jackson

Reed Bunting
Emberiza schoeniclus

This uncommon garden visitor is most likely to be encountered during late winter, when feeding conditions elsewhere can prompt individuals to turn to garden feeding stations in rural locations. The striking plumage of the breeding male, which is the plumage often shown in books, is absent in the winter, hidden beneath fresh feather tips.

Amber-listed

Spotlight

Size 16 cm; Wingspan 24 cm; Weight 21 g

Food: Seeds, also invertebrates in breeding season, taken from among sedges, reeds, rushes, etc.

Breeds: May to July

Clutch size: 4–5 eggs

Incubation: c.13 days

Young fledge: 14–16 days

Number of broods: 2 (3) per year

Population: 230,000 pairs

Max lifespan: 9 years, 11 months

Typical lifespan: 3 years

Garden reporting rate: 3%

Reed Bunting nest, by John Cranfield

Identification

Reed Buntings are not generally thought of as garden birds, but in late winter many Garden BirdWatchers report this species. At this time of year both males and females are predominantly brown with dark streaks, and can easily be confused with sparrows. However, winter-plumage Reed Buntings can be identified by the combination of a buff stripes over the eye and the pale 'submoustachial' stripe that runs from the corner of the bill down to the side of the neck. Although Reed Buntings have streaked underparts, the base colour is almost white, while Dunnocks and House Sparrows have grey underparts.

As the males come into breeding condition, the brown tips of their head feathers wear away, revealing the solid black head, white collar and white submoustachial stripe that make them so distinctive when seen on their breeding grounds. These are not new feathers, just the inner parts of the same feathers they have had throughout the winter. The males are conspicuous when on territory, singing their brief simple song – reminiscent of 'here comes the bride' – from the very top of a bush or a reed stem. They mainly feed on seeds and plant material, though they also take invertebrates to feed chicks in the nest. In gardens they will eat seed off the ground below bird feeders or on bird tables, and occasionally from hanging feeders.

Habitat preferences

As the name suggests, Reed Buntings are mainly associated with reed beds and wetlands, but they are widespread across Britain and Ireland and also breed across farmland far from water, with particularly high densities in oilseed rape crops. They are commonest in Ireland and eastern England, with a stronghold in the Fens of Norfolk, Cambridgeshire and Lincolnshire surrounding the Wash, and are only completely absent from a few areas in the south-west of England and the highlands of Scotland. As sedentary birds their summer and winter distributions are very similar, though a small number of continental immigrants do arrive in the autumn.

Reasons for change

In the early days of population monitoring in the 1960s, Reed Buntings increased rapidly, and this was associated with their spread from wetlands into drier habitats, but in the late 1970s numbers declined again, probably due to agricultural intensification. Alongside Linnets and Tree Sparrows, Reed Buntings are thought to have been affected by the general increase of herbicides on farmland, reducing the amount of farmland weeds and the seeds they provide. More recently, BTO research has shown that the critical time of year for many farmland birds, such as Yellowhammer and Reed Bunting, is early March. This is when demand for food peaks, but modern

agricultural systems mean that food supplies are not available in the wider countryside, as fields hold growing crops. This has been termed the 'hungry gap', and explains why since the 1980s Reed Buntings have started to turn to garden food supplies at this time of year; this trend was revealed by the long-running Garden Bird Feeding Survey before the start of Garden BirdWatch in 1995.

In the summer months very few Reed Buntings are seen in gardens, with under 1% of Garden BirdWatchers reporting this species from June through to November. However, every year in late winter the reporting rate rises, and reaches a peak in March before dropping off again as birds move back to their breeding grounds in farmland and wetlands.

Since the mid 1990s national numbers of Reed Buntings have shown a moderate but fluctuating increase, though never approaching the population sizes seen in the 1970s, and now there are an estimated 230,000 Reed Bunting territories in Britain.

Reed Bunting, by Allan Drewitt

Golden Pheasant, by Paul Sterry/NPL

Unusual visitors

If you're lucky, you might see a less common bird in your garden. While the list is practically inexhaustible, here are some of the more unusual birds you might see. Some of them are native birds that only occasionally visit gardens, either because they are now quite rare or because gardens are outside their normal range. Others are birds that have usually escaped from captivity in nearby aviary collections.

From top: Wryneck, by Jill Pakenham; Redstart, by John Harding; Firecrest, by Chris Knights; Garden Warbler, by Liz Cutting

Wryneck: This small, sparrow-sized relative of the woodpeckers is a regular passage migrant during the autumn, passing through to its wintering grounds in Africa. Its numbers peak in September, though a few individuals are also seen in the spring, and it is most often seen along the east and south coasts of England. Like Green Woodpeckers, they are usually seen on the ground hunting for ants on which they feed almost exclusively.

Redstart: This summer migrant arrives from Africa in April, leaving again by the end of October. They are distinctive, robin-sized birds with red tails, though females and juveniles are duller than males. They are usually found in areas of open deciduous woodland, particularly oak, and are most common in Wales, Scotland and western and northern England. They feed on invertebrates, including beetle larvae and spiders.

Firecrest: Firecrests are resident breeders in coniferous woodland but their numbers increase during the autumn and winter as passage and winter migrants arrive. They are most common in southern and eastern parts of England, and southern Wales, though they can be found along much of the British coast in the winter as passage migrants arrive. Their diet consists of insects and spiders.

Garden Warbler: Despite the name, Garden Warblers are more commonly found in scrub and open woodland than in gardens. They are summer migrants, arriving in Britain and Ireland from southern Africa from late April and leaving again by late September. They are most likely to be seen in gardens during these spring and autumn migrations. They are fairly nondescript brown-grey birds but have a lovely song similar to that of the Blackcap.

Cuckoo: Cuckoos migrate to Britain and Ireland from Africa to breed during May and June. These brood parasites are often found in areas with reed beds or scrub, depending on what their host species is, and usually feed on invertebrates such as caterpillars and beetles. It is the male that has the classic 'cuck-oo' song; females have a bubbling call. Due to an overall population decline, the species is red-listed.

Hawfinch: A resident species, Hawfinch sometimes seen in gardens during late winter and early spring, though individuals will use them in the autumn if there is not enough natural food available. They are usually found in areas of mature deciduous woodland, especially in southern England, and feed on large seeds and buds, though will take invertebrates during the summer. Due to a population decline in the UK, they are a red-listed bird of conservation concern.

Rose-coloured Starling: While Rose-coloured Starlings are very rare in the UK, when they are here they often turn up in gardens. Their home range stretches from eastern Europe to southern Asia but occasionally the population erupts and individuals turn up in Britain and Ireland, usually between June and October. They feed on insects, fruit and seeds and are often seen feeding amongst flocks of Starlings. The plain-looking juveniles (pictured) are seen more often than adults.

Whitethroat: Arriving from April, Whitethroats migrate from Africa for the summer, leaving again by the end of September. Around 1.1 million pairs of these warblers are found throughout the UK, preferring to breed in areas of scrub and heathland. During the summer, they mainly rely on insects, but move onto fruit in the autumn. They are most likely to be seen in gardens during their spring and autumn migrations.

Meadow Pipit: Seen throughout the year in a few lucky gardens, Meadow Pipits are found across Britain and Ireland. These streaked brown birds prefer to breed in areas of open rough grassland including heaths and moorland, but during the rest of the year are most common in lowland areas and along the coast as migrant birds arrive for the winter. They feed mainly on insects but will supplement these with seeds during the winter.

Skylark: Best known for their song, Skylarks are found throughout Britain and Ireland. They can be seen in gardens at any time of year, though unfortunately their population is in decline. There are around 1.4 million breeding pairs in the UK and they prefer open areas such as grassland or fields where they feed on insects or cereal and weed seeds. They are a partial migrant with birds moving away from upland areas during the winter.

Common Crossbill: Although they can be seen throughout Britain and Ireland, Common Crossbills are mostly found in northern England, Wales and Scotland. They prefer mature conifer woodland as they specialise in spruce and pine seeds, but when food is scarce they do become nomadic. They can be recorded in gardens throughout the year.

Canary: Traditionally a streaky-yellow colour, centuries of captive breeding mean that Canaries now come in a range of different colours including the 'classic' bright yellow, white and orange. These finches are native to the Canary Islands, the Azores and Madeira but their popularity as pets, thanks to the male's sweet singing voice, means that escaped birds are often seen in British and Irish gardens. Several similar species and hybrids also occur.

Zebra Finch: Native to Australia and Indonesia, wild Zebra Finches are grey and white, with a distinctive black-and-white-striped tail. In captivity there are a range of colour variations, though most can be identified by the orange-red beak and black 'tear drop' underneath the eye. As with Canaries, they are popular pets for bird enthusiasts, and therefore escape from time to time, turning up in British and Irish gardens, as do various species of waxbill.

Harris Hawk: Harris Hawks are one of the most popular birds used in falconry in Britain and Ireland. Smaller than Buzzards, they have dark brown plumage with chestnut shoulders. Originally they are from North and South America, and escaped birds have successfully bred in Britain, though there is no established population. Like Sparrowhawks, escaped birds may come into gardens attracted by pigeons and doves, though they are more likely to be seen flying over.

Diamond Dove: A small dove native to Australia, both sexes of Diamond Dove can be recognised by the white spots on their wings, orange eyes and red eye-rings, though females have more brown in their plumage and a duller eye-ring. While they regularly escape captivity, there is no established population in the UK or Ireland. Often an escaped dove will stay within the vicinity of its owners and may come into gardens attracted by bird seed.

WHAT TO DO IF YOU SEE AN UNUSUAL BIRD

If you see an unusual bird in your garden and you're not sure what it is, the best thing to do is try to take a photo of it and get in touch with the BTO via email or post. If you can't get a photo, a good description including size and plumage colour may help experts identify the bird. Contact details can be found on the website at **www.bto.org.**

Your local Bird Club or Bird Recorder will have systems in place for reporting and recording genuine rarities. An unusual bird in your garden with a colour ring and no metal ring is almost certainly an escaped captive-bred bird; in rare cases the owner can be traced through local enquiries, but this is often not possible.

Water Rail, by Edmund Fellowes

Other wildlife

MAMMALS

In Britain and Ireland, we have over 40 species of mammals including 30 native terrestrial species and 17 bats. Many of them will regularly visit our gardens, especially those in rural areas, though you may not see them due to their nocturnal behaviour. These are some of the ones, nocturnal and diurnal, that are reported most often through the BTO Garden BirdWatch survey.

Brown Long-eared Bat, by Mike Toms

Rats, mice and voles

Wood Mouse: Wood Mouse is the species of mouse most commonly seen in gardens, and even more likely to be seen in the house than the House Mouse. Note the white belly, large eyes and ears, and a long tail. Wood Mice, which are found in most habitats that are not too wet, are highly adaptable, opportunistic feeders. This means they are just as likely to be seen feeding on bird feeders as on the ground underneath them. The closely related Yellow-necked Mouse may also use gardens, though the species is restricted to southern Britain.

Common Rat: Also known as the Brown Rat, this large rodent has a relatively pointed muzzle and a long scaly tail. The species was introduced from Russia in the 1720s, and largely replaced the Ship Rat which had been present for hundreds of years. While they are adaptable and omnivorous, they are also limited to habitats where there are few competing species, or where there is additional food thanks to human activities; they do well in urban areas.

Bank Vole: Bank Vole can be distinguished from other species of vole by the rich reddish brown fur on its upperparts and a slightly longer tail. Juveniles are harder to tell apart as they are more grey. They are found throughout Britain, preferring areas of mixed deciduous woodland with a thick shrub or field layer, but they will be found in many other habitats, including in gardens. They feed mainly on fruits and seeds, but will take any herbivorous material.

Wood Mouse and Bank Vole, both by Paul Sterry/NPL; Common Rat, by John Harding

Squirrels

Grey Squirrel: Introduced from North America between the late 19th and early 20th centuries, Grey Squirrels now outnumber Red Squirrels by an average of 12 to one. Grey Squirrels are larger and heavier than their cousins, with mostly grey bodies, though they do have some brown on their backs and, in the summer, flanks and limbs. They occupy a wide range of habitats and have taken very well to gardens.

Red Squirrel: Red Squirrels are largely restricted to tracts of coniferous forest in northern England, parts of Scotland, and Anglesey, but within these areas they do make use of garden feeding stations. They have dark fur which varies from deep brown to bright chestnut, and have ear tufts from late summer through the winter.

Rabbit

Rabbit: Rabbits are more common garden mammals than you may think. They are much smaller than hares, with shorter hind legs and lack the characteristic black tips to the ears that hares have. They prefer habitats with short grasses, including heathland, and are usually found feeding close to shelter, whether it is their burrows or a hedgerow. They eat a wide range of plant materials, especially grasses, and will visit gardens with plenty of choice, especially those in rural areas.

Insectivores

Mole: People tend to see molehills more than Moles, thanks to their largely underground lifestyle. However, they do come above ground occasionally, usually after long periods of dry weather, and are recognisable by their uniformly short, black fur, spade-like forelimbs and pink, fleshy snout. They are found throughout the country, and are highly adaptable, using many habitats, including suburban ones. Moles in the garden are a sign of healthy soil, as they hunt a wide range of soil invertebrates from their tunnels.

Common Shrew: Shrews can be told from mice and voles by their pointed faces, and small eyes and ears. The Common Shrew has a brown upper surface and is larger than a Pygmy Shrew. Common Shrews are found in most habitats where there is low vegetation cover, but prefer thick grass, bushy scrub, hedgerows and deciduous woodland. They are opportunistic insectivores, eating beetles, earthworms, woodlice and spiders.

Hedgehog: A welcome addition to any garden, they are insectivores and will eat anything from beetles and earthworms to slugs, but they will also take birds' eggs and chicks if the opportunity arises. They will hibernate any time between October and March, but can be active up until December depending on how cold the weather is.

Bats

Pipistrelle Bat: It was realised only in the 1980s that our most common bat actually consists of two species, Common and Soprano, which echolocate at different frequencies and behave in slightly different ways. Both are very small, with only 18–24 cm wingspans, and they have dark brown upperparts and slightly lighter underparts. They are found throughout Britain and Ireland and have adapted to many different habitats, including suburban and urban areas. They roost mainly in human habitation, and will visit gardens to feed on small flies.

Hedgehog, by Paul Sterry/NPL; Pipistrelle, by S C Bisserot/NPL

Mole, by Geoff du Feu/NPL; Common Shrew, by Owen Newman/NPL;

Deer

Muntjac: Introduced into Bedfordshire in the early 20th century from south-east China or Taiwan, the Muntjac is the deer most reported from gardens. They are dog-sized with reddish-brown fur, a white underside and dark stripes running over their face. Males also have short simple antlers, and their upper canine teeth protrude slightly below the lip. They are widespread across much of southern England, East Anglia and the East Midlands, preferring denser habitats where they can browse undisturbed.

Red Fox and Badger

Red Fox: Found throughout Britain, foxes are unmistakeable with their reddish-brown fur, erect ears, slender muzzle and long bushy tail. They are equally at home in urban and rural areas thanks to their omnivorous diet, and highly adaptable and unspecialised habits. They visit gardens throughout the country, whether passing through or looking for food; if the garden is large enough, with suitable features, they may even breed in them.

Badger: No other mammal in the country looks like a Badger, with its powerful, stocky body, and white head with two dark stripes on either side. They are widespread across Britain, but prefer areas that contain woodland, pasture and arable land, in order to breed and feed. Their diet mostly consists of earthworms, though they eat a wide variety of plant and animal foods. Setts can be found in urban areas, and they will visit any gardens within their territories, especially those with large lawns where they can find worms. They are mostly nocturnal, and therefore if they don't leave any signs, you may not know that you have them.

REPTILES

There are six native species of reptile in Great Britain, three lizards and three snakes, though there are a few non-native species as well. The only reptile species native to Ireland is the Common Lizard. Three species are common in gardens – Common Lizard, Slow-worm and Grass Snake – but Adders do occasionally pass through.

Slow-worm, by Amy Lewis

Lizards

It may seem that lizards should be unmistakable, but Slow-worms look like snakes, and newts away from water have dry skin and can be confused with lizards. However, lizards have scaly skin and are more likely to run away fast when disturbed, while newts have smooth or 'warty' skin and are much slower.

Slow-worm: Slow-worms are found across Britain and are the most common reptile species in gardens. They may look like snakes but they are legless lizards and typically they grow to about 30 cm in length. Males are generally grey-brown and females are a warmer brown with dark sides; juveniles are thin, usually golden in colour with a stripe running down their back.

Preferring damp habitats with a lot of vegetation, Slow-worms are more likely to be found warming themselves under vegetation or objects such as bricks and metal sheets. They feed predominantly on slugs, snails and earthworms, though will take other prey items as well. They are usually seen between March and October.

Common Lizard: Common Lizards are widespread across Britain and Ireland. They are up to 15 cm long and are usually brown with patterns of spots or stripes, though different colour morphs exist. Females often have dark sides and a stripe down their back, whereas males are usually more spotty and have a yellow/orange underside. When born, the young are almost black.

Found in a range of habitats, Common Lizards are diurnal and are often seen basking in the morning and afternoon. They feed on small invertebrates ranging from flies to spiders and spend the winter sleeping under rocks or logs, or underground. In a typical year, they can be seen between March and October.

Slow-worm, by Mike Toms; Common Lizard, by Paul Sterry/NPL

Snakes

If you're lucky to see a snake in your garden, it will probably only be a fleeting glimpse. You are most likely to see Grass Snake in the garden, but small individuals could be confused with Slow-worms. Remember that the latter has a smooth, shiny appearance whereas snakes look scalier.

Grass Snake: Grass Snakes are common visitors to gardens in England and Wales in the spring and summer. Both males and females are usually grey-green with an obvious yellow and black collar (see detail). Females grow larger than males and can be over a metre long.

Found in a number of different habitats, Grass Snakes prefer areas with long grass, as their name suggests! Like most snakes they lay eggs, usually in June and July, using rotting vegetation (including in compost heaps). During the spring they usually hunt fish, moving onto newts in the summer, and will often be seen at garden ponds. Later in the summer they move on to land and hunt frogs and toads. In a typical year, they can be seen between March and October.

Adder: The only venomous snake in Britain, Adders are found throughout the country. They can easily be identified by the 'zig-zag' pattern down their back and the 'V' or 'X' marking on their head. Males are often grey-white and females brown, though there are a range of colour variations, and they can grow up to 60 cm long. Adders prefer open habitats like heathland, moorland and open woodland where they hunt small vertebrates including rodents and lizards. They are rare visitors to gardens but may be seen passing through. Unlike many other snakes, they give birth to live young, which emerge from August.

Other species: The other two native species in Britain are the Sand Lizard and the Smooth Snake. The former is a large brown-green lizard that is predominantly found on heathland in Surrey, Dorset and Hampshire, and dune systems in Merseyside. Recently, however, they have been reintroduced elsewhere in southern England and north-west Wales. Smooth Snakes are the rarest of Britain's reptiles and are only found on heathlands in Dorset, Hampshire and a few areas in Surrey.

Grass Snakes, by Paul Sterry/NPL; Adder, by Mike Toms

AMPHIBIANS

With roughly half of the UK's ponds lost during the 20th century and 80% of those remaining classed as being in poor condition, those in our gardens are becoming increasingly important for amphibians. While all of our native amphibians can be found in gardens, some are more common than others. They are most obvious when in their breeding ponds, but many spend more time on land than in the water, especially in the winter.

Palmate Newt, by Paul Sterry/NPL

Frogs & Toads

We have five native species of frog and toad, two of which – Common Frog and Common Toad – are often encountered in gardens. Another native toad – the Natterjack Toad – is found almost exclusively in coastal sand-dune systems, coastal grazing marshes and sandy heaths. Common Toads in the Channel Islands were recently found to be a different species. The remaining native species – the Pool Frog – was declared extinct in the wild in 1995 but has since been reintroduced to its former East Anglian stronghold. The Pool Frog is one of the 'green frogs', two others of which occur in the UK as introductions; these are the Edible Frog and the Marsh Frog. Both have restricted distributions and may occur in garden ponds.

Common Frog: Widespread and usually found close to fresh water, though outside the breeding season they can roam up to 500 m from breeding ponds. Up to 9 cm in length, they have smooth, moist skin. Colour variable, though usually olive-green or brown, with a dark patch behind the eye. Often have bands of darker striping on hind legs and sometimes have irregular markings on their backs.

Common Toad: Widespread, though absent from Ireland and Jersey, and prefers to breed in deeper water. Can grow up to 15 cm long. Their 'warty' skin often appears dry, and is usually uniformly brown or olive-brown. They are nocturnal, hunting invertebrates, and will remain in gardens for long periods if there are plenty of snails and slugs around. Unlike frogs, toads usually 'walk', only hopping when alarmed.

Common Frog and Common Toad, by Paul Sterry/NPL

Newts

There are three native species of newt in the UK; Smooth (or Common), Palmate and Great Crested. You may also see the introduced Alpine Newt which is becoming more widespread due to the exotic pet trade, despite the fact it is illegal to introduce them into the wild.

Smooth Newt: Also known as Common Newt; the most widespread of our newts and the only one found in Ireland. More terrestrial than other newt species and can be found in a wide variety of damp habitats. Can grow up to 11 cm long and, unlike in most amphibians, the males are usually larger than the females. Males have clear head stripes and, in the breeding season, an undulating crest running from the head to the tip of the tail. Females lack the crest and are predominantly yellowish- or olive-brown above, with indistinct stripes on the head. Both sexes have pale pinkish-orange bellies with rounded dark spots and pale spotted throats.

Great Crested Newt: Although fairly aquatic, this newt is usually found on land outside the breeding season. Prefers deeper waterbodies and mostly nocturnal during the breeding season. During the rest of the year it can be found several hundred metres from water, especially in broad-leaved woodland. Typically up to 15 cm long, though females can reach 18 cm. Has coarse skin, dark brown or blackish above with darker spots and a yellow or orange belly, with variable patterns of dark spots or blotches. Belly patterns are unique. Breeding males have a high, usually spiky, crest with white/bluish streak along its side.

Palmate Newt: A more aquatic species than Smooth Newt but can still often be found on land. They breed in a variety of still, or occasionally slow-running, shallow water ranging from large puddles to ponds. Palmate Newts can grow up to 9.5 cm long but are usually smaller. Both sexes have yellowish, olive or pale brown skin on top and pale pinkish-orange bellies. Their bellies may have a few indistinct spots but their throats are always bare. Breeding males have small crest stretching along their tail and ending in a filament. They also have dark, webbed hind feet. Females are similar to female Smooth Newts, though with less obvious belly spots.

Smooth, Great Crested and Palmate Newts, by Paul Sterry/NPL.

BUTTERFLIES

There are 59 species of butterfly in Britain and Ireland, with many regularly visiting gardens to feed and some even breeding in them. Some are widespread and use a variety of habitats; others are more specialist, only visiting specific food plants. With increasing development of land and changes in the climate, butterflies are one of the more threatened groups of wildlife and gardens are an increasingly important habitat for them.

Male Orange-tip, by John Flowerday

Whites & Yellows

Brimstone: Brimstone is a fairly large butterfly with leaf-shaped wings. The upperwings of males are yellow, with yellow-green underneath, and females are pale green. The range of the Brimstone has been expanding north but they are still relatively rare in Scotland. It is thought that this is partly due to the increased availability of the caterpillar food plants Buckthorn and Alder Buckthorn in gardens and planted hedgerows. Adults prefer areas of scrubby grassland and woodland but range widely. Brimstones overwinter as adults and usually emerge in gardens in February, with their first peak in March/April and their second in August as the new generation emerges.

Orange-tip: While male Orange-tips have white wings with bright orange tips to the forewings, females are white with black wing tips, which is why the females are often mistaken for other 'white' butterflies. The underwings are dappled green, however, which easily separates them. The species is widespread across both Britain and Ireland and their range has been expanding north into Scotland over the last 30 years, though they are still largely absent from northern Scotland. Orange-tip caterpillars prefer to feed on crucifers including Cuckooflower and Garlic Mustard. Adults prefer damp habitats including meadows and woodland clearings, but readily visit gardens. They overwinter as pupae.

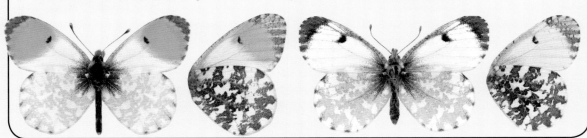

Other butterfly images by Paul Sterry/NPL

Whites & Yellows

Small White: Small White has a much shorter wingspan and smaller wing spots than the related Large White. Found throughout the country, though absent from much of northern Scotland and some Scottish islands.

Like Large Whites, Small White caterpillars prefer cultivated brassicas, especially cabbages, and *Nasturtiums*. They will also use wild crucifers such as Garlic Mustard and Hoary Cress. Adults are found in a variety of habitats, but are common in gardens and allotments. Small Whites overwinter as pupae, appearing in gardens from March. The first generation peaks in May, with the second generation peaking in August.

Green-veined White: Although the upperwings are similar to a faded Small White, the underwings have grey-green scales along their veins, giving the species its name. They are our most widespread butterfly, found throughout Britain and Ireland. The caterpillars feed on a wide range of wild crucifers, including Garlic Mustard, Cuckooflower and Wild Cabbage. Like most other 'whites' they overwinter as pupae, emerging in gardens in March.

Large White: Large Whites have white wings with black tips on the forewings. Females also have two dark spots on the forewings, which the males lack. These spots can also be seen on the undersides. They are very common butterflies and are found throughout Britain and Ireland.

Large White caterpillars feed on crucifers, with a strong preference for cabbage and Brussels sprout, earning them the alternative name of 'Cabbage White'. Adults are found in a variety of habitats, but are prominent in gardens and allotments. Large Whites usually overwinter in the pupal stage, emerging from March onwards.

Other butterfly images by Paul Sterry/NPL

Blues

Holly Blue: This is the only blue butterfly likely to be seen in most gardens, and it can be distinguished from the other blues by the powder-blue-coloured underwings, which lack any strong patterning of orange or white spots. The Holly Blue undergoes regular population cycles which are thought to be driven by a parasitic wasp, which lays its eggs in Holly Blue caterpillars. In England and Wales, Holly Blue is widespread and common. Its range is expanding north and it can now be seen in southern Scotland. They are the earliest of the 'blue' butterflies to emerge, overwintering as pupae and appearing in gardens in March. They usually have two broods with the first peak in May and another in August.

Vanessids and browns

Comma: This species can be readily recognised by the ragged outline to its wings, with males usually a little darker in colouration than females. Colour also varies with season; those individuals emerging in early summer paler than the generation that overwinters in the adult form. They are widespread throughout England and Wales and are expanding their range into Scotland.

Meadow Brown: Both sexes have a black eyespot on the forewing tip with one white spot inside. They are a widespread species in Britain and Ireland, though colonies have been lost in the past to agricultural intensification. They overwinter as caterpillars, emerging as adults in May and usually peaking in July.

Ringlet: When fresh, the Ringlet has velvety dark brown upperwings with a narrow white fringe along the edge. Underneath it has distinctive ringed eyespots which give it its name. These vary in number and size. The Ringlet population is widespread across Britain and Ireland except in some parts of western England and northern Scotland. Ringlets overwinter as caterpillars, with adults starting to emerge in May and peaking in July.

All butterfly images by Paul Sterry/NPL, except underside of Meadow Brown, by Hugh Clark/NPL

Vanessids and browns

Peacock: Peacock butterflies have striking red wings with black markings and four eyespots with yellow, blue and purple in them which have evolved to startle predators. Their undersides are very dark and make them resemble dead leaves. They are widespread throughout England, Wales and Ireland, with their range continuing to expand north through Scotland. They overwinter as adults, usually emerging in February. Generally they only have one brood with a peak in gardens in August, but in good years a small second brood may appear.

Small Tortoiseshell: Small Tortoiseshells have orange and black wings with a white patch on the forewing, and blue patches around the edges of the wings. The latter separates them from other brown and orange butterflies. Widespread throughout Britain and Ireland, they overwinter as adults and may be found in houses and outbuildings. They emerge in February and have their first peak in March/April. Except in northern areas, they usually have two broods, and peak again in August.

Red Admiral: The black upperwings of the Red Admiral have a red band on the forewing and the hindwing and white spots near the tips of the forewings. Red Admiral is predominantly a migrant butterfly, arriving here from North Africa and continental Europe. They are widespread throughout the country and, while they start appearing in gardens from February, they are not numerous until May. They have a single brood and peak in gardens in September.

Painted Lady: The population varies from year to year because this is a migrant butterfly, arriving from North Africa and the Middle East. Overall, however, the population seems to be increasing. They can be seen throughout Britain and Ireland, and their migration can take them to the far north of Scotland. They usually start appearing in gardens from April and tend to have one brood peaking in early August, though depending on the weather may have a second.

All butterfly images by Paul Sterry/NPL

DRAGONFLIES

Whether you live in an urban centre or the middle of the countryside, dragonflies may still visit your garden. Garden ponds are becoming increasingly important for dragonflies as a third of our species are now threatened by habitat destruction and climate change. Dragonflies and damselflies spend 95% of their lives under water as larvae, which is why we only see them for a short period of time during the summer.

Banded Demoiselle, by Mike Toms

Damselflies

Azure Damselfly: The male Azure Damselfly is bright blue with black rings between its segments. Its main distinguishing feature is a black 'U-shape' on the second segment of its abdomen. Females are green or pale blue with black markings. Azure Damselflies are usually seen between May and early September, near small ponds or streams. They are common throughout Britain and Ireland, but are scarce in northern Scotland.

Common Blue Damselfly: Male Common Blue Damselflies are bright blue with thin black segments, with a black oval shape on the second segment of their abdomen which separates them from other blue damselflies. Females are blue or dull green with black markings. They usually fly between mid May and late September and are found near most types of water, though may avoid smaller ponds. They are widespread and common throughout Britain and Ireland.

Blue-tailed Damselfly: Both male and female Blue-tailed Damselflies have blue 'tail' segments. Males have blue bodies and black abdomens, and while females can vary in colour, they often have this colouration when mature. Usually seen between May and September, Blue-tailed Damselflies are amongst the first species to colonise new ponds. They are found throughout Britain and Ireland in lowland habitats.

Large Red Damselfly: Large Red Damselfly males are mostly red with a black end to their abdomen. Both sexes have red eyes. Often the first damselfly to emerge, Large Red Damselflies can be seen on the wing between mid April and early September. They are widespread and common throughout Britain and Ireland, and are usually seen near ponds, canals and ditches. They are one of the species most reported by Garden BirdWatchers.

Large Red Damselfly, by Graham Jarvis; Blue-tailed Damselfly, by Paul Sterry/NPL; Common Blue Damselflies, by Moss Taylor; Azure Damselfly, by Andrew Merrick/NPL; cut-outs by Paul Sterry/NPL.

Dragonflies

Broad-bodied Chaser: Broad-bodied Chasers are easily identified by their broad, flattened abdomens. Both sexes have yellow spots on the sides of the abdomen – males have a light blue abdomen while females are yellow-brown. The species can also be identified by the brown patches at the base of the wings. They normally fly between May and late July, though they have been recorded by Garden BirdWatchers as late as October.

Common Darter: Both male and female Common Darters have brown thoraxes and yellow legs. Males have an orange-red abdomen and females a yellow or light brown abdomen. They usually fly between mid June and late October, though can be seen as late as November if the weather remains mild. While they are not seen in the Scottish Highlands, they are common and widespread throughout the rest of Britain and Ireland.

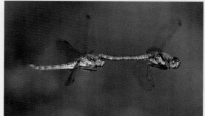

Ruddy Darter: Male Ruddy Darters can be told from other species by their 'waisted' appearance, red-brown thorax and bright red abdomen. Females are duller, usually yellow-brown with black stripes down their sides. Usually flying between late May and early October, Ruddy Darters are most likely to be seen in gardens with ponds that have dense vegetation. They are most common in south-east England and southern Ireland.

Brown Hawker: Both sexes of the Brown Hawker are brown with golden-brown wings and yellow stripes along the sides of the thorax, but males also have blue dots on the sides of their abdomens. Flying between late June and early October, they breed in standing or slow-flowing water. They do, however, hunt well away from water and tend to be seen passing through gardens. Most common and widespread in south and east.

Southern Hawker: Southern Hawker males are black with bright green markings and blue stripes towards the end of their abdomens. Females are chocolate-brown with green and yellow markings. They are often seen in gardens during their flight period of July to October as they like well-vegetated small ponds, and they are one of the most reported dragonfly species by Garden BirdWatchers. They are not present in Ireland.

Migrant Hawker: Migrant Hawkers are relatively small for a hawker species. Both sexes are brown, though males are usually darker with small blue paired dots along the abdomen and blue eyes. Females have dull yellow-green spots and have brown eyes. Both sexes have a small yellow triangle at the top of the abdomen. While they are rare in gardens, Migrant Hawkers are found well away from breeding sites and do pass through.

Broad-bodied Chaser, by Moss Taylor; Brown Hawker, by Paul Sterry/NPL; all others by Richard Revels/NPL

BUMBLEBEES

There are 24 species of bumblebee in Britain and Ireland and many will make use of resources in gardens. Many species are now declining, due to changes in land use reducing the availability of flowers, and two species have become extinct since 1940. The first bumblebees you see in the spring will be new queens that have spent the winter in hibernation. These feed up on flowers and then search for somewhere to nest.

Buff-tailed Bumblebee, by Moss Taylor

Bumblebees

Buff-tailed Bumblebee: All Buff-tailed Bumblebees have a golden yellow collar near their head and another on the abdomen. Queens have a buff tail but workers and males have a white tail with a thin buff line separating it from the rest of the abdomen. Males have black facial hair which separates them from many other species. Buff-tailed Bumblebees are common throughout Britain and Ireland, though are scarcer in north-west Scotland.

White-tailed Bumblebee: White-tailed Bumblebees have two lemon-yellow bands, one on the thorax and one on the abdomen. They all have clean white tails, though these may fade as they age. Males have yellow facial hair and extra yellow on the thorax and abdomen. They are common throughout Britain and Ireland and their queens are among the earliest to emerge, usually in mid March in southern Britain. Most colonies die out by late August.

Early Bumblebee: This small species has yellow bands on the thorax and abdomen, though the latter is more subtle or sometimes missing in workers. In males, the thorax band is very broad and they have yellow facial hair. All of them have dark rust-red tails, though these fade with time. Common on mainland Britain and in Ireland, they are missing from parts of north-west Scotland and most Scottish islands. They usually emerge in March in southern England.

Garden Bumblebee: Garden Bumblebees have bright white tails and three yellow bands; one each at the front and end of the thorax and one at the front of the abdomen. If you can get up close, they can be told from other similar species like Heath Bumblebee by the fact that they have longer faces. They are common in Britain and Ireland and can be seen between late March and mid July though occasionally will be around until September.

Buff-tailed and White-tailed Bumblebees, by Roger Tidman/NPL; Early Bumblebee, by Andrew Merrick/NPL; Garden Bumblebee, by Paul Sterry/NPL

Red-tailed and Tree Bumblebees, by Roger Tidman/NPL; Heath Bumblebee, by NatureGuides – www.natureguides.com; Common Carder Bee, by Paul Sterry/NPL; Forest Cuckoo Bumblebee, by Roger Tidman/NPL

Bumblebees

Red-tailed Bumblebee: Red-tailed Bumblebees have black bodies with orange-red tails. Unlike queens and workers, males have yellow facial hair and a yellow band on the thorax. They are common bees in England, Wales and Ireland but are scarcer in Scotland. Queens usually emerge from March and the species will be seen until late August. They use a wide range of flowers in a number of habitats.

Tree Bumblebee: Tree Bumblebees are easily identifiable in gardens thanks to their ginger thorax, black head and abdomen, and white tail. They are a relatively new species in the UK having first been found in 2001. Their range is expanding fast and they are now found throughout much of England and Wales. They usually emerge in late March and fly until late September. They often forage in gardens and may nest in bird boxes.

Heath Bumblebee: Heath Bumblebees have three yellow bands, one at the front of the abdomen and two on the thorax. Their tail colour, however, depends on where they are found; in most areas they have white tails but on the Western Isles and Shetland it is buff. Found throughout Britain and Ireland but with very local distributions. The queens usually emerge in late March and the species may be seen until mid September.

Common Carder Bee: While the shade may vary, all Common Carder Bees are completely ginger or brown and relatively small for bumblebees. They are common throughout Britain and Ireland, usually emerging in late March. Their colonies are among the latest to break up and can often be seen until early October. Garden flowers are particularly important for queens when they first emerge, and for workers later in the summer.

Cuckoo Bumblebees

There are six species of cuckoo bumblebee in Britain and Ireland, three of which commonly occur in gardens: Southern, Field and Forest Cuckoo Bumblebee. Cuckoo bumblebees can be told from 'true' bumblebees by their back legs being covered in hair, with no pollen baskets as they do not collect pollen. Their wings also appear darker. Like their bird namesake, they lay their eggs in the nests of other bumblebees.

Forest Cuckoo Bumblebee: Both male and female Forest Cuckoo Bumblebees usually have a yellow stripe on their thorax and no stripe on their abdomen. They have white tails with black tips, though the black is more obvious in the males, which also have a tiny orange tip to the tail. They are found throughout much of England and Wales and in some parts of Scotland, taking over the nests of Early and Heath Bumblebees.

OTHER INVERTEBRATES

A wide range of different invertebrates visit our gardens, many of which even experts struggle to identify. For this reason, Garden BirdWatch only takes records of a few species. It's worth considering garden visitors such as beetles, moths and bees when gardening for wildlife, and should you rise to the challenge of identification there are national recording schemes in place for all groups.

Hornet, by Richard Revels/NPL

Beetles

There are over 300,000 recorded species of beetle in the world, making them the largest order of insects. In Britain and Ireland there are over 4,000 known species in over 100 different families, including ladybirds, tiger, and longhorn beetles. Most beetles can be told from other insects by the fact that they have protective wing cases (formerly the forewings) covering the hind wings which alone are used for flight. This gives them their classic armoured look. Learn more about beetles and recording them here: www.coleoptera.org.uk.

Stag Beetle: The largest beetle in Britain and Ireland is the Stag Beetle, which is one of the two species that can be recorded for BTO Garden BirdWatch. It is named for the male's large mandibles which look like antlers (right). Males are very large (35–70 mm, with long mandibles), females (below right) somewhat smaller (30–50 mm long) with small mandibles. Adults emerge from mid May and die by the end of August. Widespread in southern England, especially in areas with light soils. Can also be found in some areas of south-west England, Wales and East Anglia. Not present in Scotland or Ireland.

Cockchafer: Also known as the May Bug, most people will see Cockchafers at night crashing into lights. Due to this and their large size, they are easy to recognise and are the other beetle recorded for Garden BirdWatch. Males have seven 'feathers' on their antennae, females have six. Adults usually emerge in late April/early May and are most likely to be seen between May and July. The species is found throughout Britain and Ireland. Cockchafer larvae, which can spend up to three years underground, feed on the roots of a wide range of plants and are considered an agricultural pest. Adults, which live for only six weeks, feed on the leaves of a number of different deciduous trees.

Stag Beetles and Cockchafer, by Paul Sterry/NPL

Moths

Over 2,400 species of moth have been recorded in Britain and Ireland including both macro and micro moths. They are an important part of the garden ecosystem, providing pollination and a source of food for other animals. In the last 100 years, however, 65 species of moth have become extinct and studies have found that the overall numbers of moths have declined by 28% since 1968. The reasons behind this are complex, but the loss of habitats through intensive land use for agriculture and urban development is a large issue. Learn more about moths and how to record them here: www.mothscount.org.

Hummingbird Hawk-moth: This day-flying moth feeds while hovering on rapidly-beating wings. Its behaviour makes it an easy moth to recognise, and it is the only moth that can be recorded for Garden BirdWatch. This moth has orange-brown hindwings, grey-brown forewings, a black-and-white-spotted body and a long proboscis. This is a migrant, arriving here between June and August, and can be seen throughout Britain and Ireland, though it is most common in southern and eastern England, south Wales and the Midlands. It uses a wide range of habitats and is common in gardens. Although still mostly a migrant, it is thought that some adults have started to survive the winter in the south of England due to warmer winter temperatures. Adults like flowers with deep tubes such as honeysuckle and Red Valerian.

Bees and wasps

While bumblebees can be identified to species with a little care, these represent just a small proportion of the bee and wasp species that can be found in your garden. In Britain and Ireland there are around 6,700 species of Hymenoptera (which includes ants, wasps, bees and sawflies). Of these, over 200 species are solitary bees, 2,400 are solitary wasps and only seven are social wasps – those that live in colonies. All the species of social wasp found in Britain and Ireland look similar, with yellow and black patterns, but their size and patterns vary. Solitary bees and wasps do not have colonies; instead they usually lay their eggs in a nest and leave the young to survive alone. Find out more about bees and wasps and how to record them here: www.bwars.com.

Hornet: The largest and most easily identifiable of our social wasps is the Hornet, a species that can be recorded for Garden BirdWatch. Hornet nests can contain hundreds or thousands of individuals. Queens emerge from April and active nests can persist until November if the weather conditions are favourable. Although the species is most common in southern England its range extends as far north as Yorkshire. Despite generally being cautious and passive, Hornets have a bad name partly because they sting and partly because they are increasingly found nesting in wall cavities, buildings and chimneys. Traditionally, however, they prefer to use hollow trees in woodland. The diet of both adults and larvae consists mainly of insects but queens may also eat tree sap, windfall fruit and nectar before hibernating.

Nuthatch, by Richard Winston

Resources

The following books, websites and scientific papers provide you with the opportunity to find out more about your birds and other garden wildlife. You can also find useful advice on wildlife-friendly gardening and read and learn about the scientific papers that have emerged from citizen science projects such as Garden BirdWatch.

Books

The Birds of the Western Palearctic
Cramp, Stanley *et al.* (1977–1994)

Bird Atlas 2007–11
Dawn Balmer, Simon Gillings, Brian Caffrey, Bob Swann, Iain Downie and Rob Fuller (2013)

Birds Britannica
Mark Cocker and Richard Mabey (2005)

The BTO Nestbox Guide
Chris du Feu (2003)

Collins Bird Guide
Lars Svensson *et al.* (1999)

Collins BTO Guide to British Birds
Paul Sterry and Paul Stancliffe (2015)

Collins BTO Guide to Rare British Birds
Paul Sterry and Paul Stancliffe (2015)

Collins Butterfly Guide
Tom Tolman and Richard Lewington (2009)

A Field Guide to Monitoring Nests
James Ferguson-Lees, Richard Castell and Dave Leech (2011)

Gardening for Birdwatchers
Mike Toms, Ian Wilson & Barley Wilson (2008)

Garden Birds and Wildlife
Mike Toms and Paul Sterry (2008)

Insects of Britain and Western Europe
Michael Chinery (2012)

Mammals of the British Isles: Handbook
Stephen Harris and Derek Yalden (2008)

Reptiles and Amphibians of Britain and Europe
Denys Ovenden and Nick Arnold (2002)

The State of Butterflies in Britain and Ireland
Richard Fox, Jim Asher, Tom Brereton, David Roy and Martin Warren (2006)

The Migration Atlas: movements of the birds of Britain & Ireland.
Chris Wernham, Mike Toms, John Marchant, Jacquie Clark, Gavin Siriwardena and Stephen Baillie (2002)

Websites

British Trust for Ornithology
www.bto.org

Garden Wildlife Health
www.gardenwildlifehealth.org

Amphibian and Reptile Conservation
www.arc-trust.org

Bat Conservation Trust
www.bats.org.uk

Bees, Wasps & Ants Recording Society
www.bwars.com

British Dragonfly Society
www.british-dragonflies.org.uk
Buglife
www.buglife.org.uk
Bumblebee Conservation Trust
www.bumblebeeconservation.org
Butterfly Conservation
www.butterfly-conservation.org
Froglife
www.froglife.org
The Mammal Society
www.mammal.org.uk
Moths Count
www.mothscount.org
People's Trust for Endangered Species
www.ptes.org
Royal Horticultural Society
www.rhs.org.uk
Wildlife Gardening with Jenny Steel
www.wildlife-gardening.co.uk

Scientific papers

Scientific papers allow research to be peer-reviewed by other scientists, thus ensuring quality. While many of these papers will be freely viewable online, some are not, however, but copies can be requested from the authors.

Bland, R.L, Tully, J. & Greenwood, J.J.D. (2004) Birds breeding in British gardens: an underestimated population? *Bird Study* **51**: 97–106.

Cannon, A.R., Chamberlain, D.E., Toms, M.P., Hatchwell, B.J. & Gaston, K.J. (2005) Trends in the use of private gardens by wild birds in Great Britain 1995–2002. *Journal of Applied Ecology* **42**: 659–671.

Chamberlain, D.E., Cannon, A.R. & Toms, M.P. (2004) Associations of garden birds with gradients in garden habitat and local habitat. *Ecography* **27**: 589–600.

Chamberlain, D.E., Toms, M.P., Cleary-McHarg, R. & Banks, A.N. (2007) House Sparrow *Passer domesticus* habitat use in urbanized landscapes. *Journal of Ornithology* **148**: 453–462.

Clewley, G.D., Plummer, K.E., Robinson, R.A., Simm, C.H. & Toms, M.P. (2016) The effect of artificial lighting on the arrival time of birds using garden feeding stations in winter: a missed opportunity? *Urban Ecosystems* **19**: 535–546.

Lawson, B., Robinson, R.A., Neimanis, A., Handeland, K., Isomursu, M., Agren, E.O., Hamnes, I.S., Tyler, K.M., Chantrey, J., Hughes, L.A., Pennycott, T.W., Simpson, V.R., John, S.K., Peck, K.M., Toms, M.P., Bennett, M., Kirkwood, J.K. & Cunningham, A.A. (2011) Evidence of spread of the emerging infectious disease, finch trichomonosis, by migrating birds. *EcoHealth* **8**: 143–153.

McKenzie, A.J., Petty, S.J., Toms, M.P. & Furness, R.W. (2007) Importance of Sitka Spruce *Picea sitchensis* seed and garden bird-feeders for Siskins *Carduelis spinus* and Coal Tits *Periparus ater*. *Bird Study* **54**: 236–247.

Morrison, C.A., Robinson, R.A., Leech, D.I., Dadam, D. & Toms, M. (2014) Using citizen science to investigate the role of productivity in House Sparrow *Passer domesticus* population trends. *Bird Study* **61**: 91–100.

Musgrove, A., Aebischer, N., Eaton, M., Hearn, R., Newson, S., Noble, D., Parsons, M., Risely, K. & Stroud, D. (2013) Population estimates of birds in Great Britain and the United Kingdom. *British Birds* **106**: 64–100.

Ockendon, N., Davis, S.E., Miyar, T. and Toms, M.P. (2009) Urbanization and time of arrival of common birds at garden feeding stations. *Bird Study* **56**: 405–410.

Ockendon, N., Davis, E., Toms, M.P. & Mukherjee, S. (2009) Eye size and the time of arrival of birds at garden feeding stations in winter. *Journal of Ornithology* **150**: 903–908.

Plummer, K.E., Siriwardena, G.M., Conway, G.J., Risely, K. & Toms, M.P. (2015) Is supplementary feeding in gardens a driver of evolutionary change in a migratory bird species? *Global Change Biology* **21**: 4353–4363.

Robinson, R.A., Lawson, B., Toms, M.P., Peck, K.M., Kirkwood, J.K., Chantrey, J., Clatworthy, I.R., *et al.* (2010) Emerging infectious disease leads to rapid population decline of common British birds. *PLoS ONE* **5** e12215

Salisbury, A., Armitage, J., Bostock, H., Perry, J., Tatchell, M. & Thompson, K. (2015) Enhancing gardens as habitats for flower-visiting aerial insects (pollinators): should we plant native or exotic species? *Journal of Applied Ecology* **52**: 1156–1164.

Yellow-necked Mouse, by John Harding

Index

This index includes the species and topics mentioned within the book and should be used alongside the contents list. Page references shown in **bold** indicate sections where the species or topic is covered in the greatest detail. Plants are listed by their common name, except where reference is being made to several species within a single genus - e.g. *Cotoneaster*.